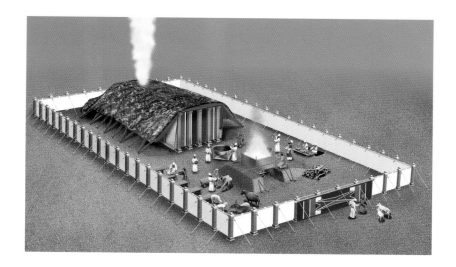

The Tabernacle: To dwell among the people of Israel, Jehovah told Moses to build the Tabernacle. The people of Israel could then meet God by receiving the remission of their sins by giving their offerings according to the requirements of the sacrificial system that He had given them. This Tabernacle was a detailed portrait of Jesus Christ who would come to us in the New Testament's time as our Messiah.

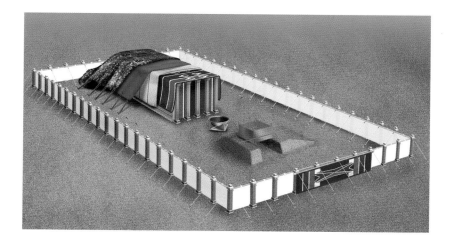

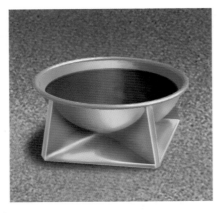 

The laver of bronze: The laver of bronze manifests that Jesus Christ, who came to this earth in the flesh of a man, took upon all the sins of mankind and washed them all away by being baptized by John the Baptist.

The altar of burnt offering: The altar of burnt offering shows us that Jesus Christ, taking upon all the sins of mankind onto His body, shed His blood and died on the Cross to be condemned vicariously for theses sins.

The TABERNACLE:
A Detailed Portrait of Jesus Christ
(I)

The TABERNACLE:
A Detailed Portrait of Jesus Christ
(I)

PAUL C. JONG

Hephzibah Publishing House
A Ministry of THE NEW LIFE MISSION
SEOUL, KOREA

The TABERNACLE: A Detailed Portrait of Jesus Christ (I)
Copyright © 2003 by Hephzibah Publishing House
Scripture quotations are from *the New King James Version.*

ISBN 89-8314-299-5
Cover Art by Min-soo Kim
Illustration by Young-ae Kim
Printed in Korea

Hephzibah Publishing House
A Ministry of THE NEW LIFE MISSION
48 Bon-dong, Dongjack-gu
Seoul, Korea 156-060

♠ Website: http://www.bjnewlife.org
♠ E-mail: newlife@bjnewlife.org
♠ Phone: 82(Korea)-16-392-2954
♠ Fax: 82-33-651-2954

Acknowledgement

This book is the first of the two-volume series on the Tabernacle that follows my earlier publication of another two-volume series on Revelation. Needless to say, it is only by the grace of God this book is seeing its light. The more I write, the more I realize from the depth of my heart just how biblically sound the gospel of the water and the Spirit given to us by the Lord really is, how precious this gospel is, as well as how immensely thankful I am for having received the remission of my sins by believing in this gospel of the water and the Spirit.

Words fail me to express my profound gratitude to all the staffs and the coworkers of The New Life Mission who have labored tirelessly together in faith to bring this book out, and who have united their hearts to serve the gospel. I am sure that their precious, hard works will produce bountiful fruits all over the world. It is by the dedicated services of these faithful souls that this book could see its light, and it is by their services that I could follow the Great Commission of our Lord to spread the gospel to the ends of the earth. And I would also like to give my sincere thanks to Mr. Youngwon Cho for assisting us diligently with the translation of this book.

I give all glory and thanks to God for saving us all, and for permitting us the coworkers and His Church to serve the Lord's works. ✉

PAUL C. JONG

CONTENTS

CONTENTS

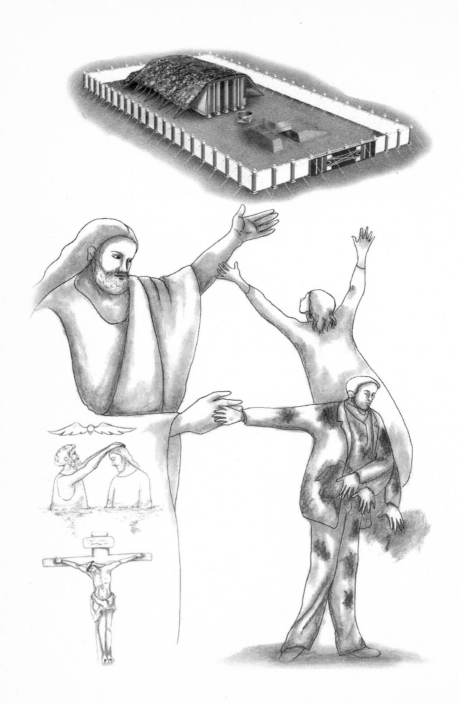

Foreword

The Tabernacle system that God spoke of in the Old Testament has long been an object of great interest for everyone who has sought to study the Scriptural Word. But even the truth seekers in Christianity have not been able to discover its exact spiritual lessons, for the revelation of God manifested through the Tabernacle has been hidden from them, like the summit of the Mountain Sinai was hidden in clouds to the common Israelites while God showed Moses its pattern clearly there.

This was God's will. As He said, *"Go and tell this people: 'Keep on hearing, but do not understand; keep on seeing, but do not perceive'" (Isaiah 6:9).* All the Word of God is the Word of revelation that, without hearing it with a heart that reveres God, a humble heart that truly recognizes one's own sinfulness, and a heart that believes in and is thankful for how He has saved such a hell-bound being, can never be understood, nor ever realized—that is, it is the Word of revelation that can be seen only when God Himself unveils and shows it to us.

Like this, it is only when illuminated by the gospel of the water and the Spirit that all the Word of the Scriptures can be perceived correctly, and it is only then that this Word can give life to us and work in our lives. As for myself, it was only after I was born again through the gospel of the water and the Spirit that I, too, could come to understand and know the true meaning and significance of the Tabernacle system revealed in the Word of God.

Before this, the Tabernacle had remained to me only as a fossilized relic that had appeared once and then disappeared from the historiography of the people of Israel, but it has now been planted firmly at the center of my life of faith as the place of grace where the living God meets me in person. This has been as wonderful and marvelous an experience as that of the blind man whose eyes were opened when he met the Lord. How exactly and elaborately the Word of the Tabernacle shows us Jesus Christ our Savior and His works of salvation! How lively and presently our Lord speaks to us through the Tabernacle system!

I wrote this book out of my sincere heart that ardently desires each and every one of you to enter into the gate of the court of the Tabernacle with the true faith, and to thereby enter into the house of gold that the Lord has given you. I am convinced that this Tabernacle, a detailed portrait of Jesus Christ, will also be engraved in the heart of everyone who reads this book. I am also certain, beyond any doubt, that with this engraving, and through the gospel of the water and the Spirit, you will also encounter the perfect works of salvation that Jesus fulfilled while on this earth.

In science, the very basics are more important than anything else. Just as mastering the fundamentals of science is essential for attaining advanced scientific knowledge, the same principle applies when we are trying to grasp the gospel of the water and the Spirit and believe in it properly. On the Tabernacle, too, the reality of today's Christians is that many of them, in general, do not possess even the basic understanding of the fundamental truth of the blue, purple, and scarlet thread and the fine woven linen shown in the Tabernacle. We see, as a result, that their souls are deeply troubled by many problems of sin. As such, the true knowledge of the remission of sin can be attained only when we understand the gospel of salvation revealed through the

Tabernacle's blue, purple, and scarlet thread and fine woven linen.

It saddens me deeply to see that most of today's Christians have no proper knowledge of the gospel of the water and the Spirit. My goal here, therefore, is to explain, based on the Word of the Old and New Testaments, this gospel of the Tabernacle's blue, purple, and scarlet thread and fine woven linen, and to testify what the truth of the remission of sin really is.

What, nowadays, do those who are not born again say about the meaning of the blue thread used for the Tabernacle? Some of them limit the significance of the blue thread by saying, "As the sky is blue, the blue thread means that Jesus is God." But the proper interpretation of the blue thread is that Jesus became our perfect Savior by taking upon the sins of the world upon Himself through His baptism received from John the Baptist. Owing to His ministry of the blue thread, it was possible for Him to atone all our sins with His bloodshed on the Cross, that is, His ministry of the scarlet tread.

Now is the time for us to realize and believe in the truth of the gospel revealed in this blue thread. Knowing the truth of the blue thread is intimately related to the knowledge of our salvation from sin. The gospel of the remission of sin completed by the Tabernacle's blue, purple, and scarlet thread and fine woven linen gives us a great conviction of faith in our Lord as our Savior, and it permits us to clearly realize what the truth of redemption is.

What Is the Mystery of the Blue Thread of the Gate of the Tabernacle's Court?

The mystery of the blue thread used for the gate of the court of the Tabernacle is the truth revealed in the New Testament that Jesus took upon the sins of the world through His baptism received from John. First of all, we have to pay attention to the passages below: *"For the gate of the court there shall be a screen twenty cubits long, woven of blue, purple, and scarlet thread, and fine woven linen, made by a weaver. It shall have four pillars and four sockets,"* (Exodus 27:16) and *"But Jesus answered and said to him, 'Permit it to be so now, for thus it is fitting for us to fulfill all righteousness.' Then he allowed Him"* (Matthew 3:15).

In other words, the truth manifested by the blue thread is that the baptism Jesus received from John was the inevitable process by which He took upon the sins of the world according to the will of God the Father. This truth of the blue thread is also revealed in 1 Peter 3:21, which tells us, *"There is also an antitype which now saves us—baptism (not the removal of the filth of the flesh, but the answer of a good conscience toward God), through the resurrection of Jesus Christ."* As such, the truth of the blue thread used for the Old Testament's Tabernacle refers to the baptism that Jesus received from John (Matthew 3:15-16).

When you understand the Word of truth manifested in the blue, purple, and scarlet thread and the fine woven linen used for the gate of the court of the Tabernacle, it will be a great help for you to understand the truth of salvation. Do you know that Jesus' baptism from John is the absolute truth for washing away all your sins? Even if you believe in Jesus as your Savior, you still need to correctly realize the reason why Jesus was baptized by John, and believe in it. If you do not know this truth, Jesus would bring no benefit to your souls. Through the four ministries manifested by the blue, purple, and scarlet thread and the fine woven linen, our Lord has saved us from our sins wholly. We must now all realize the remission of sin fulfilled through these blue, purple, and scarlet thread and fine woven linen, and truly believe in it.

But What about Your Faith?

If you think that your own faith is only proper and correct, you will have no wish to find out the truth of blue, purple, and scarlet thread. But if you feel that your faith is not standing upright, you must come out before God with your faith in the gospel of the remission of sin fulfilled through the blue, purple, and scarlet thread. The works of our Lord manifested by the blue, purple, and scarlet thread used for the gate of the court of the Tabernacle will straighten out your mistaken faith and knowledge, and it will lead you to the complete faith that believes in the perfect gospel.

Do you not, by any chance, have your own conviction of salvation that you have established by yourself? Does your faith really dwell in the gospel of the water and the Spirit? If not, then it can only mean that you have been locked in the confines of your own thoughts, believing in Jesus by yourself, and loving Him in unrequited affection. This is why there are so many among today's Christians who, confined by their own thoughts, regard themselves to be righteous, even when they in fact still remain sinful. What I am saying here is that many people are now convinced that Jesus is their Savior, but their conviction is based only on their own thoughts.

In the confines of the thoughts of their flesh, they may regard Jesus is their Savior and may even be convinced, in their own way, of this fact, but they must realize that if sin is still present in their hearts, they still remain as sinners, who will ultimately be punished for their sins. When believing in Jesus as one's Savior, if the person thinks that he/she is still a good Christian without even recognizing the truth of the gospel of blue, purple, and scarlet thread, then this person's faith is dangerously mistaken. For us to have the true faith, we must seek the true salvation by believing in the gospel of the water and the Spirit manifested by the blue, purple, and scarlet thread. If we were to delude ourselves by insisting that we are good Christians without even realizing this truth of the real gospel, then none of us would ever be unable to escape the fearful wrath of God.

These Are the People with Wrong Faith

In these days, among those who believe in Jesus as their Savior, there are many who have misunderstood and misbelieved in Jesus. Their faith is one that does not believe in the truth that Jesus took upon the sins of the world with His baptism received from John. They believe that their salvation from all their sins comes by just believing in the blood of Jesus alone, even though they do not believe in the truth that Christ took upon all their sins when He was baptized by John. Such faith is fundamentally different from the gospel of the water and the Spirit revealed in the Bible.

There are many in this world who have this wrong faith. Although they misunderstand and misbelieve that they are delivered from all their sins just by believing in the blood that

Jesus shed on the Cross as their salvation, in fact, their hearts still remain sinful. In their stubbornness, they keep insisting that they can be saved from all their sins even if Jesus had not taken upon the sins of the world by being baptized by John. As such, they are convinced that only Jesus' blood on the Cross can save everyone of this world, but the reality is that they themselves have not been able to be freed from their own sins with such a faith. Nevertheless, God tells us that we must be saved by realizing the truth of the gospel manifested in the gate of the Tabernacle's outer court, woven with blue, purple, and scarlet thread and fine woven linen, and by believing in this truth.

Some people deceive their own hearts, thinking that they are sinless, when, in fact, their hearts still remain sinful. But they cannot deceive God, for sin is still found in their hearts. Because their hearts remain sinful, God cannot truly dwell in these people. Because we have to turn away from this wrong faith and believe in the true gospel, we must believe in the Word of God revealed to us through the blue, purple, and scarlet thread and the fine woven linen of the gate of the Tabernacle's outer court, and thereby be saved from all our sins.

Why Is Abraham's Faith Right?

In Genesis 17, God made His covenant of blessings with Abraham through circumcision. On the other hand, with His sacrificial system, God made Abraham's descendants, the Israelites, to pass their sins on their sacrificial offering by putting their hands on its head, and then shedding its blood (Leviticus 1:1-4). Through this sacrificial offering, God wanted to give the remission of sin to His people, and to be with them forever. This is why He gave them the sacrificial system.

The promise of God that Abraham believed in was the following: *"I will make you exceedingly fruitful; and I will make nations of you, and kings shall come from you" (Genesis 17:6)*. The covenant that God made with Abraham and his descendants was the promised blessing of salvation attained through the sign of circumcision (Genesis 17:5-10).

By being circumcised, the sign of the covenant between God and Abraham, Abraham and his descendents, the people of Israel, were blessed to become the people of God. This circumcision of the Old Testament was completed in the New Testament's times by the baptism that Jesus received from John. This is the spiritual circumcision (Romans 2:29), one in which all the sins of our hearts are cut off from us by passing them onto Jesus with our faith in His baptism. In this spiritual circumcision is found the salvation manifesting not the righteousness of man, but the righteousness of God.

For us, who are now living in the New Testament's times, the covenant that God made with Abraham is fulfilled only through our true faith that believes in the spiritual circumcision achieved by the baptism of Jesus. To be forgiven of their sins, the Israelites passed their sins to the sacrificial offering by laying their hands on its head, and thus washed away their sins. Because this sacrificial offering bore the Israelites' sins with the laying on of hands, it had to shed its blood of sacrifice. The Israelites, therefore, could wash away all their sins by believing in the laying on of hands and the blood of the sacrificial offering. In other words, in the Old Testament, all sins were passed onto the sacrificial animal with the laying on of hands, and in the New Testament, they are washed away by believing in the baptism of Jesus and His blood on the Cross.

The truth of the remission of sin given by God is closely correlated with circumcision. To believe in God's love, therefore, it is absolutely necessary to realize the truth of salvation coming through the gospel of the water and the Spirit, the essential substance of circumcision. God spoke of the Tabernacle from Exodus 25; His purpose for giving this Tabernacle to the people of Israel was to cleanse away their sins with their faith in circumcision. Circumcision was the forever-unchanging truth that brought the remission of sin, and this was all planned even before the creation.

God approved Abraham's faith that believed in His Word. Noah, too, gave sacrificial offerings to God, even when the sacrificial system of the Tabernacle was yet to be given. But along with the sacrificial system of the Tabernacle, in the New Testament's time God has given the mankind the gospel of the water and the Spirit, the essential substance of His covenant with Abraham. As such, we must realize that the faith of Abraham and the sacrificial system of the Tabernacle are all intimately related to and match with the gospel of the water and the Spirit that Jesus has given us in the New Testament's time.

In this book, therefore, we will look how exactly the details of the Tabernacle are interrelated with Abraham's faith and the gospel of the water and the Spirit, and from our discovery, we should all accept into our hearts the truth of salvation manifested by the Tabernacle and believe in it.

The Tabernacle

The Tabernacle was a place where God dwelt. Also, it was the shadow of Jesus Christ the Lord God who came in the flesh of a man.

The Tabernacle itself was a small structure built with 48 boards of acacia wood, and the outer court of the Tabernacle had 60 pillars. The fence of the Tabernacle's outer court was surrounded by curtains of white linen, supported by these 60 pillars, with a gate that was woven with blue, purple, and scarlet thread and fine woven linen, measuring 2.5 m in height and 10 m in width. This gate was located to the east of the court.

Entering into this gate of the Tabernacle's court, which was woven with blue, purple, and scarlet thread and fine woven linen, and hung at the eastside, we would first see the altar of burnt offering. Passing the altar of burnt offering, and before entering into the Holy Place, we would then see the laver of bronze. Past the laver and into the Holy Place, to the left was the lampstand, to the right the table of showbread, with the altar of incense at the center. Past the altar of incense and behind the veil concealing the Most Holy was the mercy seat covering the Ark of the Testimony.

The Tabernacle was the shadow of Jesus Christ who has forgiven the sins of the Israelites and everyone who believes in Him. Our Lord was the very owner of the Tabernacle. And He was the Savior who has blotted out everyone's sins all at once, and at the same time, the sacrificial offering itself for all mankind.

Although the people of Israel sinned everyday, by laying their hands on of the head of the unblemished sacrificial animal in the Tabernacle's court according to the sacrificial system, they could pass their sins onto the offering. This is how anyone who believed in ministry of the priests and the sacrificial offering given according to the sacrificial system could all receive the remission of sin, washing away their sins and turned as white as snow. Likewise, by believing in the baptism and sacrifice of Jesus, the true substance of the Tabernacle, the people of Israel and those of us who are Gentiles have all been clothed in the blessing of the remission of all our sins and of living with the Lord forever.

Not only the Israelites, but all the Gentiles also can be freed from all their sins only by believing in Jesus, the Lord of the Tabernacle. The Tabernacle teaches us what the gift of the remission of sin that God has given to everyone is. As such, the Tabernacle itself was the very substance of Jesus Christ.

Jesus has become the Savior of sinners. Every sinner, whoever he/she is, can become sinless just by believing in the baptism of Jesus, His blood on the Cross, and the truth that He is God Himself. We can be delivered from God's judgment by our faith in the blue, purple, and scarlet thread—in other words, by believing in the baptism of Jesus, His blood, and His divinity. Jesus is the gate to the Kingdom of Heaven.

Acts 4:12 says, *"Nor is there salvation in any other, for there is no other name under heaven given among men by which we must be saved."* No one else but Jesus can save all the people from their sins. There is no Savior apart from Jesus. John 10:9 says, *"I am the door. If anyone enters by Me, he will be saved, and will go in and out and find pasture."* 1 Timothy 2:5 says, *"For there is one God and one Mediator between God and men, the Man Christ Jesus;"* and Matthew 3:15 says, *"But Jesus answered and said to him, 'Permit it to be so now, for thus it is fitting for us to fulfill all righteousness.'"* All these verses testify to this truth.

Jesus came to this earth in the flesh of a man, and by receiving His baptism (blue thread) and shedding His blood (scarlet thread), He has save sinners. As such, Jesus has become the door of salvation for all sinners. Just as the gate of the Tabernacle's court was woven of blue, purple, and scarlet thread, Jesus, coming to this earth, first of all took the sins of the world upon Himself with His baptism received from John the Baptist. He, therefore, became the sacrificial offering, the Lamb of God (John 1:29).

Second, after thus taking upon the iniquities of all the sinners with His baptism, He died in their place and has given new life to those who believe. Third, this Jesus was God Himself. Genesis 1:1 says, *"In the beginning God created the heavens and the earth,"* and Genesis 1:3 says, *"Then God said, 'Let there be light'; and there was light."* Jesus was none other than this very God of logos, the One who created the whole universe and everything in it with His Word.

God told Moses to make the gate of the Tabernacle's court with blue, purple, and scarlet thread and fine woven linen. Jesus, who is God Himself, completed His work of making sinners righteous by coming to this earth in the flesh of a man and saving His people from all their sins through His baptism and His death on the Cross. These three ministries are the way by which Christ has saved sinners, and they are the evidence of this truth.

The Apostle Paul said in Ephesians 4:4-6, *"There is one body and one Spirit, just as you were called in one hope of your calling; one Lord, one faith, one baptism; one God and Father of all, who is above all, and through all, and in you all."* This Word refers to the salvation from sin made of the blue, purple, and scarlet thread and the fine woven linen.

Through our exploration of the Tabernacle, we must realize its correct truth, and thereby be blessed to be forgiven of all our sins. May the holiness of God be with you. ✉

SERMON

1

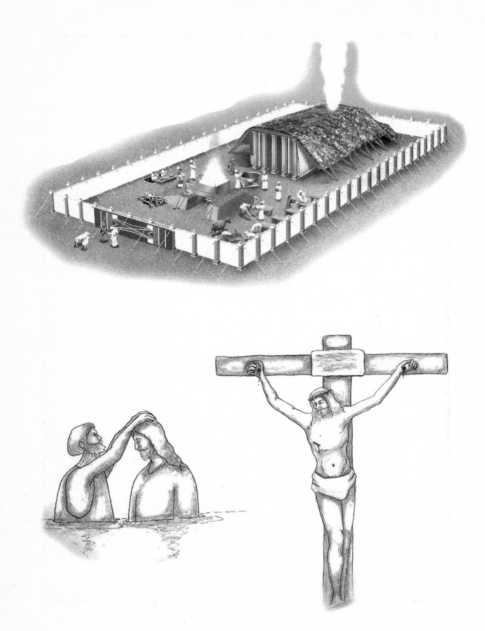

The Salvation of Sinners Revealed in the Tabernacle

< Exodus 27:9-21 >

"You shall also make the court of the tabernacle. For the south side there shall be hangings for the court made of fine woven linen, one hundred cubits long for one side. And its twenty pillars and their twenty sockets shall be bronze. The hooks of the pillars and their bands shall be silver. Likewise along the length of the north side there shall be hangings one hundred cubits long, with its twenty pillars and their twenty sockets of bronze, and the hooks of the pillars and their bands of silver. And along the width of the court on the west side shall be hangings of fifty cubits, with their ten pillars and their ten sockets. The width of the court on the east side shall be fifty cubits. The hangings on one side of the gate shall be fifteen cubits, with their three pillars and their three sockets. And on the other side shall be hangings of fifteen cubits, with their three pillars and their three sockets. For the gate of the court there shall be a screen twenty cubits long, woven of blue, purple, and scarlet thread, and fine woven linen, made by a weaver. It shall have four pillars and four sockets. All the pillars around the court shall have bands of silver; their hooks shall be of silver and their sockets of bronze. The length of the court shall be one hundred cubits, the width fifty throughout, and the height five cubits, made of fine woven linen, and its sockets of bronze. All the utensils of the tabernacle for all its service, all its pegs, and all the pegs of

the court, shall be of bronze. And you shall command the children of Israel that they bring you pure oil of pressed olives for the light, to cause the lamp to burn continually. In the tabernacle of meeting, outside the veil which is before the Testimony, Aaron and his sons shall tend it from evening until morning before the LORD. It shall be a statute forever to their generations on behalf of the children of Israel."

The fence of the rectangular court of the Tabernacle measured 100 cubits in length. In the Bible, a cubit was set as the length extending from one's elbow to the tip of his finger, about 45 cm in today's measurement. As such, that the fence of the court of the Tabernacle was 100 cubits long means that it was about 45 m, and that its width was 50 cubits means that it was approximately 22.5 m wide. So this was the size of the House in which God dwelt among the people of Israel in the Old Testament's time.

The Outer Court of the Tabernacle Was Surrounded by a Fence

Have you seen a model of the Tabernacle in a picture or painting by any chance? Broadly speaking, the Tabernacle was divided into its court and the Tabernacle itself, the House of God. In this House of God, the Tabernacle, there was a small structure called the Sanctuary. The Sanctuary was covered by four different coverings: a covering woven of fine woven linen and blue, purple, and scarlet thread; another of goats' hair; that of lam skins dyed red; and a covering of badger skins.

At the eastside of the court of the Tabernacle was found its gate, woven of blue, purple, and scarlet thread and fine woven linen. Entering into this gate, we would have seen the altar of burnt offering and the laver. Passing the laver, we would have then seen the Tabernacle itself. The Tabernacle was divided into the Holy Place and the Most Holy, where God's Ark of the Testimony was found. The fence of the court of the Tabernacle was built with 60 pillars with hangings of fine white linen. The Tabernacle itself, on the other hand, was built with 48 boards and 9 pillars. We need to have at least a general idea of the external features of the Tabernacle in order to be able to understand what God is speaking to us through its format.

God dwelt inside the Tabernacle built with 48 boards. God manifested His presence to the people of Israel with the pillar of cloud by day and that of fire by night above the Tabernacle. And inside the Sanctuary, where God Himself dwelt, the glory of God filled the place. Inside the Holy Place, there were the table of showbread, the lampstand, and the altar of incense, and inside the Most Holy, there were the Ark of the Testimony and the mercy seat. These were off-limit places for the common people of Israel; only the priests and the High Priest could enter the places according to the system of the Tabernacle. It is written, *"Now when these things had been thus prepared, the priests always went into the first part of the tabernacle, performing the services. But into the second part the high priest went alone once a year, not without blood, which he offered for himself and for the people's sins committed in ignorance" (Hebrews 9:6-7).* This tells us that in today's age, only those who have the faith of gold that believes in the gospel of the water and the Spirit can live their lives with God while serving Him.

What is the meaning of the bread placed on the table of showbread? It means the Word of God. What does the altar of incense mean then? It tells us of prayers. Inside the Most Holy, there was the Ark of the Testimony, and the mercy seat, made of pure gold, was put above the Ark. The cherubim stretched out their wings above, covering the mercy seat with their wings, and they faced one another toward the mercy seat. This was the mercy seat, the place where God's grace was bestowed. Inside the Ark of the Testimony, the two stone tablets into which the Ten Commandments were carved, the sprouted staff of Aaron, and a jar filled with manna were placed. The Ark was covered by a gold covering (the mercy seat), and above it the cherubim were looking down toward the mercy seat.

Where Do Those Who Received the Remission of Sin Live?

The place where those who received the remission of sin live is inside the Sanctuary. The Sanctuary was built with 48 boards, all of which were overlaid with gold. Think about it. When you are looking at the golden wall not of just a handful, but of 48 golden boards, how brilliantly would it shine? As the interior of the Sanctuary and all its utensils were made of pure gold in this way, they shined brilliantly.

The altar of burnt offering and the laver in the outer court of the Tabernacle were all made of bronze, and the fence of the court was made of the pillars overlaid with silver and fine white linen. In contrast, all the utensils inside the Sanctuary were made of gold; the lampstand was golden, and so was the table of showbread. As all the items in the Sanctuary and its three-sided walls were thus made of pure gold, the inside of the

Sanctuary always shined brilliantly in golden radiance.

That the inside of the Sanctuary thus shined brilliantly in golden radiance tells us that the saved saints live their precious lives of faith inside God's Church. The saints who live in their faith in the gospel of the water and the Spirit are like the pure gold found in the Sanctuary. The life that such saints live inside the Sanctuary is the blessed life that dwells in the Church, feeds on the Word of God, prays to and praises Him, and goes before the throne of God and is clothed in His grace everyday, all through the Church. This is the life of faith inside the Sanctuary. You must take it to your hearts that only the righteous who have been saved through the gospel of the water and the Spirit can live this precious life of faith inside the Sanctuary.

God Divided the Inside and Outside of the Sanctuary Clearly

As most houses have fences, the court of the Tabernacle also had a fence made of 60 pillars and surrounded by the hangings of fine white linen. At the east of the court, a gate made of blue, purple, and scarlet thread and fine woven linen was placed for all to see, measuring as long as 9 m in width.

In studying the Tabernacle, we must realize clearly what is the brilliant faith that God wants from us, what kind of faith is the faith of the saved, and, through the materials used for the Tabernacle, how our Lord has saved us. To learn what is the golden and brilliant faith captured inside the Sanctuary, we must first look carefully at the laver, the altar of burnt offering, and the fence that were placed in the outer court of the Tabernacle, and all the materials used for them. By doing so, we can find out with what kind of faith we can enter into the brilliantly golden and radiant Sanctuary.

What were in the outer court of the Tabernacle? There were the laver and the altar of burnt offering. And it was surrounded by 60 wooden pillars, and on these pillars the hangings of fine linen were placed as the court's fence. The pillars of this fence was made of acacia wood, which, despite its hardiness, was very light. The pillars made of this wood was approximately 2.25 m high, making it impossible for most people with normal heights to peek into the inside of the Tabernacle from the outside of the fence of the outer court. If something was deliberately placed to step on, one could possibly see inside the court, but without such help, it was impossible to peek inside. This tells us that through our own man-made efforts, we can never enter into the Kingdom of God.

At the bottom ends of the wooden pillars of the outer court, bronze sockets were placed, and their tops were capped with silver capitals. As the pillars could not stand on their own, silver bands clasped steadily the adjacent pillars to each other. And to support the pillars firmly in cross-directions, the silver hooks placed in the silver cover of the pillars were tied to the bronze pegs with the cords (Exodus 35:18).

What Were the Materials Used for the Gate of the Court of the Tabernacle?

The materials used for the gate of the court of the Tabernacle were blue, purple, and scarlet thread and fine woven linen. The height of the gate was 2.25 m, and its width was about 9 m. It was a screen woven of blue, purple, and scarlet thread and fine woven linen, which was hung on four pillars. As such, whenever one tried to enter into the court of the Tabernacle, he/she could easily find its gate.

The materials of blue, purple, and scarlet thread and fine woven linen used for the gate of the Tabernacle manifest that God would save us from all our sins through the four works of His Son Jesus. All the 60 wooden pillars and the fine linen of the fence of the court of the Tabernacle also manifest clearly through what method God would save you and me from our sins through His Son Jesus.

Through the gate of the outer court of the Tabernacle, in other words, God is revealing the mystery of salvation to us clearly. Let us once again go over the materials used for the gate of the court of the Tabernacle: blue, purple, and scarlet thread and fine woven linen. These four threads are critically important for us to be saved by believing in Jesus. If these materials were not important, the Bible would not have recorded them in so much detail.

All the materials used for the gate of the court of the Tabernacle were absolutely necessary for God to save you and me. However, the fact that the gate was woven of the blue, purple, and scarlet thread and the fine woven linen without fail is of utmost importance for God to save sinners, because these four threads were the very revelation of God's perfect salvation. This is how God determined. This is why God showed the model of the Tabernacle to Moses on the Mountain Sinai and told him to make the gate of the court of the Tabernacle accordingly.

What Are the Meanings of the Blue, Purple, and Scarlet Thread and the Fine Woven Linen?

The gate of the Holy Place was made of a curtain woven of blue, purple, and scarlet thread and fine woven linen, and the veil between the Holy Place and the Most Holy was also woven of these four threads. Not only this, but the ephod and the breastplate of the High Priest were also woven of blue, purple, and scarlet thread and fine woven linen. What, then, do the blue, purple, and scarlet thread and the fine woven linen tell us? What exactly do these blue, purple, and scarlet thread and fine woven linen, which were absolutely necessary for our Lord to save us, say to us? We must make sure to examine this issue closely.

First of all, the blue thread tells us of the baptism of Jesus Christ. Those who are ignorant of the significance of baptism do not know that the blue thread refers to the baptism of Jesus Christ. As such, those who are not born again generally claim that the meaning of the blue thread is, "Jesus Christ is God Himself, and He came to this earth in the flesh of a man." Others, on the other hand, claim, "the blue thread just means the Word." However, the Bible tells us that the blue thread means "Jesus' baptism through which He accepted the sins of the world onto Himself after coming this earth." The Scripture shows us clearly that the blue thread refers to the water baptism that Jesus received from John the Baptist. Reading the Word on the Tabernacle, I came to realize, "Aha, God wants to shows us the importance of our faith in the baptism of Jesus."

The robe worn by the high priest while giving offerings was also woven of blue thread. A plate of gold was hung on the turban that the High Priest wore on his head, and the cord that tied the plate to the turban was also blue. And on this plate of gold, the phrase, *"Holiness to the Lord,"* was engraved. We can see that the blue cord that tied the gold plate on the High Priest's turban clearly manifests the baptism of Jesus that gives holiness to the Lord.

In this way, through the blue chord that tied the plate of gold to the turban, God speaks to us of our true salvation. In other words, the linchpin that gives us holiness is blue, and this is Jesus' baptism. Although the color blue generally reminds us of the blue sky, blue does not refer to only God. Of the blue, purple, and scarlet thread and the fine woven linen, the blue thread surely means the baptism of Jesus Christ. Put differently, the blue thread tells us that Jesus Christ took the sins of all the sinners of this world by being baptized (Matthew 3:15). Had Jesus not taken everyone's sins by being baptized, we the believers would not be able to give "holiness to the Lord." Were it not for the baptism that Jesus received, we could never be clothed in holiness before God.

Do you know the spiritual meaning of God's command to weave the gate of the court of the Tabernacle with blue thread according to the format shown to Moses? The gate of the court leading into the Tabernacle where God dwelt refers to Jesus Christ. No one can enter the Kingdom of Heaven, but through Jesus Christ. The gate of the court, which refers to Jesus, was woven of blue, purple, and scarlet thread and fine woven linen, clearly because God wanted to reveal the truth that leads us to our salvation. The purple thread refers to the Holy Spirit, telling us, "Jesus is the King of kings." The scarlet thread refers to the blood that Jesus shed on the Cross. The blue thread, as just mentioned, refers to the baptism that Jesus received from John the Baptist.

The blue, purple, and scarlet threads therefore tell us of Jesus' baptism, God's incarnation, and His death on the Cross.

The works of Jesus manifested in these three threads give us the faith that enables us to go before Jehovah in holiness. That Jesus, God Himself, came to this earth in the flesh of a man, took the iniquities of sinners upon His own body by being baptized, and vicariously bore the condemnation of all sins and curses by shedding His blood—this is the very spiritual mystery of the blue, purple, and scarlet thread.

Perhaps you had thus far thought of the blue thread only as manifesting God or His Word. But you must now know clearly that the blue thread actually refers to the baptism of Jesus Christ. The baptism through which Jesus accepted all our sins passed onto Him is critically important and cannot left out of His works; as such, from the Tabernacle of the Old Testament, God is telling us of its importance.

Baptism Was the Means by Which Jesus Bore Our Sins

The pillars of the fence of the Tabernacle were made of acacia woods. Bronze sockets were placed at the bottom of these pillars, and silver capitals were capped on top of them. This tells us first that sinners must be judged for their sins. Only those who have been judged once for their sins can be saved. Those who have not been judged yet and therefore are not saved cannot avoid but be condemned to bear the eternal punishment for their sins when they go before God.

As it is written, *"For the wages of sin is death,"* (Romans 6:23) sinners will most certainly be subjected to God's fearful judgment for their sins. Sinners must therefore be judged by God once for their sins, and then live again by being clothed in His grace. This is what being born again is. The faith of the blue thread, that Jesus Christ took all our sins upon Himself through baptism, and the faith of the scarlet thread, that Jesus has delivered all sinners by being judged on the Cross—none other than this faith is what make us die once to our sins and be born again. You must realize that only the eternal condemnation awaits those who, because of their disbelief, cannot pass through the judgment in faith.

The baptism of Jesus was the means by which Christ bore all our sins to save us from our sins. Jesus was baptized by John the Baptist in order to take all our sins upon Himself. Jesus is God Himself, and yet to save us, He came to this earth in the flesh of a man, took all the iniquities of sinners upon Himself by being baptized by John the Baptist, the representative of mankind, and was condemned vicariously on sinners' behalf by giving up His own body on the Cross and shedding water and blood. The gate of the court of the Tabernacle is telling us in elaborate detail about the works that Jesus fulfilled as our Savior. Through the gate of the court of the Tabernacle, God is telling us clearly that Jesus has become the Savior of sinners.

The fine woven linen refers to the Word of the Old and New Testaments, which is this much detailed, and matches one another. How intricately would each strand be knitted to make this fine woven linen? Through the fine woven linen, God is telling us in detail how He has saved us.

When we look at carpets, we see that they are knitted by weaving different threads. Like this, God told the Israelites to make the gate of the court of the Tabernacle by weaving blue, purple, and scarlet thread on fine woven linen. This tell us that Jesus who came to us through the water (baptism), the blood (the Cross), and the Holy Spirit (Jesus is God), which are hidden in the intricate Word of God, is the very door of our salvation. By having the proper faith in Jesus Christ that is revealed in the intricate Word of God and by being clothed in His love, we have now been saved wholly through faith.

Jesus Christ did not save us haphazardly. We can see this when we look at the Tabernacle. Jesus has saved sinners elaborately. We can realize how elaborately He has saved us when we look at only the pillars of the fence. Why, of all numbers, is the number of the pillars of the fence 60? It is because the number 6 refers to man, while the number 3 refers to God. In Revelation 13, the mark of 666 appears, and God tells us that this number is the number of the Beast, and that the wise know the mystery of this number. Therefore, the number 666 means that man acts like God. What is the wish of mankind? Is it not to become like a perfect divine being? If we truly want to become like a divine being, then we must be born again by believing in Jesus and become the children of God. The 60 pillars refer to this implication elaborately.

However, instead of having faith, people commit the boastful, evil act of trying to be partakers of the divine nature through their own efforts. None other than this is the reason why people reinterpret all the Word according to the lust of man and misbelieve in their own man-made thoughts, for they do not have faith but only the lust that stands against God. Because of this lust of the flesh that tries to become whole by themselves and to reach the perfection of their flesh, they end up far removed from the Word of God.

The Word of Salvation Revealed in All the Items of the Tabernacle

For Jesus Christ to save sinners and pull them into the

Sanctuary, all the utensils and materials of the Tabernacle were necessary. The altar of burnt offering was necessary, the laver was necessary, and the pillars, bronze sockets, silver capitals, hooks and silver bands were also all necessary. All these things are the utensils found outside the Sanctuary, and their materials were all necessary to turn a sinner into a righteous.

All these things were necessary to enable sinners to enter and live in the Kingdom of God, but the most important among them was the blue thread (Jesus' baptism). The blue, purple, and scarlet threads were used to make the gate of the court of the Tabernacle. These threads refer to the three works of Jesus that are needed by us when believing in God. First, Jesus came to this earth and took all our sins upon Himself with His baptism; second, Jesus is God (Spirit); and third, Jesus died on the Cross to bear the condemnation of all the sins that He accepted onto Himself through John at the Jordan River. This is the correct order of true faith that is needed for sinners to be saved and become the righteous.

When we read the Bible, we can realize just how intricate our Lord is. We can clearly find out that the One who has saved us so elaborately, strand by strand like the fine woven linen, is none other than God Himself. Furthermore, God made the Israelites to build the gate of the court of the Tabernacle by weaving blue, purple, and scarlet thread on fine linen that was as long as 9 m. As such, God made sure that anyone looking at the Tabernacle, even from far away, could discern the gate of the court of the Tabernacle.

The hangings of the fine white linen hung over the pillars of the court of the Tabernacle manifests God's holiness. As such, we can realize that sinners cannot dare to approach the Tabernacle, and that they can enter into its court only when they are saved by believing in the ministries of Jesus manifested in the blue, purple, and scarlet thread woven into the gate of the court of the Tabernacle. In this way, God has enabled sinners to know that Jesus Christ has blotted out all their sins and saved them through the water, the blood, and the Holy Spirit.

Not only this, but the materials of all the items that make up the Tabernacle, including the gate of its court, also show us the intricate Word needed for God to turns sinners into the righteous. Because God told the Israelites to make the gate of the court of the Tabernacle large enough for everyone to find, and because this gate was made by intricately weaving blue, purple, and scarlet thread on fine linen, God enabled all to understand clearly the important Word that can turn sinners into the righteous.

The gate of the court of the Tabernacle tells us that God has wholly saved us, who were like acacia wood, from sins through the blue thread (Jesus' baptism), the scarlet thread (the blood of the Cross), and the purple thread (Jesus is God). God has determined that only those who clearly believe in this can enter into the Sanctuary, the House of God.

Jesus Christ Is Telling Us

God tells us that to live the golden, brilliantly shining life of faith, we must be washed of all our sins through Jesus' baptism and go before the Lord. This is why God Himself showed the model of the Tabernacle to Moses, built it through Moses, and made the people of Israel to receive the remission of sin through the institution of this Tabernacle. Let us recapitulate the faith that took us through the court of the Tabernacle and into the Sanctuary. Through the court of the

Tabernacle, God continues to speak to us of our faith in the truth that Jesus has saved us through the water, the blood, and the Holy Spirit. The faith in the gate of the court, that it was woven of blue, purple, and scarlet thread, in the High Priest's laying on of hands on the sacrificial lamb and the bloodshed of this sacrificial lamb, and the faith with which the High Priest washed his hands and feet at the laver—all these things let us know that only our faith in the gospel of the water and the Spirit is the faith of pure gold that enables us to enter into the Sanctuary and live there in glory.

Through the Tabernacle, God has permitted all of us to receive the grace of salvation and His blessing. Through the Tabernacle, we can know the blessings that God has bestowed on us. We can realize and believe in the grace of salvation that has enabled us to go before the throne of the grace of God and be saved all at once. Can you realize this? Through the Tabernacle, we can see just how elaborately our Lord has saved you and me, how intricately He planned our salvation, and how definitely He fulfilled it according this plan and has turned us the sinners into the righteous.

Have you, by any chance, been believing in Jesus only vaguely all this time? Did you believe that the color blue only means the sky? Were you only aware of the faith of purple and scarlet colors, that Jesus Christ, the King of kings, came to this earth and saved us on the Cross, and did you believe accordingly? If so, now is the time to find the true faith. I hope that you would all clearly know the baptism of Jesus, the faith of blue color, and thereby realize and believe in the immeasurable grace of salvation that God has given you.

God has not saved us only through the blood and the Holy Spirit. Why? Because God clearly speaks to us of the blue, purple, and scarlet colors, and through these three threads He is telling us exactly how Jesus has saved us. Through the Tabernacle, our God has shown us Jesus' works of salvation in detail. After telling through Moses to build the Tabernacle, through this Tabernacle, God promised that He would save us in this way. As promised, Jesus Christ came in the flesh of a man and took our sins upon Himself by being baptized in the water (blue) of the Jordan River. Through His baptism, Jesus has actually saved sinners from all sins. How intricate, how exactly correct, and how certain our salvation is then!

When we enter into the Holy Place, we can see the lampstand, the table of showbread, and the altar of incense. Before entering the Most Holy, we come to live for a while in this Holy Place that shines brilliantly in gold, being fed with the bread of the Word to our hearts' content. How blessed is this? Before entering the Kingdom of God, we live in His Church as the ones who have been wholly saved by being born again through the gospel of the water and the Spirit. God's Church that gives us the bread of life is the Holy Place.

In the Holy Place—that is, God's Church—there were the lampstand, the table of showbread, and the altar of incense. The lampstand, with its shaft, branches, bowls, ornamental knobs, and flowers, was made in a single piece by hammering a talent of pure gold. The lampstand that was made by hammering a talent of pure gold in this way tells us that we the righteous must unite with God's Church.

On the table of showbread, unleavened bread was placed, symbolizing the bread of the pure Word of God that is free from the evil and filthy teachings of the world. The Sanctuary of God—that is, God's Church—preaches this pure Word of God that is without any leaven, and lives by the pure faith without doing evil before God.

In front of the veil to the Most Holy, the altar of incense

was placed. The altar of incense was where prayers were given to God. Through the utensils in the Sanctuary, God is telling us that when we go before Him, we must have unity, faith in His pure Word, and prayers. Only the righteous can pray, for God listens to only the righteous' prayers (Isaiah 59:1-2, James 5:16). And only those who pray before God can meet Him.

Like this, the Holy Place tells us how glorious it is for us to be saved in God's Church. The key materials used for the Tabernacle—the blue thread (Jesus was baptized), the scarlet thread (Taking all our sins upon Himself through His baptism, Jesus died on the Cross and bore the condemnation of our sins), and the purple thread (Jesus is God)—refer to the faith that we absolutely cannot fail to have. These three constitute the whole of our faith. When we believe that Jesus is the Son of God and God Himself in essence, and that He has saved us, we can then enter into the Holy Place shinning in gold, where God dwells. If we do not believe in the works of Jesus that are manifested in these three threads, then we can never enter into the Holy Place, no matter how ardently we believe in Jesus. Not all Christian can enter into the Most Holy.

Those Who Stay in the Court of the Tabernacle with Mistaken Faith

Today, there are many Christians who are unable to enter into the Holy Place even as they profess their faith. There are, in other words, many people who try to be saved with their blind faith. None other than those who think that they can be saved just by believing in the blood of Jesus Christ, and that He is God Himself and the King of kings, are precisely such people. They believe in Jesus simplistically. Believing only in the blood of Jesus, they stand before the altar of burnt offering and pray blindly, "Lord, I'm still a sinner today. Forgive me, Lord. I give You all my thanks, Lord, for being crucified and dying in my place. Oh, Lord, I love You!"

After doing this in the morning, they go back to their lives, and then return to the altar of burnt offering again in the evening and give the same prayer. People who haunt the altar of burnt offering every morning, evening, and month cannot be born again, but fall into the fallacy of believing according to their own thoughts.

They put the sacrificial offering on the altar of burnt offering scorching with red flames and give their offering by fire. Because the flesh is burnt in the flames there, the smell of burning flesh spreads, and black and white smoke continues to rise. The altar of burnt offering is not a place where we cry asking God to make our sins disappear, but it is, in fact, a place that reminds us of the fearful fire of hell.

However, people go to this place every morning and evening, and say, "Lord, I've sinned. Please forgive my sins." They then go back home, satisfied on their own as if they had really been forgiven of their sins. They may even be so happy as to sing, "♫I've been forgiven, ♪you've been forgiven, ♫we've all been forgiven." But such feelings are only ephemeral. In no time, they sin again and find themselves standing before the altar of burnt offering once again, confessing, "Lord, I'm a sinner." Those who commute to and from the altar of burnt offering everyday are, regardless of their professed faith in Jesus, still sinners. Such people can never enter the Holy Kingdom of God.

Who, then, can wholly receive the remission of sin and enter into the Holy Place of God? They are the ones know and believe in the mystery of the blue, purple, and scarlet thread set by God. Those who believe in this can pass by the altar of burnt offering by their faith in the death of Jesus who accepted their sins passed onto Him, wash their hands and feet at the laver and remind themselves that all their sins were passed onto Jesus through His baptism, and then enter into the Holy Place of God. Those who believe in the gospel of the water and the Spirit and have received the remission of sin enter the Kingdom of Heave by their faith, for their faith is approved by God.

I hope that you would all realize and believe that the biblical meaning of the blue thread is the baptism of Jesus. There are many who profess to believe in Jesus today, but few go as far as to believe in the water (the blue thread), the baptism of Jesus. This is a deeply saddening phenomenon. It is a cause for a great distress that so many people leave out the most important faith of baptism from their Christian belief, even when Jesus did not merely come to this earth as God and only died on the Cross. I hope and pray that even now, you would all know and believe in the faith of the blue, purple, and scarlet thread, and thereby become the ones who enter the Kingdom of God.

We Must Believe in the Lord Manifested in the Blue, Purple, and Scarlet Thread of the Tabernacle, Its Actual Substance That Has Saved Us

Our Lord has save you and me. When we look at the Tabernacle, we can find out with how elaborate a method the Lord has saved us. We cannot thank Him enough for this. How grateful we are that the Lord has saved us through the blue, purple, and scarlet thread, and that He has also given us the faith that believes in these blue, purple, and scarlet threads!

Sinners can never enter into the Holy Place without being clothed in God's grace and going through His fearful judgment of their sins. How can one who has not been judged of his/her sins ever open the door of the Tabernacle and enter into the Holy Place? They cannot! When such people enter into the Holy Place, they will be cursed to turn blind at a first flash. "Wow, it's so bright in here! Uh-oh, how come I can't see anything? When I was outside, I thought I could see everything in the Holy Place if I were just to enter into the place. Why can't I see anything at all, and why it is so completely dark in here? I could see well when I was outside the Holy Place... I was told that the Holy Place is bright; how come it is even darker?" They cannot see because they have turned spiritually blind, for they do not have the faith of the blue, purple, and scarlet thread. Like this, sinners can never enter into the Holy Place.

Our Lord has enabled us to not be blinded in the Holy Place, but to receive the blessing of living in the Holy Place forever. Through the blue, purple, and scarlet thread and the fine woven linen found in every quarter of the Tabernacle, God has told us exactly the method of our salvation, and according to this Word of prophecy, He has indeed delivered us from all our sins.

Our Lord has saved us through the water, the blood, and the Holy Spirit (1 John 5:4-8), so that we would not turn blind but live forever in His shinning grace. He has saved us through the blue, purple, and scarlet thread and the fine woven linen. Our Lord promised us with the intricate Word of God, and He has told us that He has saved us by fulfilling this promise.

Do you believe that you and I have been saved through the intricate works of Jesus manifested in the blue, purple, and scarlet thread and the fine woven linen? Yes! Have we been saved only haphazardly? No! We cannot be saved without believing in the blue, purple, and scarlet thread.

The blue thread does not refer to God. It refers to the baptism of Jesus with which He took all the sins of every sinner of the world at the Jordan River.

It is possible, incidentally, to stand before the altar of burnt offering without believing in the blue thread, the baptism of Jesus. People may even reach as far as the laver next to the altar of burnt offering, but they cannot enter the Holy Place where God dwells. Those who can open the door of the Tabernacle and enter the Holy Place are only the children of God who have received the remission of sin by wholly believing in the gospel of the water and the Spirit. But the sinful, no matter who, can never enter the Holy Place. How far, then, do we have to enter to reach our salvation? We are saved not when we just enter into the court of the Tabernacle, but when we enter into the Holy Place where God is.

The Difference between the Faith inside the Tabernacle and the Faith outside the Tabernacle

The altar of burnt offering and the laver in the outer court of the Tabernacle were all made of bronze, and the fence was made of wood, silver, and bronze. But when we enter into the Tabernacle, the materials are completely differently. A key characteristic of the Tabernacle is that it is a "house of gold." The three-sided walls were built with 48 boards of acacia wood, all overlaid with gold. The table of showbread and the altar of incense were also made by acacia, and overlaid with gold, and the lampstand was made by hammering a talent of gold. As such, all the utensils inside the Holy Place were made of or overlaid with pure gold.

On the other hand, what were the sockets underneath the boards made of? They were made of silver. While the sockets for the pillars of the fence of the Tabernacle's court were made of bronze, the sockets for the boards of the Tabernacle were made of silver. And while the pillars of the fence of the court were made of wood, the boards of the Tabernacle were made of acacia wood overlaid with gold. But the sockets for the five pillars of the door of the Tabernacle were made of bronze.

Although the sockets for the boards of the Tabernacle were made of silver, the sockets for the pillars of the door of the Tabernacle were cast in bronze. What does this mean? It means that whoever comes into God's presence must be judged for his/her sins. How, then, can we go before God when we are judged and put to death? If we ourselves die, we would not be able to go before God.

Through the bronze used for the sockets of the five pillars of the Tabernacle's door, God is therefore telling us that although we had to be judged for our sins, Jesus took our sins upon Himself through His baptism and was condemned for these sins in our place. We were the ones who had to be condemned for our sins. But someone else bore this condemnation of all our sins in our place. Instead of us, someone else died for us. The One who was vicariously condemned and died in our place is none other than Jesus Christ.

The faith that is manifested by the blue thread is the faith that believes that Jesus Christ accepted all our sins passed onto Him through His baptism and has forgiven us of all sins. As God took the life of Jesus Christ for the condemnation of all our sins passed onto Him through His baptism and has thereby solved away all our sins, we are no longer facing any condemnation for our sins. The faith manifested by the scarlet thread is the faith in the blood that Jesus shed on the Cross. This faith believes that Jesus Christ vicariously bore the condemnation of our sins that we ourselves were supposed to face.

Only those who passed all their sins onto Jesus by believing in His baptism, and have been judged for all their sins by believing in the blood that Jesus shed on the Cross with the death of His flesh because of all these sins, can enter into the Holy Place. This is the reason why the sockets of the door of the Tabernacle was made of bronze. As such, we must believe in the blood of Christ who took all our sins upon Himself through His baptism and was condemned in our place.

God has determined that only those who are convinced of the fact that Jesus Christ who has saved them is God Himself (the purple thread), of the baptism of Jesus (the blue thread), and of the truth that Jesus was vicariously condemned for their sins in their place (the scarlet thread) would be able to enter into the Holy Place. God has permitted only those who have once been judged for all their sins by believing in Jesus, and who believe that Jesus has saved them from all their sins, to enter into the Holy Place.

The sockets of the pillars of the Tabernacle's door were cast in bronze. The bronze sockets have the spiritual meaning that God has allowed sinners who are born as the descendants of Adam to enter into the Holy Place of His dwelling only when they, no matter who they are, have the faith of the blue thread (the baptism of Jesus), the scarlet thread (Jesus' vicarious judgment in sinners' place), and the purple thread (Jesus is God Himself). That the five sockets of the pillars of the door were all made of bronze tells us of the gospel of God, that as written in Romans 6:23, *"For the wages of sin is death, but the gift of God is eternal life in Christ Jesus our Lord,"* Jesus has forgiven all our sins with the water, the blood and the Spirit.

We Must Not Ignore But Believe in the Word and God

Believing in Jesus does not mean that you are unconditionally saved. Nor does attending your church mean that you have unconditionally been born again. Our Lord says in John 3 that only those who are born again of water and the Spirit can see and enter the Kingdom of God. Jesus decisively told Nicodemus, a leader of Jews and a faithful believer of God, "You are a teacher of Jews, and yet do not how to be born again? Only when one is born again of water and the Spirit can he/she see and enter the Kingdom of God." People who believe in Jesus can be born again only when they have the faith of the blue thread (Jesus took all our sins upon Himself at once when He was baptized), the scarlet thread (Jesus died for our sins), and the purple thread (Jesus is the Savior, God Himself, and the Son of God). As such, through the blue, purple, and scarlet thread found in every quarter of the Tabernacle, all sinners must believe that Jesus is the Savior of sinners.

It is because many people believe in Jesus without believing in this truth that they are neither able to be born again nor know the Word of being born again. Our Lord has clearly told us that even if we profess to believe in Jesus, if we are not born again, then we can never enter the Holy Place, the Kingdom of the Father, nor live a proper life of faith.

In our man-made thoughts, we may wonder how nice it

would be if all Christians were approved to be born again no matter how they believe. Is it not so? If we could be saved just by calling on the name of Jesus and professing our faith in Him just in words without even knowing the details of what He did to save the mankind, people would find it amazingly easy to believe in Jesus. We may thank Him whenever we meet a new Christian, singing, "♫I've been forgiven; ♪you've been forgiven; ♫we've all been forgiven." "Since there are so many believers, what's the point of witnessing? Things are just fine as they are. Isn't this just wonderful?" If this were indeed the case, people would think of salvation too easily, since whoever calls on the name of the Lord can be saved, and their salvation would come even if they live in whatever way they wish. But God told us that we can never be born again with such blind faith. On the contrary, He told us that those who claim to have been saved without even knowing the gospel of the water and the Spirit are all practicing lawlessness.

What Is Born again Is Your Spirit, Not Your Flesh

Jesus became a man, came to this earth, and has saved us through the gospel of the water and the Spirit. Joseph, Jesus' father in the flesh was a carpenter (Matthew 13:55), and Jesus served His family under this carpenter father, Himself working as a carpenter for the first 29 years of His life. But when He turned 30, He had to begin His divine works, that is, carry out His public ministries.

As Jesus thus had both divine and human nature, we the born again righteous also have two different natures. We have both the flesh and the spirit. However, when one professes to believe in Jesus even as his/her spirit is not born again, then this person is not born again—that is, he/she has no born-again spirit. If one tries to believe in Jesus without being born again in his/her spirit, then this person is merely someone who is trying to be born again in the flesh like Nicodemus, and is never someone who is born again. Although Jesus was God Himself in His substance, He nevertheless was also in the flesh of a man full of weaknesses. As such, when we say that we have been born again, it means that our spirits have been born again, not our flesh.

If all those who profess to believe in Jesus somehow were indeed born again, I would have tried to be known as a benevolent pastor. Why? Because I would not have been so exasperated by those who do not believe in the truth, and therefore I would not have been so blunt in my sermons hoping that they would come to know the truth. I would be known as a well-mannered, noble, benevolent, tender and humorous pastor, explaining how people can become holy in their flesh. Of course, I can beautify my image to be so, but I never do that. It is not because I have no ability to plant in your minds the impression, "This pastor really takes after the holy and merciful image of Jesus." It is because the flesh of a man cannot change, and because being a little kind, benevolent, and merciful in the flesh does not mean that this person is a born-again righteous. No one can be born again in the flesh. It is the spirit, another human element, that must be born again by believing in the Word of God.

When you believe in Jesus, you must know the truth. *"You shall know the truth, and the truth shall make you free" (John 8:32).* Only the truth of God makes us born again, frees our souls from the bondage of sin, and makes us born again as the righteous. Only when we know, believe, and preach the Bible properly can we enter into the Holy Place and live our lives of true faith, as well as go to the mercy seat of the Most Holy. The gospel of the water and the Spirit that makes our souls born again is the truth, and our faith in this has forgiven us of all our sins and allows us to live in the realm of faith with God. The gospel of the water and the Spirit that is in our hearts enables us to live as the born-again children of God in the spiritual and shinning realm with the Lord in happiness.

Believing in Jesus blindly is not the proper faith. Looking from a human perspective, I have many shortcomings. I am not just saying this with my lips, but whenever I do something, I actually come to realize that I have many shortcomings. For instance, when I am preparing for a Bible camp so that the participating saints and new comers would hear the Word in comfort, be inspired in their hearts by the grace of God, receive the blessing of being born again, and return after having rested in both their bodies and hearts, I find out that there are so many things that I failed to think of and to prepare beforehand. Things that would been easily taken care of by giving just a little bit more attention and care always appear when the preparation time is over and the camp is about to begin. I wonder to myself why I had not thought of such things before and prepared them in advance, when if I had been just a little more attentive and careful in my planning of the Bible camp, the saints and the new souls would have heard the Word well, been saved, and spent a good time. Also, even when I work the whole day, because of the lack of efficiency on my part, there are many times when the results do not match my efforts. I myself am well-aware of the fact that I have far too many shortcomings.

"Why can't I do this? Why didn't I think of this? All that I have to do is be just a bit more attentive, and yet why is it that I can't do this?" When I am actually serving the gospel, I realize my shortcomings very often. So I recognize myself and admit, "This is who I am. This is how insufficient I am." I am not just saying this only with my lips, and I am not pretending to be modest, but I am, in fact, someone who cannot tie the loose ends of even small affairs properly but go about haphazardly. Looking at myself, I really feel my many shortcomings.

We Receive Holiness through the Faith of the Blue Thread

When people think of themselves, they feel like they can do everything well without making any mistakes. But when they actually tackle a task, their true competence and shortcomings are clearly revealed. They find out that they are truly insufficient and that they cannot help but sin and make mistakes. Also, when people think that they are doing okay, they delude themselves thinking that they are going to the Kingdom of God because of how good their faith is.

But the flesh never changes. There is no flesh without shortcomings, and it always does wrong and reveals its shortcomings. If, by any chance, you think that you can go to the Kingdom of our Lord because of some good that your flesh has done, you must realize that no matter what it is that your flesh had done well, it is absolutely useless before God. The only thing that enables us to enter the Lord's Kingdom is our faith in the Word of truth—the blue, purple, and scarlet thread, that the Lord has saved us. Because our Lord has saved us through the blue, purple, and scarlet thread, we can enter the Holy Place only by believing in this.

Had God not saved us through the blue, purple, and scarlet thread, we would all never be able to enter the Holy Place. No matter how strong our faith might be, we cannot enter it. Why? Because if this were the case, it would mean that our faith of the flesh must be good everyday for us to be able to enter. If we can enter the Kingdom of God only when our faith is good enough everyday, how can we, who have such weak flesh, ever make our faith good everyday and be able to enter it? When there is no way for us to receive the remission of sin by ourselves, and when we have no faith to turn around everyday whenever we sin, how can we ever make our faith good enough to enter the Kingdom of God? Our bodies would have to be holy bodies that do not sin at all to begin with, or we would have to give our prayers of repentance and fasting everyday, but whose body is ever holy and who can ever do this?

Had God not saved us through the blue, purple, and scarlet thread, there would be no one among us who would be able to enter the Kingdom of Heaven. We are such that our faith may be good one moment but disappear the next moment. When our faith becomes good only to disappear again repeatedly, we get confused whether or not we really have faith, and end up losing even the faith that we first had. Ultimately, we become even more sinful long after first believing in Jesus. But Jesus has perfectly saved us, the insufficient sinners, according to His plan of salvation manifested in the blue, purple, and scarlet thread and the fine woven linen. He has given us the remission of our sins.

Only when we have this evidence can we put the golden plate, "holiness to the Lord," to our turban like the High Priest (Exodus 28:36-38). We can then carry out our priesthood. Those who can testify their "holiness to the Lord" to people while they serve Him as His priests are the ones who have the evidence in their hearts that they have received the remission of sin through the gospel of the water and the Spirit.

A golden plate was attached to the High Priest's turban, and what tied this golden plate to the turban was also a blue cord. Why, then, did God say that the turban should be tied with this blue cord? What was needed for our Lord to save us was the blue thread, and this blue thread refers to the baptism that Jesus received to take all our sins upon Himself. Had the Lord not blotted out our sins by taking them upon Himself in the New Testament through His baptism, the same form as the Old Testament's laying on of hands, we cannot receive holiness from Jehovah no matter how well we believe in Jesus. This is why the golden plate was tied to the turban with a blue cord. And everyone who sees the High Priest with the golden plate into which "holiness to the Lord" is engraved can remind him/herself that they must be holy before God by receiving the remission of their sins. And it makes people think how they can be holy before God.

We, too, must then recall how we have become the righteous. How have we become the righteous? Let's read Matthew 3:15. *"But Jesus answered and said to him [John], 'Permit it to be so now, for thus it is fitting for us to fulfill all righteousness.' Then he allowed Him."* Jesus has saved us all from our sins by being baptized. Because Jesus took our sins upon Himself with His baptism, those who believe in this are sinless. Had Jesus not been baptized, how could we even dare to say that we are sinless? Did you receive the remission of sin only by your confession of faith in Jesus' death on the Cross with your sincere tears in your eyes? There are so many people who, finding it difficult to be saddened by the death of Jesus, someone whom they have no relation whatsoever, try to squeeze tears by thinking of the death of their grandparents, the difficulties they had when they fell ill, or the hardships and sufferings of their own past. Whether you feign to cry like this, or you are truly saddened by the crucifixion of Jesus, your sins can never be blotted out in this way regardless.

As the golden plate with the engraving of "holiness to the Lord" was tied with a blue cord to the High Priest's turban, what blots out our sins and makes us holy is the baptism of Jesus. Our hearts received the remission of sin because Jesus took all our sins upon Himself with His baptism, because Jehovah burdened all our sins onto Him, and because all the sins of the world were passed onto Jesus through His baptism. No matter how devoid of emotion our hearts might be, and no matter how insufficient we might be in our acts, we have become the righteous and been save perfectly by the Word of the blue thread written in the Bible. When we look at our flesh, we cannot be dignified, but because the faith of the blue, purple, and scarlet thread is in our hearts—that is, because we have the perfect gospel of the water and the Spirit that tells us that Jesus took all our sins upon Himself through baptism and bore our condemnation on the Cross—we can boldly and fearlessly speak of the gospel. It is because we have the gospel of the water and the Spirit that we can live by our faith as the righteous, and also preach this righteous faith to people.

We cannot thank enough for the grace of our Lord. As our salvation did not come by haphazardly, we are even more thankful for it. The salvation that we received is not a trivial one that just about anyone can receive even if he/she does not believe properly. Calling upon the Lord at one's own whim, saying, "Lord, Lord," does not mean that everyone who does so can be saved. Because we have in our hearts the evidence that our sins have disappeared through the gospel of the water and the Spirit, that the Lord has saved us elaborately with the blue, purple, and scarlet thread and the fine woven linen, we are so thankful for this great salvation.

The Bible tells us that everyone who believes in Jesus Christ the Son of God has the witness in his/her heart (1 John 5:10). If there is no witness in our hearts, we would be turning God into a liar, and so we must all have the conclusive evidence in our hearts. As such, there is no reason to be recoiled if some people challenges you and demands, "Show me the proof that you have been saved. You say that when people receive the remission of sin, they receive the Holy Spirit as a gift, and that there is a clear evidence of salvation. Show me this evidence." You can show the evidence boldly as the following: "I have in me the gospel of the water and the Spirit with which Jesus has saved me wholly. Because I have been saved perfectly by Him, I have no sin."

If you do not have the evidence of your salvation in your hearts, then you are not saved. No matter how ardently people might believe in Jesus, this in itself does not constitute their salvation. This is only an unrequited love. It is a love that has no regard for how the other person might be feeling. When someone whom we cannot love has a fluttering heart, expects something from us, feels love, and looks at us as if he/she is dying to be loved, it does not mean we have to love this person in return. Likewise, God does not embrace into His arms those who have not received the remission of their sins just because their hearts are aching for Him. None other than this is the unrequited love of sinners for God.

When we love God, we must love Him by believing in His Word in the truth. Our love for Him must not be one-sided. We must tell Him our love for Him, and we must first find out whether He truly loves us or not before we love Him. If we give all our love to the other person who really does not love us, all that we end up with is a broken heart.

Our Lord has clothed us in the glory of salvation from our

sins so that we would not be condemned for them. He has allowed us to enter the Kingdom of God and to live with God, and He has given us the gift that enables us to receive the remission of sin through the grace of God. God's salvation has brought to us countless spiritual blessings of Heaven. This salvation alone that God has given us, in other words, has enabled us to receive all these blessings from Him.

The Salvation that Jesus Himself Has Brought to Us

Our Lord has saved us through the blue, purple, and scarlet thread. He has given us salvation made of three different threads. This salvation of the blue, purple, and scarlet thread is none other than the gift of salvation given by God. It is this gift of salvation that enables us to enter and live in the Holy Place.

The gospel of the water and the Spirit has turned you and me into the righteous. It allowed us to come into God's Church and live a life of purity. And the true gospel also enabled us to feed on the spiritual Word of God and receive His grace. It has also allowed us to go before the throne of the grace of God and pray, and thereby given us the faith with which we can take the abundant grace bestowed by God as our own. By our salvation alone, God has made such great blessings ours. This is why salvation is so precious.

Jesus told us to build our houses of faith on the rock (Matthew 7:24). This rock is none other than our salvation coming through the gospel of the water and the Spirit. As such, we must all live our lives of faith by being saved—become the righteous by being saved, enjoy eternal life by being saved, and enter Heaven by being saved.

The end times of this world are nearing us. In this age, therefore, people have even more reason to be saved by the exact Word. There are some people who say that one can be saved just by believing in Jesus roughly without knowing the faith of the blue, purple, and scarlet thread, and that there is no need to talk about the life of faith, for it suffices to be saved in this way.

However, the reason why I repeatedly say this is because only those who have received the remission of sin in their hearts can live their lives of faith that God approves. Because the heart of every saint who received the remission of sin is the holy temple where the Holy Spirit dwells, he/she must live his/her life of faith in order not to defile this holiness.

How the righteous live their lives is on a whole different dimension from how sinners live. From God's standpoint, how sinners live is completely below His standard. Their lives are filled by only hypocrisy. They try very hard to live according to the Law. They set their own standards of how they should walk, how they should live their lives, how they should talk, and how they should laugh.

But this is far removed from the life of faith that the righteous live. God tells the righteous in detail, "Love the Lord your God with all your heart and strength and love your neighbors as you love your own body." This is the mode of life that God has given to the righteous. It is proper for us the righteous to live our lives by loving God with all our hearts, and by following His will with all our strength and will. To save our neighbors, we must make countless investments in His works. This is the life of Christians.

If we remain at a level where we think that all that matters is that we ourselves do not sin, then we cannot follow the faithful life of the born-again Christians. Before I was born again, I had led a legalistic life of faith in a conservative Presbyterian denomination, and so as far as the life of the Law was concerned, I tried to keep it thoroughly. Nowadays, people tend to no longer do so, but because I have been leading my religious life from long ago, I had been very apt at keeping the Law in my everyday life. I was so thoroughly obedient to the Law that I never worked on the Lord's day, as the Law commands that the Sabbath should be remembered and kept holy, to the extent that I didn't even get into a car ever on Sundays. If I were to demand you to live like I did, there would be virtually no one who could live such a legalistic life. This was how legalistic my life had been before I was born again. However, no matter how piously I had spent my religious days, that had nothing to do with God's will and was absolutely of no use.

Readers, do you have the faith of the blue, purple, and scarlet thread? Because Jesus' salvation is contained in these three threads, we can enter into the Holy Place by our faith. Our salvation was fulfilled over 2,000 years ago. Jesus Christ, even before we came to know Him, already took upon all our sins upon Himself by being baptized and bore the condemnation of our sins by dying on the Cross.

Salvation from Sin Is Set in Jesus Christ

When those who are not born again enter into the Tabernacle, they do not enter through the gate of its court, but they climb over the fence illegally. They say, "Why is the fine linen of the fence so white? It's so burdensome. They should have colored it with some red and blue. It's what's fashionable nowadays. But this fence is just too white! It sticks out too much. And why is it so high? It's over 2.25 m. My own height does not even reach 2 m; how am I supposed to get inside when the fence is so high? Well, I can climb over using a ladder!"

Such people are trying to enter with their good deeds. They climb up the fence of the court of the Tabernacle with their offerings, charitable works, and patience, and they jump off the fence, saying, "I can surely leap down 2.25 m in any way." So having climbed into the court of the Tabernacle, they look back and see the altar of burnt offering. They then take their eyes off the altar and look toward the Holy Place, and the first thing that they see is the laver laying in front of it.

The height of the pillars of the fence of the Tabernacle's court is 2.25 m, but the height of the pillars and the screen of the door of the Holy Place where God dwells is 4.5 m. People can enter into the court of the Tabernacle by their will if they have enough determination. But even if they leap over the 2.25 m high fence and enter into the court of the Tabernacle, when they try to enter into where God dwells, they will encounter the 4.5 m high pillars and a screen of the door of the Holy Place. People can leap over 2.5 m with their own effort. But they cannot leap over 4.5 m set by God. This is their limit.

This means that when we first believe in Jesus, we can believe merely as a religion. Also, some people can believe in Jesus as their Savior by their own will, and believe that the Savior is only one of the four great sages. Regardless of how people believe, they can have their own faith of whatever way they choose, but they cannot be truly born again through such faith.

To be truly born again, they must pass through the gate of the blue, purple, and scarlet thread by their faith. We are born again before God by believing that Jesus is our Savior and the door of the truth, and that He has saved us through the water, the blood, and the Spirit. The faith that believes in the works of Jesus manifested in the three threads is none other than the faith of the water, the blood, and the Spirit. People are free to believe in something else, but there is absolutely no proof positive that they can be saved and greatly blessed by believing so. Only with our faith in the gospel of the water and the Spirit can we receive the approval of God and the great grace and blessings of God's salvation. The objective of this faith in the gospel of the water and the Spirit is to clothe us in God's grace.

Do you regard the Tabernacle as merely a rectangular shaped court, with a house standing in it? This cannot bring any benefit to your faith. The Tabernacle is telling us about the whole faith, and we must know exactly what this faith is.

Not knowing the Tabernacle well, you might think that the height of the Tabernacle is about the height of its fence, 2.25 m. But this is not the case. Even if we were not to enter into the court but look at the Tabernacle from outside the fence, we would be able to see that the Tabernacle is twice higher than the fence. Though we would not be able to see the bottom of the Tabernacle, we would still see its door clearly, telling us that the Tabernacle stands higher than the fence of its court.

Those who have receive the remission of their sins by believing in Jesus and thereby entered into the gate of the court of the Tabernacle must confirm their proper faith at the altar of burnt offering and the laver, and then enter into the Holy Place. To enter into the Holy Place, there must be self-denial without fail. The utensils inside the Holy Place must be distinguished from all the utensils found outside the Holy Place.

Do you know what Satan hates the most? He loathes that the demarcation line between the inside and outside of the Holy

Place is drawn. Because God works among those who divide the inside and outside of the Holy Place, Satan hates that such a line is drawn and tries to prevent people from drawing this line. But remember this: God clearly works through those who draw this demarcation line of faith. God is please by such people who draw this dividing line, and He bestows His blessings on them so that they can live inside the Holy Place with their brilliant faith.

Believe that all the utensils in the outer court of the Tabernacle and all the materials used for them have been prepared and prearranged by God so that people can receive the remission of their sins. And when you enter into the Holy Place by believing in this, God will bestow on you even greater grace and blessings.

The Mercy Seat Is the Place Where the Grace of Salvation Is Received

In the Most Holy, two cherubim stretching their wings looked down from above the lid that covered the Ark of the Testimony. The space between the two cherubim is called the mercy seat. The mercy seat is where God bestows His grace on us. The covering of the Ark of the Testimony was stained by blood, as the High Priest sprinkled the blood of the sacrifice given for the people of Israel on this mercy seat for seven times. God thus descended on the mercy seat and bestowed His mercy on the people of Israel. To those who believe in this, God's blessings, protection, and guidance begin. From then on, they become the true people of God and are eligible to enter into the Holy Place.

Among the many Christians of this world, there are some

whose faith has allowed them enter into the Holy Place, while others do not have such faith with which they can enter into the Holy Place. What kind of faith do you have? We need the faith that can draw the clear line of salvation and enter into the Holy Place of God, for by only doing so can we be greatly blessed by God.

But it is not that easy to have this kind of faith. Because Satan hates when people draw the clear line of salvation, he constantly attempts to blur this line. "You don't have to believe in that way. Not everyone else believes like that, so why do you place so much importance on it and keep repeating yourself? Take it easy; go with the flow." Saying such things, Satan tries to obscure this clear line of salvation. Also, Satan reveals our weaknesses of the flesh and tries to turn them into troubles. Would you be the ones who listen to the deceptive words of Satan trying to separate us from God? Or would you live your lives by reminding yourself of your salvation daily, uniting with the Church, following the Word of God, leading a life of prayer, and receiving the grace that God bestows on you?

Actually, those who have received the remission of sin like to remind themselves of their salvation. They like to dwell on the gospel of the water and the Spirit over and over. Meditating on the gospel is good and essential to you. Are you not like this? "Gosh, is it that story again, when we have been saved? The story material and the plot might be different, but it's still the same old story. I'm getting so tired of it!"

Is there anyone who might be saying this? I would be sorry if I were to tell the same story about myself everyday, but when the Bible tells us that we should ruminate over our salvation everyday, what can I do? When both the Old and New Testaments speak to us of the gospel of the water and the

Spirit, what is evil before God is for people to actually preach something else other than this. All the Word of the Bible speaks of the gospel of the water and the Spirit. "Salvation, life of faith, faith, spiritual living, fight against Satan, Heaven, glory, grace, blessing, resurrection, eternal life, hope, and the Holy Spirit"—all these key concepts of the saints are related to this true gospel. Speaking of something else other than these is none other than heresy and false teachings. What looks similar but is different in substance is none other than false teachings. Gospels that appear similar outside but are different inside from the gospel of the water and the Spirit are merely the pseudo-gospels of false religions.

How wonderful is it that God's Church spreads the Word of God everyday, not the deceptive words of false religions? It is a blessing that we are united to God's Church, hear and believe in the pure Word of God. By always preaching the gospel of the water and the Spirit, God's Church enables the saints to think of the grace of God everyday, to pray to Him, and revere Him, and to live a life that does not pursue evil. Are you not happy that you have heard once again and believed in the Word of truth that allows you receive the remission of sin? I, too, am very happy.

If I were to be coerced to preach something else other than this gospel of the water and the Spirit, I would suffer greatly. If I were coerced to spread not the Word of salvation but some other man-made teachings, I would want to escape. It is not, of course, because I have nothing else to talk about. There are plenty of other humanistic issues that I can address, but these are all unnecessary and are merely the teachings of corrupting leaven for those of us who are born again.

Only this gospel of the water and the Spirit through which Jesus, God Himself, has saved us is the precious Word of God that gives out its sweetness even as we chew on it over and over again. There are so many other stories that I could tell you, but I like it the most when I am speaking of the gospel of the water and the Spirit that saves us. I get most elated then. I am happiest when I am speaking of this salvation, for this is when I can reminisce about old memories, remind myself of how the Lord has saved me, thank Him once more, and feed again on the bread of salvation.

I am sure that you, too, like it the most when you hear this Word of salvation. Perhaps you might complain that it's the same story everyday, but deep inside, you think, "Now that I heard it again, it's even better. At first, it wasn't that great, but when I continue to hear it, I can see that there is no other story that is as worthy of listening as this one. I thought today's story might be somewhat special, but the conclusion tells me that it was the same story again. But still, I'm happy." I am sure that this is how your hearts feel.

Brothers and sisters, what I am preaching here is the Word of Jesus. Preachers must preach the Word of Jesus. Preaching what Jesus has done for us and spreading the truth of the water and the Spirit through the written Word are none other than what God's Church is supposed to do. We are now leading our lives of faith in the Church. Entering into the Holy Place, lighting under the lampstand with seven branches made by hammering a talent of gold, eating bread in the house of pure gold, praying at the altar of incense, going to the Temple of God, worshipping Him, and living in this house of gold—none other than these are our lives of faith.

You and I are now leading the lives of faith given by God. Receiving the remission of sin and living the lives of faith are what the life inside the golden House of God is all about. *"Even though our outward man is perishing, yet the inward man is being renewed day by day" (2 Corinthians 4:16).* With our faith in the blue, purple, and scarlet thread and the fine woven linen manifested in the Tabernacle, our souls are living in the House of God shinning in gold.

I give my thanks to God forever for saving us from all our sins and condemnation. Hallelujah! ✉

SERMON

2

Our Lord Who Suffered for Us

< Isaiah 52:13-53:9 >
"Behold, My Servant shall deal prudently;
He shall be exalted and extolled and be very high.
Just as many were astonished at you,
So His visage was marred more than any man,
And His form more than the sons of men;
So shall He sprinkle many nations.
Kings shall shut their mouths at Him;
For what had not been told them they shall see,
And what they had not heard they shall consider.
Who has believed our report?
And to whom has the arm of the LORD been revealed?
For He shall grow up before Him as a tender plant,
And as a root out of dry ground.
He has no form or comeliness;
And when we see Him,
There is no beauty that we should desire Him.
He is despised and rejected by men,
A Man of sorrows and acquainted with grief.
And we hid, as it were, our faces from Him;
He was despised, and we did not esteem Him.
Surely He has borne our griefs
And carried our sorrows;
Yet we esteemed Him stricken,
Smitten by God, and afflicted.
But He was wounded for our transgressions,

He was bruised for our iniquities;
The chastisement for our peace was upon Him,
And by His stripes we are healed.
All we like sheep have gone astray;
We have turned, every one, to his own way;
And the LORD has laid on Him the iniquity of us all.
He was oppressed and He was afflicted,
Yet He opened not His mouth;
He was led as a lamb to the slaughter,
And as a sheep before its shearers is silent,
So He opened not His mouth.
He was taken from prison and from judgment,
And who will declare His generation?
For He was cut off from the land of the living;
For the transgressions of My people He was stricken.
And they made His grave with the wicked—
But with the rich at His death,
Because He had done no violence,
Nor was any deceit in His mouth."

The Gospel Is Now Spreading throughout the Entire World

This age is indeed heading toward the end. From politics to economics, everything is running toward the end. In particular, the wind of war is looming large, as the superpowers still try to extend their influence over the rest of the world. Closer to my own home, North Korea recently announced that it was developing nuclear weapons, causing a great upheaval throughout the international community. In such a time of crisis-ridden world, I can only hope that everyone involved in these disputes would be able to resolve all their issues with wisdom, not in foolishness, and come to terms with each other so that all may prosper together.

We must pray everyday, so that God would give us more time to still allow us to spread the gospel more and further. It's not because I am afraid of dying. It is because there still are countries where the true gospel has not been preached yet, and there also are countries where the genuine gospel is now about to blossom. My desire is to continue to spread the original gospel even more, when it is sprouting and blossoming, for the gospel still needs to be preached more and further.

Of course, God makes all things work together for good, but what I am worried about is that the human beings can be so foolish. There are in fact people who threaten others' life even as they have no idea when and how they themselves would face their own death; some of them go even as far as trying to massacre everyone.

I believe that God surely rules the hearts of all the leaders of the world. And I also believe that He would give us peace.

In this age, the people of Israel are still waiting for the Messiah promised to them. They must realize that their Messiah is none other than Jesus. They must recognize Jesus as the Messiah whom they have been waiting for, and believe in Him as such. In not too distant future, the gospel that pleases our Lord will soon enter Israel, as well as other countries where the door of the gospel has not been opened yet. In fact, the gospel is being spread through the whole world so well that it is blossoming fully in this age of the end times.

I've been told that a theological seminary in Bangladesh has made our English publications a required reading for its students to earn their degrees. Having come across the gospel of the water and the Spirit for the first time, the students at this seminary will now all receive the remission of their sins, before they even have a chance to be marveled.

Like this, I hope first of all that all the theologians of the world would receive the remission of sin by knowing and believing in the gospel of the water and the Spirit. And those of us who have received the remission of sin prior to them must pray endlessly for this to happen. Not only must we pray, but we must also live our lives by faith.

The Messiah Came to This Earth about 700 Years after the Prophecy of Isaiah

Isaiah was a prophet who lived about 700 years before the birth of Jesus Christ on this earth. Though he actually preceded the coming of Jesus Christ by 700 years, because he knew many things about the Messiah, Isaiah prophesied all about how the Messiah would come and how He would do His work of salvation, as if he had seen the Messiah with his own eyes. From Isaiah 52:13 and throughout chapters 53 and 54, Isaiah continuously prophesied, in detail, how the Messiah would save the mankind from sin. It is simply marvelous that he had so accurately prophesied that Jesus Christ would indeed come to this earth, take upon all the sins with His baptism, shed His blood on the Cross, and thereby bring salvation to all. And after 700 years passed by since Isaiah's prophecy was made, Jesus Christ in fact came to this earth and fulfilled all His works exactly as prophesied by Isaiah.

Isaiah prophesied that the Messiah would come to this earth and act in wisdom. As prophesied in Isaiah 52:13, *"Behold, My Servant shall deal prudently; He shall be exalted and extolled and be very high."* Because Jesus Christ came to this earth in the flesh of a man and actually took upon all the sins of the world Himself with His baptism, He could give up His life on the Cross, and thereby be judged for all the sins of the entire mankind. Just as Isaiah had prophesied, everything was indeed dealt prudently. Because of Jesus Christ, all the sins of mankind have indeed disappeared, dealt prudently, and His name has in fact become very high, exalted and extolled, all in accordance to what had been prophesied before. What Isaiah had prophesied about Christ actually came true.

However, when our Lord came to this earth, the people of Israel did not recognize Him properly. Even though our Lord came to this earth and actually took upon the sins of the world including those of the Israelites, died on the Cross, and rose from the dead again, the people of Israel did not even believe in the baptism of the Messiah, nor in His blood. In fact, the Israelites did not recognize that this Messiah was already born in their nation, and that with His baptism and Cross He has taken care of not only the sins of the Israelites, but also the sins of the entire mankind. They did not realize that this Jesus Christ was in fact the Son of God, the actual Messiah of the people of Israel. The Israelites must now properly realize that Jesus is indeed the Messiah whom they have been waiting for all these years.

The Sufferings of Jesus Were to Make the Sins of the World Disappear

When Jesus came to this earth, He in fact suffered an extreme affront beyond any description. As shown in Isaiah 53, the Messiah indeed seemed to be a man of sorrow. By taking upon so many sins of ours, He was afflicted greatly—so much so that the Bible tells us that we even hid, as it were, our faces from Him.

But few actually recognized Jesus as the Messiah. Because He had been afflicted too much by the people of His age, many failed to recognize and believe in Jesus Christ the Messiah as the Savior. Our Lord indeed came to this earth in obedience to the Father's will to fulfill His work of saving the mankind from the sins of the world, and to do this work, He was in fact greatly oppressed. It was not enough for Him to come to this world of His own creation in the flesh of a man, whom He Himself had made in His own image, but He was even despised, ridiculed, stricken, and oppressed, so much so that the Scripture tells us that we hid our faces from Him, for it was too much too bear. Far from being revered as the Messiah on this earth, He was treated and oppressed as if He were insane, whose humility could not even begin to be described with words. As we turn our faces away when we see someone profoundly humiliated and embarrassed, the Messiah was oppressed before His own creations, so much so that the Israelites at that time hid their faces from Him.

When Jesus came to this earth, what did He look like? When the Messiah came to this earth, He in fact was like a tender plant, as a root out of dry ground. There was not much to speak of, in other words, in His outside appearance. In fact, even when we compare our Lord to ourselves, there was little that was handsome or attractive in this Messiah. Our Messiah's outward appearance was such that there really was nothing to boast of.

When the Messiah did come to this earth, there was indeed no beauty in His appearance that we might desire or revere Him. But regardless of this appearance, as our Messiah, He dealt prudently, received the laying on of hands from John to take all our sins onto His body according to the sacrificial system, was crucified and shed His blood, rose from the dead again, and thereby saved us from all our sins. Because this Messiah took all our sins upon Himself by actually being baptized by John, He could be crucified and shed His blood for us.

As Isaiah 53:3 says, *"He is despised and rejected by men, A Man of sorrows and acquainted with grief. And we hid, as it were, our faces from Him; He was despised, and we did not esteem Him."* Because our Messiah had to come to this earth and make all the sins of the world disappear by receiving the laying of hands and shedding His blood, He had to actually be suppressed in such a manner by the people of Israel and Roman soldiers.

The Oppression of the Messiah Was Prophesied about 700 Years Ago

That the Messiah would have to in fact come to this earth, be baptized by John, shed His blood on the Cross, and rise from the dead again had already been prophesied by the prophet Isaiah about 700 years prior to the birth of Christ. As the Prophet Isaiah had prophesied about the coming Messiah, Jesus Christ did indeed come to this earth exactly as prophesied. That is, the Messiah Jesus was born to a virgin on a manger in humbleness, took upon the sins of the world with His baptism received from John the Baptist, went to the Cross, where He shed His blood and died for our salvation, and in three days rose from the dead again.

Just as hands were laid on the head of the sacrificial offering and its blood was shed on the Day of Atonement

(Leviticus 16), when a year's sins were thus atoned, Jesus indeed took upon all our sins with His baptism received from John and shed His blood and died on the Cross, all in accordance to the actual Word of prophecy. After bearing all the sins of the world with His baptism, Jesus in fact faced three years of suffering during His public life. The reason why Jesus the Messiah was crucified is because, with His baptism from John the Baptist, all the sins of the world were passed onto Him, and this is also why He thus was despised, persecuted, and oppressed by everyone.

In fact, people did not only deny that Jesus was the Messiah, but also some of the Jews and the Romans hated and persecuted Jesus beyond any description. He was hated and rejected by them to an extreme.

Jesus in fact took upon all the sins of mankind all at once by receiving His baptism from John the Baptist at the Jordan River, and He then shed His blood on the Cross. The Messiah was baptized by John and shed His blood on the Cross to fulfill His Father's will. He was stripped naked on the Cross and was spat at. All the surrounding people at that time ridiculed Jesus, taunting Him, "If you really are the Son of God, then come down and save yourself!"

When Jesus began His public life with His baptism, He in fact had to go through many sufferings brought by the mankind. Though Jesus Christ had actually shouldered the sins of the world with His baptism for the sake of mankind, people of those days, unable to fathom this, hated Jesus, who came as their own Messiah, persecuted Him continuously, brought great sufferings to Him, denounced and insulted Him. In fact, Jesus the Messiah was hated so much that the Scripture tells us that He was treated like a worm while on this earth.

Indeed, you have no idea just how much the Pharisees

hated Jesus. These Pharisees could not leave the Messiah alone, who seemed to threaten their leadership and popularity. So they hated the Messiah, always trying to find faults with Him, and did not hesitate to launch all kinds of personal attacks against Him every time their schemes failed. The Messiah was subjected to all kinds of insults and denouncements filled with hatred and evilness. Isaiah thus had prophesied just how the Messiah would be oppressed. We can therefore confirm, from the detailed prophecies of the Prophet Isaiah made over 700 years prior to the coming of the Messiah, just what kind of treatment Jesus would receive in this world.

Did the People Believe in Jesus Christ the Messiah Who Came by Water and Blood?

However, regardless of this oppression, Jesus the Messiah quietly did and completed His works. Now the people of Israel and everyone throughout the whole world must realize and believe that this Messiah is Jesus Christ. To make the sins of the Israelites and of everyone throughout the entire world disappear, the Messiah did indeed receive His baptism in the form of the laying on of hands, was in fact crucified, and thus suffered all His oppressions to an extreme—and by doing so, He has perfectly saved the believers in His ministries from all their sins, and has approved the faith of these believers as whole. Despite the fact that the Messiah came to this world in His humble form, and despite the fact that He was baptized, died on the Cross, and rose from the dead again to make all the sins of everyone disappear, those who believed in Him numbered only a few. For us to live, we must believe that Jesus indeed is our true Savior and Messiah, that He is the Messiah for not only the Israelites, but also for the entire mankind.

Even though Jesus actually took upon our own sins with His baptism and assumed our own sorrows, our own diseases, and our own curses, some people may think, "What sin did He commit to face so much oppression?" But Jesus is, in fact, the sinless Son of God. By bearing all our sins, the Messiah vicariously suffered, in our place, all the curses, sorrows, and oppressions of our sins. Through all the oppressions that Jesus had faced throughout His 33 years of life since coming to this earth, He has saved us from all our sins.

Back then, hearing the Word of God spoken through the Prophet Isaiah, did the people of the time believe in Jesus Christ the Messiah, who came by the water and the Spirit? Who believed in this gospel of the water and the Spirit that we are now preaching? Even now, there are many people who have no interest in the gospel of the water and the Spirit, even though they claim to believe in Jesus.

Here, in the main passage, the Prophet Isaiah is now prophesying that the Son of God would come to this earth, act wisely, take upon all our sins, be judged for them, and thereby save us. But not many have accepted the truth He accomplished. However, I am sure that from now on, all the people of all the nations would recognize Jesus Christ as their Messiah and exalt Him high. Do you now realize that Jesus the Messiah was oppressed because of the sins of the people of Israel, because of the sins of you and me, and because of the sins of the entire mankind? The Prophet Isaiah, who would have wanted you to know and believe in this, thus prophesied the ministry of the Messiah in this way.

The Messiah Was Like a Root out of Dry Ground

This is how the Prophet Isaiah foretold of the coming of Jesus Christ the Messiah, that when He comes to this earth, He would come in such a pitiful form. Isaiah said that the Messiah would *"grow up before Him as a tender plant, And as a root out of dry ground" (Isaiah 53:2).* When Jesus Christ came to this earth in the flesh of a man, He was not someone whom people would actually see anything desirable. He was not a muscular, tall and well-built man, like Arnold Schwarzenegger or Sylvester Stallone. In fact, He was so diminutive that if we had looked at Him, we would actually have felt sorry for Him, pitying and sympathizing with Him. Nevertheless, His Word was like a sharp double-edged sword.

Jesus the Messiah was not only rather poor-looking in His appearance, but He was also poor materially. Joseph, His father of the flesh, was a mere carpenter. A family whose needs were provided by a carpenter, then as now, was not that well-off, far from living in abundance. Only with hard work could carpenters barely get by.

Nor did the Messiah, having come to this earth, attend a school. And so the Pharisees tried to deride Him for it, but they could not do so, since it would only reveal that Jesus Christ the Messiah was indeed the Son of God. Jesus never even set a foot in the Gamaliel's School, the most reputable Jewish school of the time, where one of the greatest scholars of the Law, Gamaliel, had been teaching the Law. In this school, students could learn from the great teachers of the Law, trained not only in the knowledge of this world, but also in the Law itself. But Jesus was not trained in such a school. There is no record whatsoever that He attended a school. Yet despite this, there was nothing about the Law of the Old Testament that the

Messiah did not know, and where the Old Testament taught about the Messiah, He was even more widely knowledgeable and had greater faith than any. There was nothing in what He said that ever was illogical or departed from the Law of God.

Why Did the Messiah Have to Be So Oppressed, Humiliated, and Despised?

To actually become the real Messiah to the people of Israel, and to save them from all their sins and make them God's people, our Messiah came to this earth and willingly embraced all His sufferings, insults, derisions, and scorns. The suffering and contempt that the Messiah actually went through for the sake of the people of Israel were extremely sacrificing and oppressive. The oppression that the Messiah suffered for our sake was such a great suffering that we would have hidden our face from Him. Because Jesus was the Messiah who would save us from our sins and judgment, He did indeed deliver us from our sins by being oppressed and despised beyond any description before all kinds of people. Jesus thus was oppressed in this world.

Because Jesus the Messiah was so greatly oppressed and despised, people of those days could not bear the sight of Him. We must never forget that although Jesus came as your and my Messiah, indeed, as the Messiah of all the mankind, to fulfill and complete the role and the works of this Messiah, He was oppressed greatly, and by being so He has delivered us from our sins and the condemnation of sin.

Even as the Messiah was crucified, people did not cease to mock Him: "Why don't You come down from there? If You are really the Son of God, then just come down from the Cross.

How can You possibly be the Son of God? If You really are this Son of God, then come down and save the thief hung next to You; better yet, come down and save Yourself!" They continued with their ridicule: "Oh, yeah, why don't You turn this stone into bread? If you are the Son of God, give us the proof! Show us the proof so that we can believe. If You can't even do that, what kind of Messiah are You? How pathetic!"

People thus insulted the Messiah, denounced Him, and ridiculed Him endlessly. They stripped Him naked, slapped His face, and spat at Him. Christ suffered the greatest mockery, humiliation, and insults, the likes of which had never been seen before, nor ever seen again. He also was condemned with the punishment of crucifixion, a punishment reserved for the worst kind of criminals at the time. Our Messiah was whipped by the soldiers, both His hands and feet were nailed on the Cross, and spilled out all the blood that He had in His body.

Jesus really bore all such contempt, pain and oppression, so that He could fulfill His ministry as the Messiah, for our own sake. By being crucified, He took upon all our sins, all our curses, all our diseases, and all our punishment of sin. He took in our place all the oppressions that you and I were supposed to bear, and for our own sake He even gave up His own life. This Messiah has now become the Savior for those of us who believe that Jesus indeed is our Savior. He willingly became our Messiah. He came to this earth according to His Father's will, and took upon our sins and the punishment of sin on the Cross for our sake, and rose from the death again—all to save us!

My brothers and sisters, do you think it was easy for Jesus to go through all such suffering and humiliation before all these strangers? If we were in His place, if it had been we who faced all this contempt, of being stripped naked, insulted, tortured, and crucified, not just before our own family or husbands or wives, or even our loved ones, but before our own enemies, we would have gone insane before dying! Christ was crucified, so that everyone could see His humiliation, not in some obscure corner, but high above, so that all could point their fingers and spit at Him.

Even greater suffering, sorrow, and hardship came to Christ before His crucifixion. Before nailing Jesus on the Cross, people made sure that He would go through all kinds of sufferings. He was brought before the multitude and judged in their presence, was spat at, and His face was even slapped by a servant of the high priest. He was spat at! People slapped His face, whipped Him, and stoned Him! Jesus the Messiah went through all this oppression for none other than our own sake!

The Scripture tells us that He was thus oppressed for our sake, saying, *"He was wounded for our transgressions, He was bruised for our iniquities" (Isaiah 53:5).* The Messiah went through such sufferings so that He could deliver all the people including the Israelites from their sins and the condemnation of their sins. This Messiah took care of the sins of the world and the punishment of sin by receiving baptism from John, and completed His ministry as the Messiah by being oppressed by His own people, the Roman soldiers, and the people of many other nations.

God prophesied that the Messiah would save these very people who stood against Him from all their sins—indeed, from all the sins ever committed by the entire mankind—and just as it had thus been prophesied, Jesus Christ indeed came to this earth as this Messiah, actually went through all this oppression, and saved you and me from our sins and the condemnation of our sins by shedding His precious blood.

That we have been saved from sin and the condemnation

of sin by believing in the Messiah did not in fact come without paying the price of sacrifice. It is because Jesus Christ came to this earth and faced all such oppression that we could have now become sinless, and it is because this Messiah was judged for all our sins that we could, just by believing with our hearts, have received the gift of salvation and of the remission of sin, and become the children of God. It is because of our Messiah that we could have become such happy people.

We must thank the Messiah for giving us this happiness and for bestowing us with His blessings. The salvation that the Messiah has given us came to us only through our faith, for though we have not given Him any offering of our own, He Himself gave His priceless offering before God the Father. We must believe that God Himself has indeed saved us by suffering all this oppression, and we must thank Him for it.

Hear, O Israel, Turn around and Believe in Jesus Christ

The people of Israel must repent now and believe in Jesus the Messiah as their Savior. Even until this very moment, the Israelites still do not recognize that their Messiah has already come. Just as it had all been prophesied by the Prophet Isaiah that the Messiah, the Servant of God, would come to this earth, and just as this Word of prophecy foretold us that this Messiah would, coming to this earth, save us all by taking upon all the sins of mankind with His baptism and being crucified on the Cross, Jesus Christ has indeed fulfilled all His works of salvation. The people of Israel must now turn around, and know and believe in this truth. They must admit the sin that their own people committed by crucifying Jesus. And they must recognize their true selves to be simply a mass of sin from their birth, and by believing in this Messiah now they must be saved from all their sins and the condemnation of sin.

There is now no other Messiah. Because Jesus Christ already came as the Messiah, there is no other Messiah. How could there actually be any other Messiah? How could there be another Savior? When the people of Israel go through even more difficulties in the future, would they hope that some kind of Hollywood action hero, like the Superman, would emerge and become their Messiah?

Even from now, the Israelites must recognize Jesus Christ as their Messiah. They must believe that Jesus Christ is indeed their own true Messiah. Their Messiah had already come to this earth 2,000 years ago, and to take upon their sins and to make them the true children of Abraham, He was baptized, just as they had to be circumcised, and was crucified, all so that they would receive the spiritual circumcision. The Messiah became the true Savior of the people of Israel by taking upon their sins with His baptism from John, carrying the Cross and shedding His blood to be oppressed, and rising from the dead again.

The Israelites must repent to believe in the Messiah. They must now believe in Jesus Christ as their Messiah. All that remains to be fulfilled now is for the people of Israel to believe in Jesus Christ as the Savior. They must realize that the Messiah prophesied by Isaiah is this very Jesus Christ. They must realize and believe that this prophesied One is none other than Jesus Himself. The prophecies of the Old Testament have been all fulfilled through Jesus Christ, leaving out neither the smallest letter nor the slightest stroke. In the main passage, it is also said that many nations would be sprinkled.

Isaiah 52:14-15 state, *"Just as many were astonished at you, So His visage was marred more than any man, And His form more than the sons of men; So shall He sprinkle many nations. Kings shall shut their mouths at Him; For what had not been told them they shall see, And what they had not heard they shall consider."*

Coming to this earth, Jesus Christ faced sufferings that were far greater than that of any criminals of this world condemned to death. He sacrificed Himself by taking on more pain and oppression than any criminals of this world, all in order to make the entire mankind His own people. He has saved His people who would receive the remission of sin by believing in Him. This is how He has saved them.

People will hear the wonderful news of salvation, which they had neither heard nor seen before. All those who still have not even heard that the Messiah was Jesus Christ will indeed hear it and believe in it eventually.

Jesus Is the Messiah, Who Once Came and Will Come Again

Today, we are now approaching the end times. It will be an age of death and tribulations. Those who believe in the Messiah, however, actually have no fear of death. On the contrary, they are waiting even more for the happiness of Heaven and their resurrection that would follow their death. That the darkness is descending on the world does not mean that we, the righteous, are also darkened. When this gospel is definitely all spread, the Messiah will in fact return.

Jesus Christ, our Messiah, came to this world as the Lamb of God, as the sacrificial offering, and had His body baptized by John, and gave it up on the Cross. Like a sheep before its shearers, Jesus the Messiah quietly took upon our sins, faced great sufferings by bearing our own judgment of sin on the Cross, rose from the dead again in three days, and thus became the perfect Savior for all those who believe.

Only a few knew that the Messiah was Jesus Christ at the time. There were a few who knew that Jesus Christ became our Messiah by being quietly born unto this world about 2000 years ago, testifying the gospel of the Kingdom for three years after His baptism, dying on the Cross, and rising from the dead again. The few, who looked for and believed in God, testified that our Lord is the true Messiah who quietly fulfilled all His works.

Those servants of God spread the news throughout the whole world that the Messiah has saved us from our sins by coming to this earth and being oppressed. God Himself, in fact, is spreading the gospel of the water and the Spirit by allowing printing techniques to advance, by moving the history of the world, and by making the nations that preach this gospel strong and wealthy.

"Jesus is the Messiah. Jesus is the Messiah. Jesus is the Messiah! If you believe in Jesus as your Messiah, you will be saved. Jesus is the Son of God. Jesus is the Creator who made the whole universe. He is God. He is the Messiah our Savior." The servants of God continued to preach to the people that Jesus is the Messiah, and also about His baptism, His death on the Cross, and His resurrection.

Few Israeli youths had realized that 2,000 years ago, a young man called Jesus came to this earth, and that when He turned 30, He took upon the sins of mankind by being baptized by John. At that time, only Jesus' own disciples knew that He was the Messiah, and this knowledge was shared with only a handful of people who really feared God—all the rest remained oblivious to this truth. All in all, there were only about 500 saints (1 Corinthians 15:6) in this nation of Israel who knew that the Messiah carried the sins of the world to the Cross, that He died on it, and that He rose from the dead again. All others had no idea.

On the fiftieth day since the death of Jesus Christ and His resurrection, the Holy Spirit actually descended upon His disciples. When Christ's disciples were praying in an upper room, the Holy Spirit did indeed descend upon them, making them speak in tongues and testify that the Messiah is Jesus Christ. Then, His disciples, not fearing death, boldly testified, "Jesus is the Messiah. The Messiah is our Savior. The resurrected Jesus is our Messiah." Many people therefore came to believe at this time.

Through Jesus the Messiah, God has indeed saved you and me from all our sins and the condemnation of sin. Because He suffered such great oppression to thus save us from our sins and judgment, we absolutely must believe in Him; those who do not believe must all repent, turn around and believe also; and we must all spread this truth with faith.

The people of Israel, in fact, are now fearful under an extremely tense situation. They must therefore hear this Word of the Tabernacle that God had actually spoken to them. We also are now entering into the end times. The gospel of the water and the Spirit manifested in the sacrificial system of the Tabernacle will in fact surely make its way to the people of Israel. They, too, will come to believe that Jesus Christ is indeed the Messiah that God had spoken of to them.

God had already told the people of Israel about the sacrificial system, and they believed in it. In fact, they still desire to give offerings to God according to this Tabernacle's sacrificial system. Among the Israelites, there are still some fundamentalists who live in the wilderness. Even now, these people live in the wilderness giving offerings in this way. They are, in other words, giving the kind of offerings that were once offered in the Tabernacle before. Perhaps they are the descendants of Aaron. To keep the traditions of their families, they are living in the wilderness instead of cities. Although they are Israelites, they live as a secluded tribe, isolated from the ordinary people. To these people also, we must in fact preach the Word of the Tabernacle that the Messiah has already come to us and has saved us according to our faith.

We must thank Jesus for coming to this earth, for thus being oppressed, and for being judged in our place, all in order to save you and me, as our Savior, from our sins and the condemnation of sin.

"Love Is as Strong as Death, Jealousy as Cruel as the Grave"

That we have in fact been saved from all our sins and the judgment of sin was not achieved by a fluke, as if it came by an accidental delivery of mail. Our salvation is not some kind of chain letters that keep telling us that we have to forward them to over 20 people or else we would be doomed. Nor is our salvation of the remission of sin like one of those many fliers advertising two-for-one pizza deals, where we can simply place a call and fill our stomach to our hearts' content.

Our salvation, in fact, came by God's sending of His Son to us, by passing of all our sins onto Him, and by making Him suffer and be oppressed for all these sins of ours. This is why you and I must wholeheartedly believe in Him and thank Him. Knowing how our salvation came by, how could any of us ever throw it away as a pair of worn-out shoes, put it aside as some useless broken tool sitting in the attic, or ignore it as if it belonged to someone else?

Is there anyone among you who, though attending God's Church, has not yet received the remission of sin? Is there anyone who actually has not yet believed in the gospel of the water and the Spirit? If there indeed are such people, they must all repent and believe in the Messiah before it's too late. If you are lost, and not sure which road to take, just believe in the Word of truth with all your hearts. Those who do not believe are rejecting this love of the Son of God, the love with which He has saved them by going through all these sufferings for none other than their own sake.

Those who underestimate the value of His love and reject it will be followed by curses. The Scripture tells us, *"For love is as strong as death, Jealousy as cruel as the grave" (Song of Solomon 8:6).* God's love is so strong and great that it brings about the cruelest punishment to the people who reject it to the end. It tells us, in other words, that if one does in fact die while remaining sinful, he/she will indeed suffer the merciless pain of hell like the grave. Hatred is as cruel as the grave. When the Messiah has loved you this much, when He was thus baptized, shed His own blood, and suffered all kinds of oppression, all just to save you, if you do not believe in this love and reject it, you will surely suffer this cruel pain. This is none other than hell.

God thus said, *"And as it is appointed for men to die once, but after this the judgment" (Hebrew 9:27).* When we die, our flesh may end, but before God, it is not the end of us. To trample cruelly on those who reject the love God, God has made them live forever and never die, and will indeed bring them merciless sufferings. He will, in other words, actually cast them into the fire burning forever, and make them suffer all its pain incessantly, endlessly, and forever and ever. This cruel suffering is none other than the cruel hatred of God. Do you think God would never be able to bring Himself to do such a thing? Do not forget that nothing is impossible for God!

The great and utmost love of God for us, by suffering Himself for our sake, has saved us from all our curses, all our sins, and all our condemnation. What can solve away all your problems is this love of the Messiah. Indeed, there is nothing that is greater than the Messiah's love. Without faith in this Messiah, the love of God cannot be ours. This love is given to us only by this God, the One who has become our Messiah, and it is His Father who has sent Him to us. The Almighty triune God has loved us in this way, and has thus saved us from our sins and condemnation. This is why we must believe in the Messiah, why we must thank Him, why we must give glory to Him, and why we must be satisfied with our faith in this Messiah.

How thankful is it that the Messiah has given us the gospel of the water and the Spirit? If anyone does not know just how priceless this love is, how it can never be exchanged for anything else in this world, he/she must surely be one the most ignorant and stupid people. How terrible sufferings and afflictions did our Lord go through for us? Because we are so thankful for His love, though we are insufficient, we still dedicate all our remaining strengths to the spreading of this love to those who remain ignorant of it.

To do such works of God, we must also face hardships and sufferings. We cannot seek to prosper for only ourselves. If we have indeed been saved by receiving His love of sacrifice and being clothed in it, we must also share this love with others. Just as Jesus Christ faced all His sufferings to make our sins disappear, not with the love of the flesh, but with His true love, we must also do His works in faith, willingly embracing hardships, oppression, hatred, suffering and despise, if these mean that others would also receive the remission of their sins. We must suffer such hatred in the name of love. If you and I have truly received the remission of sin, then I believe that such love is indeed found in our hearts.

And the born-again, who really know who they were before and how great and strong Jesus' love of salvation is, bear fruits. The saved are the trees that bear the fruits of salvation, *"for a tree is known by its fruit" (Matthew 12:33)*. Before you have been saved, you were completely immersed in your sins, and thus could not even complain if you were indeed cast out to hell. Yet you believed that God has become your Savior by coming to this earth in the flesh of a man and being oppressed for your sake, and that by suffering on your behalf He has saved you from your sins and judgment. By thus believing, you have been saved. If you have indeed received this love, then you and I must surely have hearts that desire to live for others.

If anyone does not have such a heart, then he/she has not received the remission of sin. To be exact, this person is only pretending to have received the remission of sin.

Just as Christ faced all His sufferings and has saved us from all our sins and judgment because He has loved us, if we have indeed been saved by believing in this love, then this love is also found in our own hearts. Why? Because Christ now lives in our hearts. As He was oppressed for our sake and has loved us, we must also desire to live for others and to face hardships for their sake. Because those of us who have received the remission of sin no longer have any sin left in our hearts, our hearts have all been transformed, becoming like the heart of Jesus Christ.

I thank Jesus Christ for coming to this earth, for being baptized and shedding His blood on the Cross, for embracing all His sufferings for our sake, and for thereby becoming our Messiah who has delivered us from all our sins. ✉

SERMON

3

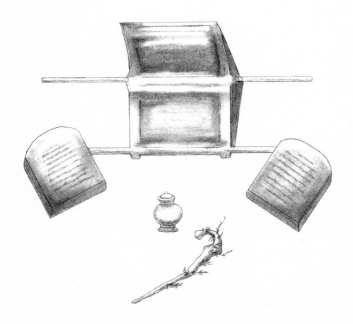

Yahweh the Living God

< Exodus 34:1-8 >

"And the LORD said to Moses, 'Cut two tablets of stone like the first ones, and I will write on these tablets the words that were on the first tablets which you broke. So be ready in the morning, and come up in the morning to Mount Sinai, and present yourself to Me there on the top of the mountain. And no man shall come up with you, and let no man be seen throughout all the mountain; let neither flocks nor herds feed before that mountain.' So he cut two tablets of stone like the first ones. Then Moses rose early in the morning and went up Mount Sinai, as the LORD had commanded him; and he took in his hand the two tablets of stone. Now the LORD descended in the cloud and stood with him there, and proclaimed the name of the LORD. And the LORD passed before him and proclaimed, 'The LORD, the LORD God, merciful and gracious, longsuffering, and abounding in goodness and truth, keeping mercy for thousands, forgiving iniquity and transgression and sin, by no means clearing the guilty, visiting the iniquity of the fathers upon the children and the children's children to the third and the fourth generation.' So Moses made haste and bowed his head toward the earth, and worshiped."

We Need to Find out Who Really Is This God in Whom We Believe

Let us begin by turning to Exodus 3:13-16: *"Then Moses said to God, 'Indeed, when I come to the children of Israel and say to them, 'The God of your fathers has sent me to you,' and they say to me, 'What is His name?' what shall I say to them?' And God said to Moses, 'I AM WHO I AM.' And He said, 'Thus you shall say to the children of Israel, 'I AM has sent me to you.'' Moreover God said to Moses, 'Thus you shall say to the children of Israel: 'The LORD God of your fathers, the God of Abraham, the God of Isaac, and the God of Jacob, has sent me to you. This is My name forever, and this is My memorial to all generations.' Go and gather the elders of Israel together, and say to them, 'The LORD God of your fathers, the God of Abraham, of Isaac, and of Jacob, appeared to me, saying, 'I have surely visited you and seen what is done to you in Egypt'''"*

Who Is Yahweh God?

The name of the Lord in Hebrew is *Yahweh* or *Yhwh*, traditionally *Jehovah*, and Yahweh means He who exists by Himself. God is, in other words, not a creation, but He who exists by Himself, the Creator who made the whole universe and everything in it.

Let's take a look at Exodus 6:2-7: *"And God spoke to Moses and said to him: 'I am the LORD. I appeared to Abraham, to Isaac, and to Jacob, as God Almighty, but by My name LORD I was not known to them. I have also established My covenant with them, to give them the land of Canaan, the land of their pilgrimage, in which they were strangers. And I have also heard the groaning of the children of Israel whom the Egyptians keep in bondage, and I have remembered My covenant. Therefore say to the children of Israel: 'I am the LORD; I will bring you out from under the burdens of the Egyptians, I will rescue you from their bondage, and I will redeem you with an outstretched arm and with great judgments. I will take you as My people, and I will be your God. Then you shall know that I am the LORD your God who brings you out from under the burdens of the Egyptians.'"*

Verse 3 above says, *"I appeared to Abraham, to Isaac, and to Jacob, as God Almighty, but by My name LORD I was not known to them."* In the *King James Version*, the clause "by my name LORD" is written as "by my name JEHOVAH." The Hebrew word JEHOVAH means "the existing One" or "the proper name of the one true God." God had not made His name of Jehovah known to the mankind before. So people at that time just called Him as God. But now, to save the people of Israel, God wanted to let His name of Jehovah be known to all the people of this world. "I am Jehovah. I am Yahweh. I am who I am, He who exists by Himself." God wanted to thus let Himself be known.

God is He who exists by Himself, "the God of Abraham, Isaac, and Jacob." He has been alive even before the most ancient times, even before the very beginning of everything. God, in other words, lives and exists eternally. God had allowed that the people of Israel, the children of Abraham, to be enslaved in Egypt for 430 years, and then He had promised that He would deliver them from their slavery and lead them into the land of Canaan. Just as He had thus promised, Jehovah God appeared after 430 years, and commanded Moses to deliver the people of Israel from the persecution of Pharaoh. "I am Jehovah. I am who I am, your God. Let My people go." For the sake of His people, He manifested Himself before Moses, and commanded Pharaoh to let His people go, for Jehovah God knew of the sufferings of the people of Israel. Because He knew that His people were moaning under their sufferings, God said that He would deliver them from their slavery.

After 430 years since He made His promise to Abraham, God came to the people of Israel and manifested Himself to them. "I am Jehovah. I am God. I have come to fulfill the promise that I made to Abraham, your father, that I would lead his children out of Egypt into the land of Canaan. And I also know all your sufferings. Now go to Pharaoh and tell him so." This is what Jehovah God said.

We must realize that God is in fact the God of Abraham, Isaac, and Jacob. God is also our own God, of you and me. What, then, is His name? His name is Yahweh, meaning He who exists by Himself. God has existed even before the creation of the universe, as He who exists by Himself, whose being came not by someone else, but by Himself.

We Must Understand the Meaning of God's Name

It is critical that we realize and believe that God is actually He who exists by Himself, the One who has made us, who rules over us, and who has delivered us from our sins. We must believe in Yahweh God as our absolute God, for this Yahweh God did in fact create the whole universe, and does continue to exist even as now.

Like the people of Israel, you and I also believe in God, and have also received His commands before His presence. Just as the people of Israel had failed to keep all the Law, we, too, have failed to live by the Law. As such, because of our sins before God, we were also the kind of beings who could not avoid but be subjected to the fearful judgment of sin. Because of our sins, in other words, we actually could not escape from being condemned by Him for our sins.

This is why every one of us should pay a ransom to God to atone for his/her own sins. To be saved from our sins, we had to give to God the Father the wages of atonement equal to our own life, with our faith. We had to actually give the sacrificial offering equivalent to our own life in order to satisfy His just judgment and to reveal the merciful love of God. Only by giving the actual atonement of life for our sins could peace be restored between God and us the mankind. It is only through faith that we can be delivered from all our sins and condemnation.

Because this indeed is the case, whenever we go before God, we had to admit, because of the sins that we have committed before Him, that we could not help but be judged and punished for these sins. When we believe in God as our Savior, we must actually recognize and admit that we are bound to hell because of our sins, and believe in the Messiah, who has paid the wages of our sins and delivered us from the judgment of sin, as our own Savior. When we go before God, we must believe in the baptism and blood of Jesus Christ, the sacrificial offering of our sins, believe in Him as the Messiah, and recognize Him as such. We must admit that we have all become sinners before God because of our failure to keep His commandments, and we must believe that Jesus Christ the Messiah has delivered us from our sins.

We must recognize that we could not avoid but be subjected to God's punishment of sin. By thus admitting our sinfulness, we became qualified to receive the blessing of the remission of sin that God has given us, and we were able to build the foundation of our faith that can garner God's mercy and receive His remission of sin.

To make us His own children, God made us in His own image, but He allowed us to be born in weaknesses. As the descendants of Adam, we all are born as sinners, but this is God's profound providence to make us His children.

We were such beings that could not avoid but be judged for our sins, but to fulfill His will, God sent His own Son to us, and has forgiven us of all our sins. Jesus, the Son of God, received His baptism and died on the Cross in obedience to God's plan. Jehovah God therefore has given new life to those of us who believe that all the sins of the world were passed onto His Son with His baptism from John, that He saved us from all our sins with His blood on the Cross, and that He thus bore all the condemnation of our sins.

The baptism of Jesus and His blood were the sacrificial offering that was more than enough to allow us, when we believe, to receive new life, to be saved from all our sins, and to become God's children. We must be saved from all our sins by believing, and with our faith in the blue, purple, and scarlet thread and the fine woven line, we must have the kind of faith that allows us to become the people of God. It is the absolute truth, in fact, that only those who have such faith can indeed become God's own people.

All the Deities of the Religions of This World Are Merely the Creatures of Mankind's Own Making

Apart from Jehovah God, Jesus Christ, and the Holy Spirit, all other deities are just worldly deities made up by the mankind itself. Except for God, there is nothing in this world that exists by itself. This is why Yahweh God said, "I am who I am."

If there, in fact, anyone who exists by himself? Buddha was born from his mother's womb, and so he is only a creature of God. So is Confucius, and so is Mohammed, for they were all born from their parents, and therefore are merely creatures made by God. The statues of Buddha that his followers have molded or carved out are also merely man's own creation, made with the stones or metals that God Himself created. Everything, from the sun to the moon, the stars, the water, the air, and the galaxies of the universe, was all made by God. There is nothing in this world that was not made by God. Even angels, the spiritual beings, were also made by God.

Only the God of Abraham, Isaac, and Jacob, in whom we believe, is Yahweh God, He who exists by Himself. Yahweh God was not made by anyone else. Only He exits by Himself, only He is the Creator of the whole universe, and only He is the One who made you and me. Only this Yahweh God has planned in His will to save us from our sins and make us His own people.

It is because God has thus planned that He made us be born into this world while crying and return empty-handed, and it is because of this plan that He has allowed us to suffer in this world, so that we could not help but search for God and meet Him.

When we say that we believe in God, we must actually admit that we are the kind of beings that, because of our sins and our failure to keep God's commandments, cannot avoid but face the punishment of death, hell, and fearful sufferings before God. Before we believe in Jesus Christ the Messiah as our Savior, we must first recognize ourselves as sinners who cannot avoid but face the fearful judgment of sin and be cast out to hell.

Yahweh God Is Omniscient and Omnipotent

Only God is the omniscient and omnipotent God who truly made us and rules over the world. After recognizing this, we must then admit before God just what kind of sinners we really are—that is, we must admit that because of our sins, we cannot avoid but be subjected to the fearful wrath of God. And we must believe in the truth that by believing in the Lamb of God who came to deliver us from all our sins, and by passing all our sins onto this sacrificial offering by laying our hands on His head, all our problems of sin are resolved. It is we who must in fact be judged and died for our sins, but because this sacrificial offering took upon all our sins with His baptism, our sins could be washed away. We must believe in this truth. We must recognize that through this sacrificial offering, God the Almighty, for whom nothing is impossible, has indeed saved us, we who could not avoid but be bound to hell, from all our sins. People who believe so are true believers of Jesus Christ the Messiah.

It is, in fact, wrong to believe in the Messiah arbitrarily. When we say that we believe in God, our faith must be established on the biblically sound foundation. And we have to set the very first and powerful foundation of truth on His Word, which said, "I am who I am. I am Jehovah."

The people of Israel failed to keep the Law that God had commanded them to follow. The commandments that God gave to the Israelites were also given to those of us who are living in today's age. If you really want to believe in God, and if you really want to become the children of Abraham with your faith, you must recognize that God has given the 613 commandments not only to the Israelites, but also to us, to everyone in this world, and to the entire universe. And we must actually recognize that we have also failed to keep the commandment, like the Israelites, and thus we are destined to death, for "the wages of sin is death" (Romans 6:23).

We must believe that God has forgiven our sins with the truth of the blue, purple, and scarlet thread. To do so, we must go out in search of the truth of salvation, by which our Lord has delivered us from our sins and the condemnation of our sins.

Despite having failed to keep God's strict commandments, if we do not realize that we are terrible sinners, and if we do not admit that we are bound to be judged for our sins, then we would never be able to believe in the Messiah. If people were to believe that they would enter Heaven even though they remain sinful, when, in fact, God has already recorded their sins in the Book of Judgment, they would then be changing God's Law on their own, committing the sin of calling God's name in vain. Such people will not ever be able to be saved from their sins. They will be eternally judged of their sins, and be condemned with the punishment of hell, for regardless of whether they believe in God or not, they have not recognized God. These people must repent at once and turn away from their unbelief.

Even at this very moment, God is in our hearts, and exists by Himself in all these spaces. And He knows everything about us.

Though God is alive, there are people who do not believe in Him, some even taunting Him. But we are all in need of sacrificial offerings for our sins. This is why God made the

Israelites give the offering of atonement with their sacrificial offerings on the Tabernacle's altar of burnt offering, in accordance to the way of salvation that God had set.

God is indeed He who exists by Himself. He is the One who was before, and is now. He is God who lived, appeared, and spoke to our forefathers of faith long before, the One who lives, appears, and speaks to us now, He who works among us, leads us, and rules over our lives.

The Truth That We Must Not Forget

Though we have been saved, there is one thing we must never forget. It is that though we could not avoid but to be judged eternally, with His baptism and by shedding His blood on the Cross, our Lord has delivered us from all such judgment of our sins. Until the day we stand before our Lord, in fact, we must never forget this truth and always believe it in our hearts. We must believe it even when we are in the Kingdom of Heaven praising God. We must thank God for allowing us, the very people who could not avoid but be cursed eternally and judged for their sins, to believe in our Lord as the Savior, and for giving us eternal life.

We must recognize the gospel of the water and the Spirit forever. What would happen if we do not admit that we are bound to be eternally judged because of our sins? There would be no reason for us to praise God. God has actually saved us, the mortal beings who could not avoid but be judged forever because of our sins. This is why we must believe and praise the Lord—because our Lord received His baptism and shed His blood for our sake. This is why you, too, must believe, and this is why we must all preach the gospel of the water and the Spirit.

Those who believe in the baptism that Jesus received and the blood that He shed for their sins have hearts that praise God. Because the Lord has saved them from their sins and death, they praise Him every day with their faith.

The problem is that some people have misunderstood Jesus. Their knowledge of Him is one-sided and half-empty. These are the kind of people whose conscience has been corrupted, who do not even realize that they are committing sin when, in fact, they are indeed engulfed in all kinds of sin. Those who commit sin and yet do not even recognize it as sin—none other than these are sinners.

Though we are actually weak beings who cannot help but sin, we must admit our sins every time we commit them, and we must confirm the baptism of our Lord and His blood on the Cross—that is, the gospel of the water and the Spirit. We therefore in fact do admit that we cannot but be sinners before God. And by actually believing in the gospel of the water and the Spirit, we can breathe in relief. Indeed, by believing in the gospel of the water and the Spirit, we have earned our peace of mind.

When I speak of being sinless, it does not mean that we would not recognize our sins even when we actually commit them. It does not mean that those who believe in the gospel of the water and the Spirit need not recognize sin as sin. Though we have in fact been delivered from all our sins, we still recognize the sins that we commit for what they are—as our sins. What we must never forget is that though we could not avoid but be judged eternally because of our sins, our Lord has saved us from all our sins and the condemnation of sin with His baptism, His blood on the Cross, and His resurrection. We must never, ever forget that our Lord has saved us with the blue, purple, and scarlet thread, but believe in it and praise Him for it. We must remember how we were before. Remember that we once were such poor beings who could not avoid but be eternally judged for our sins. And we must praise the salvation of the remission of sin given by God, and thank Him everyday for His great grace of salvation. None other than this is the faith of the believers in the gospel of the water and the Spirit.

Yahweh God Is Alive Even Now

Just as God was the God of Abraham, Isaac, and Jacob, He is now your and my God. *"God is not the author of confusion but of peace" (1 Corinthians 14:33).* He is not the God of those Christians who are of pretentious and flamboyant deeds, but He is the God of those who believe in the gospel of the water and the Spirit. We have the faith that believes in the Word of God and obeys Him with "yes." God is our God. When He actually tells us, "You are destined to hell," we say to Him, "Yes, You are right." When He tells us, "You will continue to sin until the day you die," then we also say again, "Yes, You're right." And when He says to us, "But I have actually saved you with My blue, purple, and scarlet thread and fine woven linen," we can only say, yet again, "Yes, You're very right." We have thus become the people of God who always obey Him with "yes." I thank our God for His grace that has saved us with the gospel of the water and the Spirit.

We must believe and recognize in our hearts that our Lord has indeed saved us from all our sins through the water, the blood, and the Spirit, and has thereby made us the people of the Kingdom of God. Give thanks to the Lord by believing that the gospel of the water and the Spirit is the gift of salvation that God has given you.

I praise God forever with my faith for eternally saving me, who actually could not avoid but be bound to hell because of my sins, with the gospel of the water and the Spirit. Remembering that we were in fact all of bronze—that is, we could not escape the judgment of God—and we therefore cannot but praise God for our deliverance from sin, for saving us with His blue, purple, and scarlet thread and fine woven linen. And we must thank Him by believing in the truth of the gospel hidden in these blue, purple, and scarlet thread and fine woven linen.

Only Yahweh God is the God of the whole mankind. And He has become God the Savior of the entire human race. We must all believe in Yahweh God as our own God. ✉

SERMON

4

The Reason Why God Called Moses to the Mountain Sinai

< Exodus 19:1-6 >

"In the third month after the children of Israel had gone out of the land of Egypt, on the same day, they came to the Wilderness of Sinai. For they had departed from Rephidim, had come to the Wilderness of Sinai, and camped in the wilderness. So Israel camped there before the mountain. And Moses went up to God, and the LORD called to him from the mountain, saying, 'Thus you shall say to the house of Jacob, and tell the children of Israel: 'You have seen what I did to the Egyptians, and how I bore you on eagles' wings and brought you to Myself. Now therefore, if you will indeed obey My voice and keep My covenant, then you shall be a special treasure to Me above all people; for all the earth is Mine. And you shall be to Me a kingdom of priests and a holy nation.' These are the words which you shall speak to the children of Israel.'""

Why Did God Choose the People of Israel?

The main passage comes from Exodus 19:1-6. Though the passage is not long, I have much to say about it. From this passage, I would also like to speak of the truth revealed from chapters 19 to 25 of Exodus. It had been three months since the people of Israel escaped from Egypt when the Israelites came to the Wilderness of Sinai. God made them camp in front of the Mountain Sinai, and called Moses up to the mountain.

Having thus summoned Moses, God spoke His Word to the Israelites, *"'Now therefore, if you will indeed obey My voice and keep My covenant, then you shall be a special treasure to Me above all people; for all the earth is Mine. And you shall be to Me a kingdom of priests and a holy nation.' These are the words which you shall speak to the children of Israel."* The reason why God called and raised the people of Israel was to make them His special treasure and to establish them as the priests of His kingdom.

This was the purpose with which God delivered the people of Israel from Egypt. The method by which God would make the Israelites His special treasure was giving them His Law and the sacrificial system of the Tabernacle to save them from their sins, through which He would cleanse away all their sins, make them His own people, and found them as a nation of priests. As such, the Israelites must realize this clearly, and recover the faith that God wants from them. To make their nation a kingdom of God's priests, God gave them, on the one hand, His Law composed of the 613 commandments, and on the other hand, He made them build the Tabernacle.

Therefore, if the Israelites do not believe in Jesus Christ who came as their Messiah, they must repent and believe in Him with their hearts. Jesus, who is the very substance of the sin offering of the sacrificial system of the Tabernacle, has cleansed away all their sins with His baptism received from John and His blood on the Cross. As such, the people of Israel must unambiguously accept the truth that God has made them His own people by bringing them, the descendants of Abraham, out of Egypt, and by washing away all their sins through the offerings of the Tabernacle. At that time, because the Israelites were unable to keep the Law of God, they had to be forgiven of their sins by giving sacrificial offerings to God according to the sacrificial system set by Him. These sacrificial offerings were the foreshadowing of Jesus Christ, the Savior who has now saved mankind from its sins.

Even now, the Israelites hold Moses as the greatest prophet of all. They are right in this. However, because they do not believe in Jesus Christ as the Messiah who has saved them from all their sins, they do not recognize the New Testament as the Word of God, and instead recognize only the Old Testament as God's Word. But we must remember that Jesus is not only a greater prophet than Moses, but He is the High Priest of the Kingdom of Heaven, the Messiah for whom the Israelites have been waiting and hoping. By faith, the Israelites must now realize that the very substance of the Tabernacle's sacrificial offering was none other than the Messiah Himself.

God Made the Israelites Hold Moses in Reverence, But...

Why did God raise Moses so high before the Israelites? It was to make them accept and believe in all the Word of God spoken through Moses. It was, in other words, to make Israelites believe that what Moses spoke to them was all God's own Word. God called Moses to the Mountain Sinai so that he would be raised high above before the people of Israel. This made the Israelites fear Moses and God, and the Israelites, seeing that Moses spoke with God, came to believe in him, for God talked with Moses as if he were His friend.

As such, the Word of God that Moses delivered to the people of Israel was all firmly believed by the Israelites as the actual Word that God spoke to them. However, by regarding Moses too highly, the people of Israel made a huge mistake of not accepting Jesus Christ the Messiah into their hearts as their own Savior. Ultimately, the Israelites failed to recognized their Messiah properly, and have thus ended up rejecting His love of salvation. They now have a great task before them—that is, to accept Jesus Christ, who was a greater prophet than even Moses, into their hearts as their own Savior.

God Commanded the People of Israel to Make His Tabernacle and to Give Him the Offerings of Sacrifice

Through Moses, God gave His Law and commandments to the people of Israel, and He also told them to build the Tabernacle. In the Tabernacle, God's love of mercy that truly blotted out the sins of the Israelites was revealed through its sacrificial system. Through this sacrificial system of the Tabernacle, God has also given the remission of sin to the spiritual descendants of Abraham, and He has washed away all their sins so that they may lack nothing to become God's own people.

God gave the people of Israel two stone tablets with His Ten Commandments carved into them. The Ten Commandments were composed of the upper four commandments that must be kept between God and mankind, and the lower six commandments that must be kept in human relationships. Beside these Ten Commandments, God also gave the people of Israel hundreds of commandments that they must keep in their everyday lives.

The reason why God gave the Israelites so many laws and commandments was to show in their hearts that God alone is the absolute and perfect divine Being. To the spiritual people of Israel—that is, to those who believe in Jesus as their Savior—there can be no other divine being apart from God. To clearly teach the people of Israel before entering the land of Canaan the truth that He is Jehovah, God spoke to Moses in the Mountain Sinai to give them His Law. And He made them, whenever they sinned by breaking God's commandments, be forgiven of all their sins by giving their sacrificial offering in the Tabernacle according to the sacrificial system He had established.

The People of Israel Received the Law and Commandments from God

Let us take a look at Exodus 24:3-8: *"So Moses came and told the people all the words of the LORD and all the judgments. And all the people answered with one voice and said, 'All the words which the LORD has said we will do.' And Moses wrote all the words of the LORD. And he rose early in the morning, and built an altar at the foot of the mountain, and twelve pillars according to the twelve tribes of Israel. Then he sent young men of the children of Israel, who offered burnt offerings and sacrificed peace offerings of oxen to the LORD. And Moses took half the blood and put it in basins, and half the blood he sprinkled on the altar. Then he took the Book of the Covenant and read in the hearing of the people. And they said, 'All that the LORD has said we will do, and be obedient.' And Moses took the blood, sprinkled it on the people, and said,*

'This is the blood of the covenant which the LORD has made with you according to all these words.'"

God made the covenant with blood when He gave the Law to the people of Israel through Moses. This meant, in short, that the Law of God was the Law of life. God spoke His Law of life to the Israelites, and the people of Israel had to believe in His Word.

As such, Moses told the Israelites to bring the blood of the sacrifice of the burnt offering and the peace offering. God made Moses gather his people together, read to them the Law and the commandments, God's covenant. And then Moses asked them, "Will you obey what God have commanded you?" The Israelites then answered God in one voice that they would all indeed obey Him.

"I will protect you and make you a kingdom of priests," God then promised the Israelites through Moses. Moses then sprinkled the blood of the burnt offering and the peace offering on them. This showed that when a person sins, he/she must be forgiven through the sacrificial offering. We must accept what God spoke as the Word of life. Moses took the blood of the offering, sprinkled it on his people, and said to them, *"This is the blood of the covenant which the Lord has made with you according to all these words."* This tells us that because the Word of God is the Word of life, if we have not kept it, we must then pass our sins onto the sacrificial offering by putting our hands on its head, kill it, and offer to God its sacrificial blood for our sins.

What we must realize is that in this Law of God, there is the punishment for our sins, but at the same time, there is also the sacrificial system that washes away our sins. Therefore, when we are dealing with God's Law and commandments, we must accept them into our hearts while recognizing that in these Law and commandments is found the offering that brings us the remission of our sins. This faith is absolutely necessary. Because we are blessed when we keep God's Law and are cursed when we fail to keep it, we must believe that we have to always wash away our sins with our sacrificial offering. As such, those who sinned had to receive the remission of their sins by passing their sins onto the sacrificial offering with the laying of their hands on its head, and by taking its blood of sacrifice and offering it to God. We must all realize and believe that the Law and the sacrificial system are the Law of life, through which we can receive new life from God.

Therefore, while the Law of God teaches us of our sins, the gospel of the water and the Spirit shows us in contrast that all our sins have been remitted through the baptism that Jesus Christ received from John and His blood on the Cross—it is, hence, the truth that has saved us from all the sins of the world.

In the ancient times, when tribes made promises to each other, they often brought some kind of sacrificial offerings. They brought sheep, goats, or bulls, and they marked their agreements with the blood drawn from their offerings, cutting off their throats. This captured the essential terms of the agreements, for it meant, "If you do not keep the covenant that you just made with me, you will then surely die in this manner." They established their agreements, in short, with blood.

Like this, God has also established His Law with blood. He told us, in other words, that if we fail to keep all His 613 laws and commandments, we would be killed because of this sin. But at the same time, He has also told us to receive the remission of our sins by giving Him the sin offerings with our faith, through the sacrificial system of the Tabernacle.

If we were to ever not take God's Word of the Law

seriously, we would never escape from the wrath coming from God because of our sins. But if we give to Him the offerings of sacrifice that He has set for us, God will then receive these sacrificial offerings and forgive us of all our sins. We must all believe in this Law of life, this Law of salvation that tells us God would forgive the sins of all the people of Israel through the sacrificial system of the Tabernacle, and thereby receive into our hearts the remission of our sins. Whoever ignores the Law of God is excluded from God's mercy of love, and as such, we must all believe in the Law and the sacrificial system as the truth of salvation, as our very own life.

This is why Moses read the covenant made with blood, and with this blood sprinkled on the people of Israel, they made their promise to God with blood. Therefore, realizing that we are all to die if we do not keep this Law established with blood, we must all receive the remission of all our sins by believing, along with the Law, in Jesus Christ, who is the very sacrifice of our burnt offering and peace offering to God.

All of us must realize and believe in the truth that we can be forgiven of all our sins by giving to God our sacrificial offering in accordance to the sacrificial system of the Tabernacle. Through His blue, purple, and scarlet thread and fine woven linen, God has clearly taught us the remission of the sins of all mankind. To be forgiven of their sins, all their sins had to be passed onto their sacrificial offering by putting their hands on its head, and then this offering had to shed its blood of sacrifice to be put on the horns of the altar of burnt offering and the rest of its blood to be poured on the ground.

This was the offering of sacrifice absolutely required by the law of sin and death. Therefore, with our faith, we must all accept the remission of sin promised by the sacrificial offering that blots out our sins. By giving us the sacrificial system of the

Tabernacle, God has given us the law of salvation, so that we may believe in God's Word and be forgiven of all our sins. We must all receive the blessing of the remission of sin given by God by accepting into our hearts the two laws that God has given mankind: the Law itself and the sacrificial system of the Tabernacle.

How Can We Be Saved from All Our Sins?

Through the sacrificial system that God gave to Moses, He showed the people of Israel that their salvation from all their sins is possible only by their faith in the remission of their sins through their sacrificial offering.

When we give to God our faith that believes in the sacrificial offering set by Him, He will receive our faith and save us from all our sins. Why? Because God has already saved the entire mankind from their sins, and to those who believe, He gives His blessing of sanctifying them from all their sins. Through the sacrificial system set by the One who is Absolute, God has enabled us to know the law of salvation. If one neither know nor believes in the truth that Jesus Christ has washed away his/her sins forever through His baptism and His blood on the Cross, he/she will surely be condemned. We must all believe in God's love of mercy.

God has saved us through the sacrificial system of the Tabernacle, whose method of salvation was to pass our sins onto the sacrifice by laying our hands on its head. As such, we must all believe in the gospel of mercy that has allowed all who believe in this truth to be washed of their sins. Those who do not recognize the Law and the sacrificial system before God cannot ever receive the remission of sin forever, but those who believe in the gospel of God's mercy can all receive their eternal remission of sin.

God did not just tell us not to sin, but He taught us that we were the sinful beings who could not but commit sins everyday. So, He told us to give Him our sacrificial offering to receive the remission of these sins. This is why God said, when a sinner is to give the offering of sacrifice, *"An altar of earth you shall make for Me, and you shall sacrifice on it your burnt offerings and your peace offerings, your sheep and your oxen. In every place where I record My name I will come to you, and I will bless you" (Exodus 20:24).*

The sin offering that the Israelites gave to God took the format of putting their hands on the head of the sacrifice, through which their sins were passed onto it, drawing its blood and putting it on the horns of the Altar of Burnt Offering, and putting its flesh on the Altar and burning it by fire. Believing wholeheartedly in the law of salvation given by God was essentially needed whenever they had to offer such offering. The offering that God wanted was not a ritualistic one, but it was an earnest one that passed all their sins onto the offering of sacrifice in faith, believing that they are indeed bound to hell were it not for the grace of God.

Our Lord was baptized by John and shed His blood on the Cross to make our sins disappear. He decided to blot out our sins with the same method of the sin offering. This offering of faith foreshadowed the New Testament's offering of salvation fulfilled by Jesus Christ—that is, Christ came to this earth, took upon the sins of the world with His baptism received from John, died on the Cross, and has thereby saved the whole mankind from their sins. It is by believing in this truth with all our hearts that we become God's children.

We Must Cast away Doctrinal Faith

Exodus 20:25-26 say, *"And if you make Me an altar of stone, you shall not build it of hewn stone; for if you use your tool on it, you have profaned it. Nor shall you go up by steps to My altar, that your nakedness may not be exposed on it."* We must pay particular attention to what God said in this verse. God told the Israelites that in making an altar, if they were to build to an altar of stone, they should not build it of hewn stone, but of stones that are in tact in their original shape and form. What does this mean? It means God is pleased to accept our faith in His salvation, which can never be added or altered by human thoughts.

And God is warning us, with the phrase, *"Nor shall you go up by steps to My altar, that your nakedness may not be exposed on it,"* not to worship Him with man-made, religionist faith. Every religion of the world is nothing but a belief system made by human beings. They set up a common and basic principle in their own religions that tells people into trying to become holy step by step while they live their faithful religious lives. Even the Christian religionists claim that they can be sanctified incrementally while they live virtuous lives according to God's Law.

But, is it really true? Absolutely not! People, being born as the descendants of Adam, cannot follow God's Law because of their sins, and they cannot avoid but face their certain death because of these sins. Therefore, to save all such people from the sins of the world, God established the sacrificial system of the Tabernacle, and has indeed saved them all.

Therefore, we must all accept the gospel of mercy, of the remission of our sins, of our salvation that God has set for us with the blue, purple, and scarlet thread and the fine woven linen manifested in the gate of the court of the Tabernacle. We must believe as it is actually written in the Word of the Bible, that Jesus Christ came to this earth as the God of the Word, that He did His works just as foretold by the blue, purple, and scarlet thread and the fine woven linen manifested in the Tabernacle, and He has indeed delivered us from all our sins accordingly.

But what about the people who have only religious and doctrinal faith? What are they doing to be forgiven of their daily sins? Such people try to receive their remission of sin by offering their prayers of repentance, trying, in the end, to become righteous through the doctrine of incremental sanctification. This is delusional, doctrinal faith of man's own making. Trying to meet God with one's own efforts is arrogance itself, and it is none other than the reality of the religious evilness of one's own making.

People must first admit that there is nothing that they themselves can do to make all their sins disappear before God. When we were born into this world, we were all born as the kind of beings that could not help but commit sins of our own, and this is why we are always committing so many sins. No matter how much God tells us not to sin through His Law, we are such that we cannot help but break the whole gamut of His Law and commit sins galore before God. So, we must confess before the Law of God that we are sinful. And we must believe with our hearts in the truth of salvation that God has saved us from all our sins through the works of our Lord Jesus as manifested in His blue, purple, and scarlet thread and fine woven linen.

There is no other way but to believe in the Word of God, that to deliver us from all the sins of the world, the Lord Himself became our own sacrificial offering through His baptism, and that thereby He has indeed saved us from the sins of the world. The Bible tells us that there is no other god apart from Jehovah, and that no one comes to the Father except through Christ (John 14:6). By recognizing and believing in God's Word of the Law, we become sinners, and by believing in the gospel of the water and the Spirit, we are saved from our sins. This is the truth and our real faith in God.

As such, we must all believe in His salvation as it is according to the law of the remission of sin that our Lord has set for us to save us from all our sins. Christianity is not just one of the many religions of the world, but it is the truth of salvation built on the foundation of our faith that believes in Jesus Christ who appeared in the blue, purple, and scarlet thread and the fine woven linen.

Through the Main Passage above, We Must All Realize Why God Has Called Us

We must all realize the fact that God has called you and me to make us His special treasure. You and I can never become God's people with our own deeds and efforts. Rather, you and I have become God's children because we have believed in the truth that Jesus Christ came to this earth to deliver us from the curse of the Law and the punishment and destruction of hell. By being baptized by John and shedding His blood on the Cross, He has indeed wholly saved those of us who believe. The Messiah, the Son of God, came to this earth in the flesh of a man, took upon all the sins of the mankind with His baptism all at once, carried these sins of the world to the Cross, sacrificed Himself for our sake to pay the wage of our sins by being crucified, rose from the dead again, and has thereby become the Savior to those who truly believe in Him with all their hearts.

God is telling us that He has given the mankind the perfect remission of sin through His blue, purple, and scarlet thread and fine woven linen. Our Lord is asking us, "Do you believe in My works, in what I have done for the remission of your sins, that I came to this earth and was baptized by John and shed My blood on the Cross?" Before God, all that we can say is "yes." For us to be saved, there is no other way to but believe in the remission of sin that God has given us. Not only the Israelites of the days of the Old Testament, but you and I of today—indeed, all the people of the entire world—must know why God had to call Moses to the Mountain Sinai and speak to Him this Word of the main passage.

God had given the Israelites the Ten Commandments, and then told them to build an altar of earth by faith to receive the remission of their sins (Exodus 20:24). Likewise, through our faith in the gospel of the water and the Spirit manifested in the blue, purple, and scarlet thread and the fine woven linen that God has given us, we must also be redeemed from all our sins.

What is God's own name? His name is "Yahweh." It means, "I AM WHO I AM," that is, God is He who exists by Himself. How, then, did He come to us? He came to us through the water and the Spirit (John 3:5). Our Lord came to this earth in the flesh of a man, took upon all the sins of the mankind by being baptized by John, and was sacrificed on our behalf by being crucified to death. It is because this is all true, and because we must also believe as such, that God told us to have the faith that was manifested in the blue, purple, and scarlet thread and the fine woven linen used for the gate of the Tabernacle's court. The true faith comes only when we deny our own thoughts and recognize the remission of sin given by

God. We cannot thank Him enough for giving us such an unconditional love, for we have nothing that we can be proud of before God.

We must lay our foundation of faith on the biblically sound knowledge of God. God spoke of this foundation of faith to the people of Israel, and He spoke to us also. Even now, you must all realize and believe in the truth manifested in the colors of the gate of the Tabernacle's court, the colors that constitute this very foundation of faith. We must believe in the true God. To save you and me from our sins, God Himself took upon our sins with His baptism and shed His blood on the Cross.

You, who also want to become the spiritual people of Israel, must believe in the gospel of the water and the Spirit to be saved from all your sins by reestablishing the sacrificial system destroyed by the religionized Christianity. You and I must know this gospel of the water and the Spirit manifested in the blue, purple, and scarlet thread, and once again lay the groundwork of our faith of the remission of sin so that it may stand sound and firm.

We must thank Jesus with our faith. To save those of us who could not help but be bound to hell, God the Father sent us Jesus Christ, who came as the blue, purple, and scarlet thread, through His Word of truth. By believing wholeheartedly in this truth that our Lord has saved us from all our sins with His four ministries manifested in the blue, purple, and scarlet thread and the fine woven linen, and by believing in His love of mercy, we give all our thanks to God. Only when we know properly and believe in the reason why God called Moses to the Mountain Sinai can we be called as the ones who have properly laid out the foundation of faith on the true remission of sin. You and I must realize the reason why God called us from Mountain Sinai, and believe in it: it was to forgive us of all our sins through the sacrificial offering, and to make us His own children.

From the truth manifested in the gate of the court of the Tabernacle, you will be able to encounter even more love of God's mercy. It is my sincere hope and prayer that you would all believe in this love of God's mercy and accept it into your hearts. ⊠

SERMON

5

How the Israelites Came to Give Offerings in the Tabernacle: The Historical Background

< Genesis 15:1-21 >

"After these things the word of the LORD came to Abram in a vision, saying, 'Do not be afraid, Abram. I am your shield, your exceedingly great reward.' But Abram said, 'Lord GOD, what will You give me, seeing I go childless, and the heir of my house is Eliezer of Damascus?' Then Abram said, 'Look, You have given me no offspring; indeed one born in my house is my heir!' And behold, the word of the LORD came to him, saying, 'This one shall not be your heir, but one who will come from your own body shall be your heir.' Then He brought him outside and said, 'Look now toward heaven, and count the stars if you are able to number them.' And He said to him, 'So shall your descendants be.' And he believed in the LORD, and He accounted it to him for righteousness. Then He said to him, 'I am the LORD, who brought you out of Ur of the Chaldeans, to give you this land to inherit it.' And he said, 'Lord GOD, how shall I know that I will inherit it?' So He said to him, 'Bring Me a three-year-old heifer, a three-year-old female goat, a three-year-old ram, a turtledove, and a young pigeon.' Then he brought all these to Him and cut them in two, down the middle, and placed each piece opposite the other; but he did not cut the birds in two. And when the vultures came down on the carcasses, Abram drove them away. Now when the sun was going down, a deep sleep fell upon Abram; and behold, horror and great darkness fell upon him. Then He said to Abram: 'Know certainly that your descendants will be strangers in a land that is not theirs, and will serve them, and they will afflict them four hundred years. And also the nation whom they serve I will judge; afterward they shall come out with great possessions. Now as for you, you shall go to your fathers in peace; you shall be buried at a good old age. But in the fourth generation they shall return here, for the iniquity of the Amorites is not yet complete.' And it came to pass, when the sun went down and it was dark, that behold, there appeared a smoking oven and a burning torch that passed between those pieces. On the same day the LORD made a covenant with Abram, saying: 'To your descendants I have given this land, from the river of Egypt to the great river, the River Euphrates—the Kenites, the Kenezzites, the Kadmonites, the Hittites, the Perizzites, the Rephaim, the Amorites, the Canaanites, the Girgashites, and the Jebusites.'"

Abraham's Faith in the Word of God

I have great respect and admiration for the faith of Abraham shown in the Bible. When we look at Abraham's faith, we can see all the travails of his faith through which he followed the Word of Jehovah, and we therefore cannot help but admire this faith of Abraham. God blessed Abraham greatly, as shown in Genesis 12:3, where God said, *"I will bless those who bless you, And I will curse him who curses you; And in you all the families of the earth shall be blessed."* This great blessing is also shown in Genesis 15:1, where God declared to Abraham, *"I am your shield, your exceedingly great reward."* God had such special love for Abraham that He became his own God.

After leading Abraham out from Ur of the Chaldeans, God revealed Himself before him, and said to him, *"I am your shield, your exceedingly great reward."* When God said this, Abraham asked Him in return, "What will You give me?" These words of Abraham were not the words of disbelief coming from a skeptical heart questioning what God could possibly give him, but rather they contained Abraham's earnest desire to be blessed by God. What, then, was this blessing that Abraham sought from God? This is revealed in what Abraham said to God: "What will You give me? Because I'm childless, my servant Eliezer of Damascus is my heir, as he will become my adopted son who would inherit all my belongings! What will You give me?" Here, we should understand how earnestly he yearned for his own son. Those who deliberately choose to have no children of their own perhaps cannot sympathize with Abraham's earnest desire, but he truly yearned to have to his own son as his heir.

Just as God gives all His blessings to His children who are made in His image, people also have the earnest desire to give the very best to their own children. As such, when Abraham said to God, "my servant will be my heir," we can all realize just how much he wanted to be blessed by God, so that he may have his own child as his heir. God then said to Abraham, "That's not true. The one who will come from your own body will be your heir. The one who is born from the body of your wife will be your heir, not your servant Eliezer of Damascus."

God then brought Abraham outside, and told him to look up the sky and count the stars. So Abraham looked up the stars. Countless stars and beautiful galaxies were strung across the skyline. When God told Abraham to count the stars and see if he could number them, Abraham answered that there were too many stars to count them all. God then promised Abraham that He would give him as many descendants as the stars in the sky.

Abraham believed in this Word of promise that God gave to him. This is how he became the father of faith who truly believed in all the Word of God. God thus said to him, "Your faith is right. You do indeed believe in my Word. I will therefore bless you by giving you as many descendants as the stars in the sky."

Abraham's Sacrificial Offering and God's Promise of the Land of Canaan

God led Abraham out of the land of the Chaldea and promised him that He would give him and his descendants the land of Canaan. What, then, was the evidence that God would fulfill this promise? This is shown in what God told Abraham, "Bring Me a three-year-old heifer, a three-year-old female goat, a three-year-old ram, a turtledove, and a young pigeon. These are the evidence of the covenant that I have made with you to give the land of Canaan to your descendants." This shows us that the descendants of Abraham would give the offering of sacrifice to God to be cleansed of their sins, and it was the promise of God that by this faith they would enter into the land of Canaan.

When Abraham fell into a deep sleep while offering the

sacrifices, God appeared before him and promised him, *"Know certainly that your descendants will be strangers in a land that is not theirs, and will serve them, and they will afflict them four hundred years. And also the nation whom they serve I will judge; afterward they shall come out with great possessions. Now as for you, you shall go to your fathers in peace; you shall be buried at a good old age. But in the fourth generation they shall return here" (Genesis 15:13-16).*

God, in other words, promised that He would make the people of Israel prosper in the land of Egypt, and then lead them to the land of Canaan; and to do so, He decided to make them give the offerings that blot out their sins in the Tabernacle. To show Abraham that He would fulfill this promise, God made a burning torch to pass between the pieces of flesh cut from Abraham's sacrificial offering.

In this way, God's promise to Abraham, that He would make him and his descendants His own people, came by the offering of the remission of sin implied in the sacrificial offering. God also promised Abraham, *"To your descendants I have given this land, from the river of Egypt to the great river, the River Euphrates—the Kenites, the Kenezzites, the Kadmonites, the Hittites, the Perizzites, the Rephaim, the Amorites, the Canaanites, the Girgashites, and the Jebusites."* The reason why God promised this was to show that He would wash away the sins of Abraham and his descendant through the offering of sacrifice. The process by which God fulfilled this Word promised to Abraham is shown throughout the history of the Old Testament.

God made Joseph the prime minister of Egypt and led all Jacob's family to the land of Egypt to multiply them (Genesis 41:37-45; Genesis 47). But, as time passed by, there arose a new Pharaoh who did not know Joseph's remarkable public service to Egypt, and he began to persecute the people of Israel who were then prospering in the land. Soon the Israelites were even enslaved, forced to work in bondage for Egypt (Exodus 1:8-14). Even so, the people of Israel continued to prosper, and so the Pharaoh afflicted them with even more burdens of slavery. It was when the people of Israel were suffering in Egypt with their bondage for 400 years that they finally came to look for the Savior.

Through Moses, God led them out of the land of Egypt to escape its bondage (Exodus 14:21-25). To the people of Israel who thus escaped from the land of Egypt, God gave the sacrificial system of the Tabernacle through Moses, and made them cleanse away their sins by offering Him their sacrifices. The people of Israel thus received from God the Law (Exodus 20) and the sacrificial system of the Tabernacle (Leviticus 1-4). Through the Law and the sacrificial system of the Tabernacle, the Israelites came to know of the sacrificial offering that would forgive their sins, and God made those who believed in this truth His own people, and blessed Israel to become a kingdom of priests and a holy nation of God (Exodus 19:6).

In the end, we can find out that through the sacrificial offering, God did fulfill His promise to Abraham that He would give him as many descendants as the stars in the sky and give them the land of Canaan. When the Israelites left Egypt, the number of males over 20 years of age and able to fight in war was over 600,000. God indeed kept His promise to Abraham most certainly.

Looking at Abraham's faith, that he believed in His Word of promise, God approved this faith of Abraham. God blessed Abraham because of his faith. The reason why God loved and blessed Abraham, in other words, was because of his faith in the Word of God. Because Abraham believed in His Word,

God was pleased by his faith. God therefore wanted to build the nation of Israel from Abraham, and through the sacrificial offering given by his descendant, to fulfill the promise of circumcision.

We see that Abraham's faith was approved by God as he gave his sacrificial offering to God. This faith has allowed us to also be forgiven of all our sins not by our deeds, but by our faith in the Word of God. To those who have received the spiritual circumcision that cuts off their sins through the sacrificial offering by believing in His Word as Abraham did, God has allowed the land of Canaan as His blessing. As such, God wants from us the same faith that Abraham had. He wants you and me, today, to receive the remission of sin into our hearts by believing in His Word, just like Abraham, and thereby inherit the Kingdom of God. God the Father passed our sins onto Jesus Christ through His baptism and made Him "the Lamb of God" for all mankind. And God wants us to believe in this truth as Abraham did. He wants to make such believers His own people eternally.

God shows us that just as Abraham was greatly blessed because of his faith in the Word of God, even today, you and I can also receive all God's blessings by having the faith that Abraham had. God called Moses to the Mountain Sinai, gave him the Law and the sacrificial system, and blessed those who believe in His Word to become His own people.

God has also made us His people through the remission of sins implied in the Tabernacle, even though we have failed keep His Law. Through our faith in the truth manifested in the Tabernacle, God has enabled us to receive His eternal blessings. As such, we must all become God's people by believing in this truth manifested in the Tabernacle. Only when we believe in our hearts that God has shown us Jesus Christ and given us our salvation through the Tabernacle can we receive His abundant blessings.

Just as Abraham Believed in the Word of God, So Must We Believe in God Based on His Word

Abraham was blessed not because of his good deeds, but because of his faith in the Word of God. Through the Law, God has enabled us to know our sins, and through the sacrificial system of the Tabernacle, He has enabled us to receive the remission of all our sins by passing our sins onto the unblemished sacrificial offering and giving its blood to God. In the same manner, Jesus Christ, coming to this earth, took upon all our sins with His baptism, was judged for these sins of ours with His death on the Cross, and has forgiven us of all our sins by rising again from the dead. All our sins can be forgiven and we can become God's children only by believing in this truth. The Bible tells us that only those who believe in this truth with their hearts can received all God's blessings. By believing in the Word of God, we must make His Word of salvation, the most precious blessing found nowhere else in the entire world, our very own.

Why did Abraham receive abundant blessings from God? He was blessed because he believed in what God had told him. Even today, if you and I believe in the Word of God written in the Bible, we can all have the same faith of Abraham and receive many blessings of Heaven. This is not such a difficult thing to do. If we want to have the evidence that shows that we are the people of God, what we have to do is not trying to please God with our acts of devotion, but believe in His Word with our hearts.

God promised Abraham with His Word that He would give the land of Canaan to his descendants. All of us living in today's time must believe that the four ministries of Jesus, which were manifested and prophesied by the Tabernacle's blue, purple, and scarlet thread and fine woven linen, has saved us from all our sins. And by believing thus, we must receive the remission of our sins, become God's children, and inherit the Kingdom of Heaven.

We must absolutely believe in His Word, because not a single one of God's Word is in vain, and because His Word is all true and critically important to our faith. We must surely know His Word of the water and the Spirit, and we must believe in it without fail. Why? Because it is the absolute truth! Do you now believe? If you believe the truth with your hearts, and confess it with your mouths, you will be approved by God. *"For with the heart one believes unto righteousness, and with the mouth confession is made unto salvation" (Romans 10:10).* This is why faith is so important. And it is also of utmost importance to believe in the Word of God with all our hearts. What is critical for us is not believing in what men say, but in the written Word of God; and what is important for us is not believing in the Word with our own thoughts or emotions, but believing it as it is with our sincere hearts. This is why the servants of God and those who have been saved before are preaching the Word of God as it is.

With the mark of circumcision, God made His covenant with Abraham and his descendants and gave them the sacrificial system of the Tabernacle, so that they could believe in Jesus Christ, the Messiah to come, that would forgiven all their sins with His baptism and His blood on the Cross, and so that with this faith they could enter the Kingdom of God.

I believe in God's Word of covenant. Not only Abraham

was blessed by believing in the Word of God, but all of us can also be blessed, just like him, by believing in His Word. I believe that God built the Tabernacle to save us from all our sins. This is why God led the descendants of Abraham all the way to the Mountain Sinai and gave them the Law and the sacrificial system of the Tabernacle. We must all realize that this truth is the providence of God. ⊠

SERMON

6

The Promise of God Established in His Covenant of Circumcision Is Still Effective for Us

< Genesis 17:1-14 >
"When Abram was ninety-nine years old, the LORD appeared to Abram and said to him, 'I am Almighty God; walk before Me and be blameless. And I will make My covenant between Me and you, and will multiply you exceedingly.' Then Abram fell on his face, and God talked with him, saying: 'As for Me, behold, My covenant is with you, and you shall be a father of many nations. No longer shall your name be called Abram, but your name shall be Abraham; for I have made you a father of many nations. I will make you exceedingly fruitful; and I will make nations of you, and kings shall come from you. And I will establish My covenant between Me and you and your descendants after you in their generations, for an everlasting covenant, to be God to you and your descendants after you. Also I give to you and your descendants after you the land in which you are a stranger, all the land of Canaan, as an everlasting possession; and I will be their God.' And God said to Abraham: 'As for you, you shall keep My covenant, you and your descendants after you throughout their generations. This is My covenant which you shall keep,

**between Me and you and your descendants after you:
Every male child among you shall be circumcised; and you
shall be circumcised in the flesh of your foreskins, and it
shall be a sign of the covenant between Me and you. He who
is eight days old among you shall be circumcised, every
male child in your generations, he who is born in your
house or bought with money from any foreigner who is not
your descendant. He who is born in your house and he who
is bought with your money must be circumcised, and My
covenant shall be in your flesh for an everlasting covenant.
And the uncircumcised male child, who is not circumcised
in the flesh of his foreskin, that person shall be cut off from
his people; he has broken My covenant.'"**

In chapter 17 of the Book of Genesis, the covenant of
circumcision that God established with Abraham shows us the
spiritual circumcision by which all the sins are cut off from the
Israelites by putting their hands on the head of their sacrificial
offering in the Tabernacle and thus passing their sins on to it.
In other words, the covenant that God established with
Abraham was the prefiguration of the sin offering and the burnt
offering. The promise that God made to Abraham with
circumcision, that He would be his God and the God of his
descendants, prophesied, with respect to the Tabernacle, that
Abraham's descendants were to pass their sins onto their
sacrificial offering by putting their hands on its head. We must
also realize and believe that this shows us, in addition, that in
the New Testament's time Jesus would take upon all the sins of
the world with His baptism received from John.

God promised Abraham, *"Look now toward heaven, and
count the stars if you are able to number them…. So shall your*

descendants be" (Genesis 15:5). Appearing again before Abraham, God promised once more, *"I will make you exceedingly fruitful; and I will make nations of you, and kings shall come from you. And I will establish My covenant between Me and you and your descendants after you in their generations, for an everlasting covenant, to be God to you and your descendants after you" (Genesis 17:6-7).*

The promise that God made to Abraham and his descendants came through circumcision. This circumcision coincided with the laying on of hands that would be performed when the Israelites were to give their sacrificial offering to God. It also foretold, for the New Testament's time, the remission of sin fulfilled by Jesus taking upon the sins of the world with His baptism received from John. We must realize and believe that the Old Testament's circumcision promised by God to Abraham is manifested in the New Testament by the spiritual circumcision of the washing of sin fulfilled by the baptism of Jesus. And it tells us, in addition, that the faith of Abraham was also needed by the Israelites when giving the sacrificial offering in the Tabernacle.

God told Abraham, *"You shall be circumcised in the flesh of your foreskins, and it shall be a sign of the covenant between Me and you. He who is eight days old among you shall be circumcised, every male child in your generations, he who is born in your house or bought with money from any foreigner who is not your descendant" (Genesis 17:11-12).* God, in other words, made His promise to Abraham and his descendants through circumcision. He promised that He would be Abraham's God and the God of his descendants, but in return, Abraham and his descendants were to be circumcised: *"He who is born in your house and he who is bought with your money must be circumcised, and My covenant shall be in your flesh for an everlasting covenant" (Genesis 17:13).*

This is why of all the people of the world, only the Israeli men had cut out their foreskins from the days of Abraham. Nowadays, circumcision has become much more widespread because of its health benefits, but at the time, only the Israeli males were circumcised. This was the mark of God's promise to Abraham, and God made him and the people of Israel, his descendants, to carry in their flesh this sign of the covenant that He established with them.

Genesis 17:11 says, *"you shall be circumcised in the flesh of your foreskins, and it shall be a sign of the covenant between Me and you."* So the circumcision was the mark of the covenant. To recapitulate, this is how God made His promise: "How do you know that you are My people? You know it by looking at the scars of your circumcision. From now on, every male born among you should be circumcised on his foreskin. In this way, My covenant will be in your flesh for an everlasting covenant. I promise you to be your God and the God of your descendants. And I promise you to bless you, to multiply you, to make you enter into the land of Canaan and live in it forever, and to make nations of you and raise kings from you" (Genesis 17:4-14).

God said that the covenant that He established with Abraham and his descendants would be found in their flesh. God's promise was imprinted, in other words, in the scars of the circumscribed Israeli men. God made His promise to the people of Israel through their circumcision, and, accordingly, whether men were circumcised or not determined whether they were the descendants of Abraham or not. Those who were circumcised, therefore, were recognized and blessed by God as Abraham's descendants, while the uncircumcised were not recognized as such.

Abraham Is Actually a Very Important Man for the People of Israel

For the people of Israel, the man more important than even Moses, the father of the Law, is none other than Abraham, the father of faith. Though there are many Israelites who do not remember Noah, few, if any, fail to remember Abraham. Only a handful of them may remember Shem, Seth, or Methuselah, but Abraham remains as the unforgettable father of faith for all the people of Israel. They all recognize, believe, and follow him as the father of their nation. As such, the promise that God made to the Israelites through Abraham still remains effective.

The people of Israel are wholly convinced of themselves, believing, "We are the descendants of Abraham. Our people carry the sign of circumcision in our flesh. God is therefore our God, and we are His own people." The reason why the Israelites consider themselves as the chosen people is because they still believe in the covenant that God established with Abraham through circumcision.

Abraham had two wives: his lawful wife Sarai who was named Sarah by God later, and his second wife Hagar, who had been Sarai's maidservant. Because it looked as though Sarai would bear him no child, Abraham, in his own thoughts, sought to have a child through Hagar (Genesis 16:1-4). But God said clearly that because Sarai was the lawful wife of Abraham, it would be through her own child that He would give Abraham as many descendants as the stars in the sky. Since God promised that He would recognize only those born of Sarai's body as His people, Ishmael, who was born from the second wife Hagar, was not recognized as such before God.

Were the people of Israel not to be circumcised, the promise that God made to them would become ineffective. God told them to be circumcised as the sign of His covenant so that this covenant would be in their flesh. As such, the Israelites made sure to be circumcised, since being uncircumcised would render God's promise ineffective. There is probably no one among the people of Israel who was not circumcised, for they know too well that the uncircumcised is like the Gentiles, to whom God's promise is irrelevant.

The Spiritual Circumcision

The covenant that God established with Abraham and his descendants was wholly accomplished through the remission of all sins fulfilled by Jesus Christ when He came to this earth and took upon the sins of mankind by being baptized by John the Baptist.

God told the Israelites to make the gate of the court of the Tabernacle and its covering veil by weaving them with blue, purple, and scarlet thread and fine woven linen (Exodus 26:31, 27:16). Through this detailed form of the Tabernacle, God has taught us the salvation coming through Jesus Christ. Those who believe in the truth that the Lord came to this earth, took upon the sins of the mankind with His baptism received from John at the age of 30, died on the Cross, rose from the dead again, and thereby has forgiven us of all our sins—they are all Abraham's descendants. God has become the God of those who believe in the Tabernacle's blue, purple, and scarlet thread and fine woven linen.

By believing in the baptism of Jesus, we must all be spiritually circumcised. This spiritual circumcision is none other than cutting off the sins of our hearts by believing that all our sins were passed on to Jesus Christ through His baptism

(Romans 2:29).

As such, those who have received the remission of sin today by believing in the gospel of the water and the Spirit manifested in the blue, purple, and scarlet thread and the fine woven linen are all kings of God's Kingdom and His own children. Just as God promised, *"kings shall come from you (Genesis 17:6),"* His people are indeed rising up throughout the entire world.

If we want to become Abraham's descendants, we have to believe in the baptism that Jesus received on this earth and His blood on the Cross. As such, I cannot emphasize enough just how important it is to know and believe in the baptism of Jesus. Jesus Christ is the King of kings. He is the King of kings who came wearing a purple rob (John 19:5). Jesus Christ is the King of the universe and its Creator. As He is God's only begotten Son, He came to this earth in obedience to the Father's will, and to deliver us from our sins, He took upon all our sins with His baptism all at once. To blot out our sins, He cut out all our sins from our hearts and put them onto His own body with His baptism, and was judged for all our sins by shedding His blood on the Cross. As such, all who believe in this truth can become Abraham's descendants.

Abraham, his family, and his descendants were all physically circumcised. Even the slaves bought with money from the Gentiles were circumcised. When they believed in the covenant and were circumcised, even these Gentile slaves were blessed, and God also became their God. As such, it is by faith that we become the children of God, by faith that we are blessed by God, by faith that we enter Heaven, and by faith that we live as kings on this earth. In the New Testament's time, this faith is the faith of those who believe that Jesus took upon all the sins of the world with His baptism.

However, some people claim that this baptism of Jesus is not that important, for they believe that they have been forgiven for their sins by believing only in His blood on the Cross. Although they believe in the laying on of hands on the head of the sacrificial offering performed in the age of the Tabernacle, they place little important on Jesus' own baptism. They therefore insist that because Abraham's faith was approved before the first advent of Jesus on this earth and even far before the Tabernacle of Moses, they are still saved only by believing in the Word of the blood of the Cross, even without believing in the clear Word of Jesus' baptism.

But we must remember that when God told Abraham to bring Him a three-year-old heifer, a three-year-old female goat, a three-year-old ram, a turtledove, and a young pigeon—all to make Abraham realize that He would give the land of Canaan to Abraham and his descendants as their inheritance—God had in His mind the burnt offering of sacrifice by fire. Genesis 15:17 says, *"And it came to pass, when the sun went down and it was dark, that behold, there appeared a smoking oven and a burning torch that passed between those pieces."* God had also approved the sacrificial burnt offering of Abel and his faith, but He did not approve the faith of Cain, who did not believe in this burnt offering of sacrifice.

Among today's Christians, there are too many people who mistakenly understand that they are saved just by believing in Jesus blindly, without ever being spiritually circumcised in faith. They believe only in the crucifixion of Jesus, without believing in the truth that all their sins were passed onto Jesus through His baptism. These people can never become God's own people, for believing in such a way can never blot out their sins from their hearts. As God said that the sign of His covenant is in the flesh of the circumcised, the uncircumcised therefore has nothing to do with this promise of God.

Can people be saved from sin without believing in the baptism that Jesus received from John the Baptist? Can such people become God's children? Can they enter Heaven? Can they become kings of His Kingdom? The answer to these questions is a resounding no! The main passage that we have read today provides the clear evidence for this answer. Today, the promise that God had made to Abraham is the same promise that He has made to you and me, those of us who have received the remission of sin by believing Jesus Christ as our Savior, in His baptism and His blood on the Cross. To those who thus believe, the same Word of blessings that God spoke to Abraham is applicable.

The True Believers of Jesus Do Not Follow the Doctrines of Their Own Making

The Word of God in the Bible is the definite and clear truth of salvation; the more we read and ponder over it, the more definite and the clearer it becomes. Among today's Christians, there are many whose faith is mistaken, believing in and following God based on their own thoughts, and yet unaware that what they believe in is actually false. The very foundation of such people's faith is wrong. Believing blindly that Jesus has saved them anyway may be enough to satisfy their self-consciousness, but they must realize that God does not approve their blind faith.

Our Lord said that whoever wants to follow Him must first deny him/herself and carry his/her cross. Whoever believes in the Word of God must put down his/her own thoughts and believe according to what the Word of God actually says. Today, you and I must believe in the remission of sin that Jesus Christ has given us by coming to this earth, taking upon and carrying the sins of the world with His baptism, shedding His blood on the Cross, and rising again from the dead.

In these days, there are way too many people who do not believe so, but who blindly hold onto the name of Jesus, saying that they have their own way of believing. The faith of such people has nothing to do with the gospel of the water and the Spirit given by Jesus. For example, there are some people who claim that Jesus showed up while they were praying in some deep mountains, insisting that this is how they were saved. In another example, there are those who claim that their sins all disappeared while they went to a church, fasted, and stayed up all night praying, because they were agonized by their sins, which they could not get rid of with their prayers of repentance.

These kinds of faith have nothing to do with the true salvation that comes only through the gospel of the water and the Spirit given by our Lord. Where does it say in the Word of God that He would forgive our sins if we have such kinds of faith? Nowhere! These people, vaguely aware that God is the absolute One and that Jesus is the Almighty, are borrowing the name of Christ, adding their shallow and uncertain knowledge of God onto their unreliable faith—they are thereby calling God's name in vain, forgetting their own sins, and garnering even more wrath of God. Such people have constructed their own fictitious Jesus and their own version of salvation, and believe in these figments of their own imagination.

Genesis 17:14 says, *"And the uncircumcised male child, who is not circumcised in the flesh of his foreskin, that person shall be cut off from his people; he has broken My covenant."* God has clearly promised us that He would save us from our sins through the spiritual circumcision. And God has also promised us unambiguously that only those who are born again of the water and the Spirit would become His children. As such, those who believe only in Jesus' blood on the Cross without believing in His baptism cannot ever become God's children. Such people have betrayed God, for they have not believed in the gospel promised by God, and they are therefore to be cut off from God's people and accursed by Him.

The foundation of faith that can save us from our sins is none other than the gospel of the water and the Spirit. Only when the gospel of the water and the Spirit is laid out as our foundation can we firmly and wholly believe in the Word of God. How can the spiritual Gentiles whose hearts remain spiritually uncircumcised can ever take the Word of God to their hearts? They can never do this! Because the gospel of the water and the Spirit allows us to be spiritually circumcised, enabling us to become God's children, without having this very definite foundation, the Word of God can come to us only as intellectual knowledge.

This is why the spiritual teachings of the born-again servants can be understandable and available only to those who basically believe in the gospel of the water and the Spirit. In other words, only those who are born again of the water and the Spirit can hear and understand the Word of God. When we meet people who, being ignorant of the gospel of the water and the Spirit, claim to have been born again only through the blood of the Cross, although they say that we all believe in the same God, we nevertheless feel as if we are speaking of an entirely different God. Who is the real God here? The real God is the God who gave His Word of promise to Abraham.

God promised Abraham and his descendants, *"My covenant shall be in your flesh for an everlasting covenant"*

(Genesis 17:13). Where is the sign telling us that we have received the remission of our sins? It is found in our hearts. By believing in the baptism of Jesus Christ with our hearts, we have become the children of God, whose hearts have received the spiritual circumcision by believing in the true gospel. We became His children by believing with our hearts that the Lord was baptized because of our sins to take upon all these sins of ours and that we have become spiritually circumcised.

It is by our faith in this truth that we passed all our sins onto Jesus Christ, and Jesus, in turn, carried these sins to the Cross, was crucified in our place, rose from the dead again, and thereby has saved us from all our sins. It is by faith, in other words, that we have become God's children. It is by faith that we have become sinless. Do we then have any more sin left in us? Of course not! We have no sin whatsoever! All this was fulfilled by the truly marvelous truth of the gospel.

How Can You and I Become Abraham's Descendants?

We have become Abraham's descendants because we were spiritually circumcised by believing in the works of Jesus manifested in the blue, purple, and scarlet thread of the Tabernacle. It is because we believed in the baptism of Jesus and His blood on the Cross that we have been spiritually circumcised and become God's children. It is because we believed that Jesus took upon all our sins with His baptism and was judged for all our sins on the Cross that we have received the remission of sin. This is how you and I have become Abraham's descendants spiritually.

Those who are born again of the water and the Spirit must

now recognize who they really are. You and I, we who believe in the gospel of the water and the Spirit, are all God's children and His own people, who have been spiritually circumcised by faith.

We are the kings of the coming Millennial Kingdom, who would reign over all the creations of God and enjoy His entire splendor. This is how our status has now changed. Do the people of this world know who we really are? They do not. But we are the ones whose spiritual status has changed by believing in the Word of God. As such, we can now know ourselves clearly and unambiguously.

Those who have been born again by the Word of God know who they really are. We are fundamentally different from those who are prone to advertise themselves in their worldly religious communities, who preach false doctrines even as they are completely ignorant, and who look coldly upon the born-again, the true people of God. As the people of Israel believe themselves to be the chosen people and regard the descendants of Ishmael differently, we who are the spiritual descendants of Abraham also have the right to consider ourselves as the chosen people of God.

Those of us who believe in the gospel of the water and the Spirit have fortunately become, through our faith, Abraham's descendants. We can enter the Kingdom of Heaven by our faith in the gospel of the blue, purple, and scarlet thread manifested in the Tabernacle.

And just as God promised Abraham that He would make his descendants as many as the stars in the sky, we can witness with our eyes the actual fulfillment of this covenant to us. This is the blessing that God has bestowed on us.

Through the circumcision of our hearts, God has saved us from the sins of the world. And this circumcision of faith is made of the blue, purple, and scarlet thread, and the fine woven linen used to make the gate of the Tabernacle. ⊠

SERMON

7

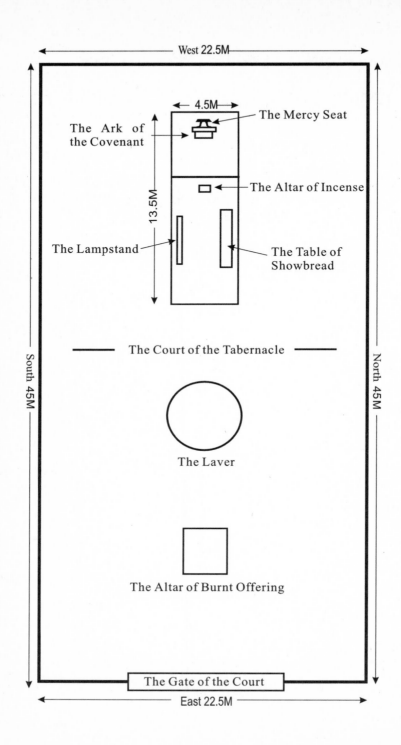

West 22.5M

4.5M

The Mercy Seat

The Ark of the Covenant

13.5M

The Altar of Incense

The Lampstand

The Table of Showbread

The Court of the Tabernacle

South 45M

North 45M

The Laver

The Altar of Burnt Offering

The Gate of the Court

East 22.5M

The Building Materials of The Tabernacle That Laid The Foundation of Faith

< Exodus 25:1-9 >

"Then the LORD spoke to Moses, saying: 'Speak to the children of Israel, that they bring Me an offering. From everyone who gives it willingly with his heart you shall take My offering. And this is the offering which you shall take from them: gold, silver, and bronze; blue, purple, and scarlet thread, fine linen, and goats' hair; ram skins dyed red, badger skins, and acacia wood; oil for the light, and spices for the anointing oil and for the sweet incense; onyx stones, and stones to be set in the ephod and in the breastplate. And let them make Me a sanctuary, that I may dwell among them. According to all that I show you, that is, the pattern of the tabernacle and the pattern of all its furnishings, just so you shall make it.'"

Poor Lives

In a poem entitled *'A Psalm of Life,'* Henry Wadsworth Longfellow wrote, "Tell me not, in mournful numbers, 'Life is but an empty dream!'"

However, if you really think about it, the lives of human beings are indeed very poor. Though everyone's life may seem to end up returning to dust in vain after a lonely and transient living in this wilderness of the world, the earth is not the final destination. The final end of every person's life will be, because of sin, the everlasting, fearful sufferings of hell.

Yet people are usually indifferent to their own death and the world beyond the grave. While living in this world, people thus live without any purpose, heading toward hell, unable to meet God who has saved them. This is life. But if this indeed were all that there is to life, how poor and pitiful would we be?

To such lives, the Messiah is waiting. If people were carelessly thrown into this open world only to roam aimlessly and disappear into the darkness, they would indeed be leading pitiful and miserable existences. We can all recognize this just by looking at those around us.

The other day, when I was in a car, I saw an old man, around 60 years old, walking along the road. Walking with his back behind me, his head was tilted down and his shoulder sagged, all around looking quite lonely. When I honked, he turned around, and I saw that his face was filled with sorrows. Seeing this old man's expression, I contemplated for a while. This old man was probably feeling how empty his life was. The desolation of the fall perhaps added even more to this feeling of emptiness, making him feel even more of the futility of his life. Not only the life of this man, but of everyone is, in fact, truly pitiful.

With time flying by them, people do not even realize that they are getting old, until they suddenly discover deep wrinkles all around them. Many of them have faced so many difficulties in their lives that they did not even have a chance to pause, turn around, and see where they had been walking. Though all the parents had lived and labored hard for their children and family, words cannot describe their sadness, for when are facing their own sunset, nothing remains of their lives.

Taken over by their emotion, they are soon overwhelmed by tears. After so much time passed by, and after so many years gone by, they finally have a chance to look back, and when they do so, all that they can feel is just how uncannily this desolated scenery of the late fall fits into their own reflections. With the fall, when all the leaves have fallen off, and facing only the dreary winter, they recognize that their lives, too, will soon disappear in this manner. They would regret, of course, that it took them so long to realize this. What hope would these people have, when they are about to pass away without even meeting the Lord? Such people who come to their end without having met the Messiah are forever pitiful.

I myself would also have led a pitiful life had I not met the Lord. What about you? Where would you be heading now, if you had not met the Lord either? There are too many people in this world who, because they were unable to meet the Lord, have reserved their own unhappiness.

It breaks my heart when I think about these people, that there are so many people who have reserved their own unhappiness. All that pigs have to do is just to feed themselves until they face their end, but our lives are different from these pigs, for we must contemplate and look beyond the present into the eternal future. Many people meet their final day full of regrets. Though they know that there is the eternal Kingdom of Heaven, they recognize that they are too unfit to enter it, for they have remained sinful. That there are so many such lives full of such regrets only makes me lament and mourn for their sorry fate.

When we think about these lives, that they are unable to go to the good place prepared by God, and that they are to disappear from this world without having fulfilled the real purpose of their lives, we can only pity these soul and lament for their fate. This is why life is often compared to a voyage over a rough and difficult ocean. In referring to life, people say that it is like living in such an ocean, trying to survive in the bitterness of human world, for from their very birth to their death, they must suffer, kicking and screaming just to survive.

When we remind ourselves that this is what life is all about, we realize with certainty that explaining the truth of this Tabernacle to all the people and helping them to meet the Lord are all works of critical importance. Why? Because through the sacrificial offering, God gives to these sinful people their salvation from sin by meeting them in His own House of God. The Tabernacle is the House of God established in the wilderness. In this House of God, the Tabernacle, God meets the sinful through the grace of the remission of sin fulfilled by the offering of sacrifice. God tells us, "I will make you build My House where I will dwell, and I will meet you inside this Tabernacle, on its mercy seat." Only in the Tabernacle, the House of God, is anyone given a chance to meet God.

This faith in the truth of the Tabernacle cannot be exchanged for anything else in this world, and it is the most precious that cannot be purchased at any price. I believe that for those of us who have the Christian faith that believes in Jesus Christ as our Savior, to have the exact knowledge of and proper faith in this Tabernacle is the way to step onto an even more blessed road.

We Live Our Blessed Lives

My heart is filled with the happy thought, wondering if there is anyone else who is living such a blessed life as we are living. Though life is such a pitiful existence, many people carry on with their lives while remaining completely oblivious to their own fate. But God wants to make them recognize just how stubborn their lives had been before Him, and to make their hearts repent. They, on the other hand, are still trying to live their lives without listening to the gospel that God has given them freely, and without opening up even the tiniest space in their hearts.

Exodus tells us about the ten plagues that God brought to Pharaoh. A total of ten plagues were brought to the land of Egypt. God had commanded Pharaoh to let go of His people living in Egypt. He told Pharaoh that if he would not obey Him, He would bring ten plagues to him. But Pharaoh did not listen to what God had told him, resisted His command in stubbornness, and ended up receiving all the ten plagues that God had promised. Pharaoh's obstinacy was wrong-footed. Also, the reason why he finally freed the people of Israel only after receiving all the punishments of God was because he was held by Satan. This refers to our own wrong recalcitrance found in each and every one of us.

Such people, however, can still receive the remission of sin set by God in His Tabernacle, and live with Him in faith. Yet these people are so obstinate that they continue to reject and not believe in God's truth with the stubbornness of a donkey. This is why there are so many people who fail to meet the God of truth, live their lives as sinners, and ultimately face their own destruction. This saddens me beyond grief. Too many people are being way too stubborn before God.

Because such people yield for a while when they face hardships, but then go right back to where they were before rejecting God's will and once again resuming their recalcitrant ways, they would face their second plague. With this second plague, they yield a little bit. But this would not last long, for they would yet again start to not obey God and challenge Him. And so they are subjected to their third plague, followed by their fourth, fifth, sixth, seventh, eighth, and ninth plagues, until they finally surrender only after the last plague and are destroyed.

When the last plague comes, there will be many people who would bear the suffering of hell for not believing in what the Messiah had done for them. How foolish are such people's lives? This is why everyone's life is so pitiful.

Though people's live are only pitiful before God, you must realize that meeting God in the Tabernacle is a great blessing for you, and dwell upon the Word of Tabernacle with this realization.

The Offerings That God Demands from Us

God commanded Moses to come up to the Mountain Sinai and gave him a whole series of His Law. First of all, He gave Moses the Ten Commandments: "You shall have no other gods before Me; you shall neither make images nor bow before them; you shall not call My name in vain; you shall remember the Sabbath and keep it holy; you shall honor your parents, you shall not murder; you shall not commit adultery; you shall not steal; you shall not bear false witness against your neighbor; and you shall not covet." In addition, God also spoke them of other laws that the Israelites had to keep in their everyday life: They were the 613 commandments and laws of God in total.

These 613 commandments covered such aspects as what to do when the Israelites lost their cattle, what to do when someone else's cattle fell into a hole, that they should not commit incest, that if they had servants they had to set them free on the seventh year, that if they had let their female servant wed their single male servant and had a child, they should let the male servant go by himself on the seventh year, and so on and so forth. God told Moses all such ethical laws that the Israelites had to keep by faith in the sight of God in their everyday life.

God then told Moses to go down the mountain, gather the elders, and declare His commandments. Hearing God's Word, the people of Israel all agreed, and swore with their blood that they would thus obey all His commandments (Exodus 24:1-4).

Then, God called Moses to the mountain once again, this time to command him to build the Tabernacle.

God spoke to Moses, *"Speak to the children of Israel, that they bring Me an offering. From everyone who gives it willingly with his heart you shall take My offering" (Exodus 25:2).* He then listed His offering: *"And this is the offering which you shall take from them: gold, silver, and bronze; blue, purple, and scarlet thread, fine linen, and goats' hair; ram skins dyed red, badger skins, and acacia wood; oil for the light, and spices for the anointing oil and for the sweet incense; onyx stones, and stones to be set in the ephod and in the breastplate" (Exodus 25:3-7).*

There was a concrete purpose behind God telling them to bring these offerings. This purpose was to build on this earth the shining House of God, where there is no sin and where God is to dwell, so that He would meet the people of Israel there and make their sins disappear. This does not mean, however, that God told them to bring money to build a memorial edifice just like today's churches. False prophets of today's Christianity are prone to misapply this passage when they are trying to build their church buildings in order to satisfy their own lusts.

In contrast, God told the Israelites to bring Him these offerings so that He would use them to build His own House and bless them abundantly there. In fact, the reason why God received these offerings was to deliver us from our sins and to save us from our judgment. It was for God Himself to meet us, we who lead pitiful lives, to wash away our sins, to make our sins disappear, and to make us His own people.

The Hidden Spiritual Meanings of the Offerings That God Commanded to Be Brought to Him

Before we proceed any further, let us first spend some time contemplating on the spiritual meanings of these offerings that God commanded to be brought to Him. After this, we will examine our faith in its light.

Gold, Silver, and Bronze

We should first of all find out where gold, silver, and bronze were used. In the Tabernacle, gold was used for the Holy Place, the Most Holy, and the items found in them, including the lampstand, the table of showbread, the altar of incense, the mercy seat, and the Ark of the Testimony. Gold refers to faith in the Word of God. And silver refers to the grace of salvation. It tells us that we must have the faith that believes in the gift of salvation given solely by the Messiah, and the faith that believes that our Lord has taken upon all our sins and was judged for us.

Bronze, in contrast, was used for the sockets of the

Tabernacle's pillars, its pegs, the laver, and the altar of burnt offering. All the bronze utensils were to be buried in or set on the ground. This refers to the judgment of people's sins, and bronze also tells us that we are to be condemned by God for failing to keep the Law and because of our sins.

What, then, are the spiritual meanings of gold, silver, and bronze? They constitute the foundations of faith in receiving the gift of salvation given by God. The Bible tells us that all of us are sinners who cannot keep the Law wholly, that we therefore are to die because of our sins, and that instead of our own death the Lord came to this earth and was condemned for our sins in our place by becoming the sacrificial offering of the sin offering that was given in the Tabernacle.

To solve the problem of their sins, sinners brought an unblemished animal to the Tabernacle and, according to the sacrificial system, passed their sins onto it by laying their hands on its head; the sacrificial offering that accepted their sins then shed its blood and was killed. By doing so, the people of Israel, who were bound to hell (bronze), could receive the remission of their sins (silver) and escape from their condemnation of sin by faith (gold).

The Blue, Purple, and Scarlet Thread and the Fine Woven Linen

Here are the other frequently used materials; blue, purple, and scarlet thread and fine woven linen. These threads were used for the gate of the court of the Tabernacle, the gate of the Holy Place, and the dividing veil between the Holy Place and the Most Holy. These four threads tell us the truth that just as prophesied in Genesis 3:15, that the Lord would come as a woman's offspring, our Lord would indeed come to this earth and save sinners from their sins by being baptized and crucified, and that God Himself would save us.

These four threads were used not only for the gates of the Tabernacle, but also for the High Priest's garments and the Tabernacle's first covering. This was God's covenant that Jesus Christ would come to this earth and save us from our sins by fulfilling His works of the blue, purple, and scarlet thread. And our Lord did in fact keep this promise and has indeed saved us from the sins of the world.

The most critical point of the gates of the Tabernacle is the blue thread. Why did Jesus Christ, coming to this earth as the Messiah, have to die on the Cross? The reason is because He was baptized. The blue thread refers to the baptism of Jesus, the purple thread tells us that Jesus is the King, and the scarlet thread refers to His crucifixion and bloodshed. The blue, purple, and scarlet thread and the fine woven linen are the essential building materials, which constitute the gift of salvation that Jesus Christ has given us by coming to this earth as the Messiah and taking all our sins upon Himself.

Many people in this world only emphasize that Jesus Christ is the Son of God, and that He is fundamentally God Himself. But God tells us clearly through the Tabernacle that such teachings cannot be the whole truth.

The Apostle Paul said in 1 Peter 3:21, *"There is also an antitype which now saves us—baptism (not the removal of the filth of the flesh, but the answer of a good conscience toward God), through the resurrection of Jesus Christ."*

This testifies to us that Jesus Christ fulfilled His promise of salvation and laid the foundations of faith wholly by receiving His baptism, the antitype that saves us. Who is our Messiah? The Messiah means the Savior, telling us that Jesus came to this earth, was baptized to take all our sins and all the sins of the world upon Himself, and did in fact take them all upon Himself with His baptism.

God told the Israelites to build the gate of the court of the Tabernacle by weaving it with blue, purple, and scarlet thread and fine woven linen. And the purpose for our Lord, who is the King of kings and the Lord of Heaven, to come to this earth in the flesh of a man was to fulfill the truth of these blue, purple, and scarlet thread and the fine woven linen. Our Lord came in the flesh of a man and received the baptism that would fulfill all the righteousness of God from John the Baptist, the representative of mankind.

This was akin to the Old Testament's sacrificial offering that accepted the sins of the Israelites passed onto it by laying on of High Priest's hands on its head and that was condemned for these sins in their place. In other words, just like the sacrificial offering of the Old Testament, Jesus came in the New Testament as the sacrificial offering for the sins of all sinners, was baptized, crucified, and thereby bore all the condemnation of the sins of the world. Jesus fulfilled the truth of the blue thread by being baptized by John as the sacrificial Lamb of God. With this baptism, Jesus took the sins of mankind upon Himself at all once.

The reason why most Christians have turned into the kind of people who are even worse than the people of other worldly religions is because they have been unable to know and believe in this truth of the blue thread, the baptism of Jesus, and have therefore not received the remission of their sins at once. When Christians do not have the correct interpretation of this baptism that Jesus received to take our sins upon Himself, their very foundations of faith cannot be laid correctly from the beginning.

To be exact, the blue thread is the method and the truth by

which the Messiah came to this earth and took our sins upon Himself. And the scarlet thread refers to the blood of Jesus. The reason why Jesus Christ was crucified, shed His blood, and died on the Cross is because all our sins had been passed onto Him through His baptism. It was because Jesus had taken our sins upon Himself with His baptism received from John that He could therefore die on the Cross, and it was because of this fact that His sacrifice on the Cross for us was not in vain. It was because Jesus Christ the Messiah bore all our condemnation of sin wholly with His baptism and crucifixion that He could complete our salvation.

The purple thread means that Jesus Christ is God and the King of kings. Although Jesus Christ is the King of kings (the purple thread), had He not been baptized by John the Baptist, the representative of mankind, and had he therefore not taken our sins upon Himself (the blue thread), no mater with how much suffering and pain He died on the Cross (the scarlet thread), His death would have been only in vain. The fine woven linen is telling us that the Word of prophecy that God spoke in the Old Testament is all fulfilled in the New Testament.

Today's Christianity Has Lost the Meaning of the Blue Tread

Yet there is a marked tendency in today's Christianity to ignore the blue thread among the four treads and to arbitrarily interpret the Word of God on one's own—this great sin will surely be condemned.

The blue, purple, and scarlet thread and the fine woven linen used for the gate of the court of the Tabernacle tell us the truth of salvation, that to save us from our sins, Jesus Christ our Messiah had to come to this earth in the flesh of a man, and be baptized and crucified. Jesus took all our sins upon Himself.

How did Jesus take our sins upon Himself? He took them through the baptism that He received from John. Only by taking our sins upon Himself could Jesus become our true Savior. This is why the gates of the Tabernacle had to be woven of these four threads, for they tell us that Jesus, who came to this earth, was baptized, shed His blood on the Cross, and rose from the dead again, is God Himself.

As such, the gate of the Tabernacle's court was made of these blue, purple, and scarlet thread and fine woven linen. Jesus is the door of salvation leading us into the Kingdom of Heaven. This door is a door woven of the blue, purple, and scarlet thread and the fine woven linen. Jesus is the Savior of sinners. The baptism of Jesus and His crucifixion are His gift of salvation that has saved sinners from their sins.

It is because today's Christianity has failed to properly understand the baptism of Jesus that it has been unable to encounter the real God and has instead ended up turning into just one of the many worldly religions. As far as our faith is concerned, therefore, we must first lay the firm foundation of faith upon the truth of the blue, purple, and scarlet thread. This foundation of faith is the fact that our Lord came to this earth and has save you and me from the sins of the world through His blue, purple, and scarlet thread and fine woven linen.

Jesus came to this earth and has completed the gift of salvation that has saved us from all our sins with His baptism and the blood of the Cross. To be more specific, Jesus came to this earth in the flesh of a man, took the sins of the world upon Himself through His baptism, atoned all our sins with His blood of the Cross, and thus bore the condemnation of our sins by dying on the Cross. This Jesus who has thus saved us through the water and the blood (1 John 5:4-8) is fundamentally the Lord of creation who made us, and the very One who has given us the gift of salvation that has saved us. This Jesus who has saved us from all our sins and condemnation has become our true Savior. This is what the building materials of the Tabernacle are telling us.

As such, we must establish our faith firmly by believing in these materials. In believing in this Jesus who came as our Messiah as our very own Savior, we must believe clearly and definitely with all our hearts in the baptism that He received, in all the condemnation that He bore for us on the Cross, and in His resurrection from the dead. The Savior who has given us the gift of our salvation from all our sins through His baptism and the blood that He shed on the Cross was not just a man, but He was the very Creator who made the mankind and the whole universe. We must confess our faith in the blue, purple, and scarlet thread. Without such a confession of faith, it is simply untenable to believe in Jesus as the Savior.

Have you ever played a silent word-relaying game? This game starts from a person who is given a card on which a sentence is written. The person first reads the sentence secretly, and then expresses the sentence silently, only with the shape of lips. Then, the next one who reads the lips then passes it onto the third person. This person then reads the lips of the second person, and then passes it onto the fourth person in the same way, until the last person is reached. The point of this game is for the last person to correctly say the original sentence that was first passed on. The reason why this game is fun is that the original sentence gets easily distorted. For instance, if the game had started with a sentence that said, "Turn on the fan," after it is relayed onto a few people, it already begins to be changed. In the end, the last person might as well say, "Turn away the donkey," ending up with a completely different sentence.

Just as this last person comes up with a totally different sentence, so does today's Christianity have a completely misplaced faith, as if had been playing this silent word-relaying game. Why is this the case? It is because it has failed to lay the foundation of faith on the faith of the blue, purple, and scarlet thread. Today's Christianity has not grounded its foundation on this faith of the blue, purple, and scarlet thread. When the foundation of faith is faltering, no matter how ardently we believe in Jesus and how much we seek to apply His teachings to our lives, we simply cannot do this.

When the Lord told the Israelites to bring Him their offerings to build the Tabernacle, He told them to first bring gold, silver, and bronze, and then to bring blue, purple, and scarlet thread and fine woven linen. These building materials all show us that Jesus has saved us through His baptism received from John, His bleeding to death on the Cross, and His resurrection.

The blue thread was used not only for all the gates of the Tabernacle, but also for the High Priest's robe and the Tabernacle's coverings. This is the gospel that is telling us how our Lord came to this earth and just how exactly He has saved you and me from our sins. As such, it tells us how important these four basic constituents of faith—that is, the blue, purple, and scarlet thread and the fine wove linen—really are for our faith. Based on this Word, we must all lay our foundation of faith firmly. Only then can we believe in God and receive our remission of sin, become His servants who spread this word thereafter, and, when the Lord returns, thereby become such people of faith who can stand confidently before God with this faith.

In Korea, it is true that there is still toadyism that considers anything foreign to be better. This tendency is present among the theologians of my country as well, who place great confidence in what western theologians have said, relying on their words even more than on the Word of God. They must be freed from this ignorance, and they must truly believe in the Word of God, trusting in and depending on Him, for the truth of the baptism of our Lord, of His blood, and of the fact that He is God Himself, has fundamentally become the door of our salvation.

Just like the Apostle Peter confessed, *"You are the Christ, the Son of the living God,"* (Matthew 16:16) if you believe in God, and if you believe that the Lord came to this earth to save us from our sins, then you must also know and believe that the Lord became our true God of salvation by taking our sins upon Himself with His baptism, dying on the Cross, and rising from the dead again. The baptism of our Lord and the blood of the Cross are the foundations of the true faith that enables us to receive the gift of salvation. If we cannot even believe in the faith of the blue, purple, and scarlet thread according to the Word of God, how could we ever call it true faith?

The Law Is the Shadow of the Good Things to Come

The building materials of the Tabernacle show us that our Lord came to this earth in the flesh of a man, took our sins upon Himself with His baptism, bore the condemnation of our sins with His crucifixion, rose from the dead again, and thereby became our Savior. With the blue, purple, and scarlet thread, our Lord promised in the Old Testament that He would give us the gift of salvation. The One who gave us this covenant was none other than Jesus Christ, the King of kings who was baptized and crucified for the sake of sinners. This God, in other words, came to us as our God the Messiah. As such, we must lay the foundation of our faith by knowing and believing in this truth wholly. By believing in the gospel of the water and the Spirit, we must all receive the gift of salvation.

Gold, silver, and bronze were also the materials used for the Tabernacle. These materials refer to the foundation of our faith. Before God, we could not help but be cast into hell because of our sins. But to such people as us, our Lord has given the gift of salvation to those of us who believe. As the sacrificial offering for all mankind, Jesus Christ was baptized by John, crucified, and has thereby saved us wholly from our sins. There was no way for us to avoid hell, for we only knew that we were bound to be condemned for our sins, and did not know how we could have the faith that makes all our sins disappear. But in God there was the gift of salvation. That Jesus came to this earth, accepted all our sins onto Himself with His baptism, died on the Cross, and thereby has solve all the problems of our sins and condemnation—this is the gift of salvation.

We are saved from our sins through our faith, by believing that God has completed His work of our salvation and has given us the gift of this salvation. This is why God said to bring to Him the faith of gold, silver, and bronze, for He has wholly saved those who could not help but be bound to hell by giving them the gift of salvation. It is because our Lord has indeed saved us by coming to this earth, taking all our sins upon Himself, and bearing all our condemnation that we have been saved wholly before God by believing in this gift of salvation.

Jesus Christ has now become our perfect Savior. We must

therefore stand firmly with our faith in His gift of salvation, for the blue, purple, and scarlet thread and the fine woven linen are the gifts of faith. God does not want us to believe arbitrarily and blindly without knowing anything at all.

Goats' Hair, Ram Skins Dyed Red, and Badger Skins

These were used to make the coverings of the Tabernacle. The first covering was woven of blue, purple, and scarlet thread and fine woven linen, on which the second covering of goats' hair was laid. This was then covered by ram skins dyed red, and, lastly, badger skins were laid on top. In this way, four different layers of coverings covered the Tabernacle.

The covering that was last laid on the Tabernacle was of badger skins. So what appeared on the surface of the Tabernacle's coverings was just these black badger skins. A badger is a sea otter. The size of its skins is about the size of a man or slightly smaller, and the skins were waterproof. This is why badger skins were used as the covering for the top layer of the Tabernacle. Because of this, the outside appearance of the Tabernacle was rather unimpressive, and it certainly was not a pleasant sight to hold. This tells us that when Jesus came to this earth for us, He indeed came in such a lowly form, with nothing desirable in His appearance.

The ram skins dyed red tell us that Jesus Christ would come to this earth and be sacrificed for our sake, while the goats' hair tells us that He would save us by being baptized as our sacrificial offering and thereby accepting our sins onto Himself, and by being sacrificed on the Cross.

The materials of these coverings of the Tabernacle, in

other words, are the fundamentals of our faith. These truths are the building materials of faith that absolutely cannot be missing at all. To give us the gift of salvation, Jesus Christ came to this earth as our own sacrificial offering. In the Old Testament, God established the sacrificial system for the remission of Israelites' sins: The unblemished sacrificial animals (goats, lambs, or bulls) accepted the sins of the Israelites passed onto them with the laying on of hands, and were killed in their place, shedding their blood and being burnt, and thereby saving them from all their sins.

Jesus Christ came to this earth as the Lamb of sacrifice and accepted our sins onto Himself through His baptism, that is, the laying on of hands. Just as the sacrificial offering was killed by shedding its blood and burnt on the altar of burnt offering for accepting the sins of the Israelites with the laying on of hands, so, too, did Jesus Christ bear all the condemnation of our sins by being baptized and dying on the Cross, and has thereby saved us from the sins of the world.

As names on the Book of Judgment were blotted out by putting the blood of the sacrificial offering on the horns of the altar of burnt offering, it was because Jesus was baptized and shed His blood that He completed our eternal atonement with this blood and has blotted out all the sins of the world. Like this, all the materials of the Tabernacle speak to us of Jesus Christ and His ministries, telling us that He has thus saved us from the sins of the world. From the Old Testament to the New Testament, the Word that Jesus Has saved us from our sins is the whole truth, completely free from any mistakes.

Many of today's Christians do not believe that Jesus Christ came to this earth as our sacrificial offering and took our sins upon Himself with His baptism, but they instead believe unconditionally only in His death on the Cross. Such Christian

faith is of a lawless gate of the Tabernacle's court woven of
only the scarlet and purple thread, leaving the blue thread out.
They only have the mistaken faith that sees no need for the
covering made of the blue, purple, and scarlet thread and the
fine woven linen, and that instead believes that all that they
need is only the two coverings of ram skins dyed red and of
badger skins.

When we look at the many paintings of the Tabernacle
depicted throughout the world, most of them are painted in
such a way that we cannot find even the slightest trace of the
blue thread. Because the people who painted these pictures are
ignorant of the gospel of the water and the Spirit, the gate of
the Tabernacle's court in their paintings is all covered in scarlet
and white colors. But such faith can never be the right faith
before God.

The thread that was most used for the gate of the court of
the Tabernacle was the blue thread, followed by the purple
thread, then by the scarlet thread, and then by the white thread.
So when looking at the gate of the court, all these four colors
must come into view at once. But because there are so many
people in this world whose faith is completely devoid of any
knowledge of the baptism of Jesus, they have all ignored the
four colored threads used for the Tabernacle and instead built
their gates of the Tabernacle with only two threads.

By doing so, they are deceiving many people, who already
have only a limited knowledge of God and are quite ignorant of
His Word. These are all false prophets. Referring to these
people, Jesus Himself described them as the tares that the Devil
sowed among the wheat (Matthew 13:25). They have become,
in other words, people who spread false lies by leaving the blue
thread out of their painting of the gate of the Tabernacle' court.
This is why so many people remain sinful even as they believe

in Jesus, and why despite their faith in Jesus they are all bound to their destruction because of their sins.

Our foundation of faith must stand firmly. What good would it serve to lead a long period of religious life for your souls when it is all grounded in a lawless foundation of faith? Wrong faith can and will crumble down at a moment's notice. No matter how beautiful our house is, what good would it serve if we build this house on a flawed foundation of faith? Regardless of how diligently you have served God, if your foundation of faith is flawed, then you have only built your house on sand; when storms come, winds rise, and floods break out, it will all crumble down at once.

But what about the faith whose foundation is solid? It never falls down, no matter how it is shaken. God told us that a house built on the rock of the truth woven of the blue, purple, and scarlet thread and the fine woven linen will never fall down. This is actually the case. What is the faith of rock? It is the faith that believes in the truth of the blue, purple, and scarlet thread and the fine woven linen. The faith of those who have built such a house of faith will never collapse. This is why it is critical for our faith to have a firm and solid foundation. If we believe without even actually grasping exactly what the Lord has done for us, then such faith would turn into false religious faith, unwanted by God.

Acacia Wood, Oil, and Spices

The pillars of the Tabernacle, the altar of burnt offering, and the boards and the items of the Sanctuary were all made of acacia wood. Wood in the Bible usually implies human beings (Judges 9:8-15, Mark 8:24). The wood here also refers to us in

our human nature; that this acacia wood was used for the
pillars, the altar of burnt offering, and the Tabernacle itself tells
us that just like the roots of acacia trees are always buried
under the ground, our fundaments are such that we cannot help
but sin all the time. People must all admit that they simply
cannot help but continue to be unrighteous and to sin always.

At the same time, the acacia wood also implies the
humanity of Jesus Christ. The Messiah who came in the flesh
of a man bore all the sins of the world, and was judged
vicariously for the sake of all mankind. He is God Himself, and
therefore, the ark, the table of showbread, the altar of incense,
and the boards of the Tabernacle were all made of acacia wood
overlaid with pure gold.

The oil for the light and the spices for the anointing oil
and for the sweet incense refer to our faith that we offer to
Jesus Christ. Jesus Christ is the Messiah who has saved you
and me. The meaning of the name "Jesus" is "the One who will
save His people from their sins," and the name "Christ" means
"the anointed One," telling us therefore that Jesus Christ is God
Himself and the High Priest of Heaven who has saved us.
Obeying the will of God, our Lord came to this earth in the
flesh of a man, was baptized, sacrificed Himself on the Cross
for our sake, and has thereby given us the gift of salvation. The
role of the High Priest taken by Jesus who has give us our
salvation was indeed the most beautiful work.

Onyx Stones and Other Stones to Be Set in the Ephod and in the Breastplate of the High Priest

Twelve different precious stones are mentioned here that
would be set in the ephod and in the breastplate of the High

Priest. The High Priest first wore tunics, then put on a blue robe, and then wore the ephod over the robe. Then, the breastplate was placed on the ephod, which was worn during the sacrificial ceremony, and on this breastplate twelve precious stones were set. This shows us that the role of the High Priest was to embrace the people of Israel as well as all other people of the whole world into his bosom, to go before God, and to give Him their sacrificial offerings.

Jesus, the eternal High Priest of Heaven, also embraced all the nations of the world into His bosom, gave up His own body to take our sins upon Himself with His baptism and to be sacrificed on our behalf, and has thereby consecrated His people to God the Father. The twelve precious stones that were placed on the breastplate refer to all the nations of this world, and the High Priest who wore them refer to Jesus Christ who has likewise saved and embraced into His bosom all the nations of the world.

So these were the offerings that our God told the Israelites to bring to build the Tabernacle for Him. There is a spiritual meaning to the fact that God told them to build the Tabernacle, His place of dwelling, with these offerings. The people of Israel always remained sinful, because they could not keep the Law that God had given them. This is why God told them through Moses to build the Tabernacle and gave them the sacrificial system, through which the remission of sin was granted by the sacrificial offerings given in the Tabernacle. God, in other words, blotted out all the sins of the Israelites by accepting their offerings, using all these offerings to build His House, and then making them give Him their sacrificial offerings in it according to the requirements of the sacrificial system. This is how God could dwell in the Tabernacle with the people of Israel.

There are, however, too many Christians on this earth who simply do not believe in the blue, purple, and scarlet thread and the fine woven linen. When God told them to bring gold, silver, and bronze to Him, why do they not believe in the truth implied by these offerings?

Were we not all bound to hell because of our sins? Have you believed in Christianity as if it were just one of the many religions of this world because you have never admitted yourselves to be bound to hell? If this is how you have believed so far, then you must repent and return to the faith of the blue, purple, and scarlet thread and the fine woven linen. And you must realize before God's strict commandments that you are a mass of sin, and that you are bound to hell because of these sins, and you must believe in the gospel of the water and the Spirit.

Now, you must believe in the gospel of the truth, that even as you were bound to hell, our Lord nevertheless came to this earth as the Messiah, accepted your sins onto Himself with His baptism, carried these sins to the Cross and sacrificed Himself by shedding His blood on it, and has thereby saved you and me from our sins and our condemnation. Without believing in the gospel of the water and the Spirit manifested in the blue, purple, and scarlet thread, we can never lay our foundation of faith wholly.

We Must Think about the Foundation of Our Faith

God tells us to have the faith of the blue, purple, and scarlet thread; we should ask ourselves whether we indeed have this faith of the blue, purple, and scarlet thread, or whether we believe in the truth manifested only in the purple and scarlet thread, leaving out the blue thread.

We need to look at ourselves and see whether or not we are taking to God the wrong kind of faith that only fits our own taste. When God tells us to bring Him the blue, purple, and scarlet thread, are we not, by any chance, giving Him black-colored nylon thread? "God, the thread that you asked for seems to be useless for the Tabernacle. It'll just rot away with rain. And it's also quite tiresome to look for it and bring it all the way here. Try this nylon thread instead. I can guarantee you that it will last at least 50 years, maybe even 100 years if You maintain it well. And even if You bury it in the ground, it won't rot away for over 200 years. Isn't this just wonderful?"

Is this not, by any chance, what we are saying to God? We must also take a good look at ourselves and consider whether we are not indeed taking this kind of narcissistic and superstitious faith to God. And if we have had such faith, we must repent right now. We must, in other words, turn around.

There are many among us who think themselves that they are really good Christians, but upon a closer look, their knowledge is mistaken and so is their faith.

Mysticism That Is Prevalent in Today's Christianity

Mysticism is what Christians ordinarily believe in the most. These people have no idea what the Word of God is actually saying. Because they do not know the Word of truth that the Messiah has given them, they believe in and follow the Lord according to their own feelings and emotions. And they are convinced that such feelings are of truth. Because they pray to God fervently by themselves, and follow faithfully their own emotions and feelings that they sense in their prayers, they cannot discern what exactly is the true faith in God.

Like this, believing in God according to one's own emotions and feelings that fluctuate widely within one's own thoughts is the faith of mysticism. People who believe in God led by the feelings they get when they fast, when they praise, when they believe, when they give early morning prayers, when they clime up a mountain to pray, when they sin, when they give prayers of repentance, and so and so forth—these people are all mystics. In other words, living a life of faith by holding onto one's own feelings is not the faith of blue, purple, and scarlet thread that the Messiah spoke of.

Perhaps as many as 99.9 percent of today's Christians have historically been mystics. It is no exaggeration, in other words, to say that except for the Early Church, the entire Christendom has all been following mysticism. Those who do not have the faith of blue, purple, and scarlet thread are deluded into thinking that their own feelings are somehow faith itself. They claim to have seen and met God in their prayers, and tell us how wonderful they feel whenever they are praising.

They say, "We gathered at this praise meeting, and we lifted up our hands and together repented our sins. We held the Cross and performed some ritual at its foot, and then our hearts were all fired up, and Christ became so intensely lovable. We felt so much thanks in our hearts for the blood that Christ shed. We believed even more fervently that the Lord has washed away all our sins, realizing even more this is why He shed His blood. We just loved the whole experience." But when their emotions subside one day, they say, "But all that feeling has just dried up, and we have sin in our hearts." None other than this kind of faith is the faith of mysticism.

Regardless of one's denominational or sectarian differences, every Christian needs the faith that believes in the truth of the blue, purple, and scarlet thread. The faith of all those who do not have this faith of the blue, purple, and scarlet thread that God spoke are mystical and superstitious. These people are giving to God not the faith of the blue, purple, and scarlet thread, but the faith of nylon thread. They are bringing to God their mystical faith, in other words, something that falls far short, something that God does not even look at.

Have you ever seen the thick ropes used to tie boats at piers? The mystics would gladly offer God this kind of material. When our Lord has told us to bring the blue, purple, and scarlet thread and the fine woven linen, some people take this thick rope to God, saying to Him, "Lord, accept this faith!" And some people take to Him even iron chains used to tie big ships to each other and to the dock. Having rolled a bundle of this thick iron chains, they offer it at the Lord's feet, asking Him to accept it.

But God has told us to bring the faith of blue, purple, and scarlet thread. He has not told us to bring to Him iron chains. Yet many people are taking to Him what looks better in their own eyes or what are easier for them to find. Though there are people who go to God with iron chains, rope, nylon thread, or even arrowroot vines, God in fact receives only the offering of the blue, purple, and scarlet thread. God hast set that the only faith that He would accept is the faith of the blue, purple, and scarlet thread. As such, we must take this faith of the blue, purple, and scarlet thread before God.

The Messiah Does Not Receive Just Any Offering

The Israelites also had to take to God gold, silver, bronze, and twelve precious stones to be set in the ephod and the breastplate. Yet there are some people who take copper or iron to God. Is Jesus running a recycling dump, as if He would accept all kinds of things? Of course not!

Jesus is not someone who accepts just any kind of garbage. He does not run a recycling dump, taking in whatever useless stuff that you bring to Him. Jesus is the Messiah who wants to bestow on us His mercy of the blue, purple, and scarlet thread that forgives our sins, and who wants to give us His true love. This is why Jesus is called as the King of love. Our Shepherd is indeed the King of love. Jesus is indeed our true Messiah. This Messiah has set the faith that He wants from us, defining certain characteristics as absolutely required. Only when we go before God with this faith, He will give us what He has promised us.

Yet we see that among those whose faith in the Messiah is based on their mistaken knowledge of Him, there are some whose stubbornness is beyond description. They are simply wicked and evil, as much as Pharaoh who had insisted on his obstinate ways before God. When Moses said to him, "Jehovah has revealed Himself; let His people go," Pharaoh retorted, "Who is this Jehovah?"

When God's existence was explained to him, he would certainly have been better off to quickly surrender and yield to Him after calculating the costs and benefits of his recalcitrance. If he still absolutely could not believe and had to insist on his stubbornness, he could have tried to hold out for a while, but after a couple of plagues, he should have given up. How foolish and pitiful was it for Pharaoh to still hold out in his stubbornness and disobey the Word of God, even as he was plagued by frogs covering his whole nation?

Not only frogs, but lice also plagued Pharaoh's palace. Left and right, wherever one turned, everywhere in the whole land of Egypt became filled by lice, and yet Pharaoh did not surrender. How could anyone live when everywhere is filled by lice? In this situation, he should have realized, "Because I have disobeyed God, He is showing me who the real King is. I may be a king of my empire on this earth, but I am nothing compared to Him. Though I am the king of the greatest nation on the face of this earth, and though I have power over the whole world, God is even more powerful than I am, and He is bringing me these plagues because of my disobedience." This is how he should have surrendered.

The wise thing for Pharaoh to do would have been to quickly surrender after seeing for himself what the cost of his resistance would be. Regardless of how powerful Pharaoh was, if he reached the conclusion that there was no way for him to stand against God, all that he had to was to surrender to Him, saying, "Okay, God, You take the first place; I'll take the second place." But because Pharaoh refused to thus yield, his whole nation and people were plagued by lice.

Because of this, no Egyptian could do anything at all. When everyone was tormented relentlessly by lice, how could anyone do anything else but try to get rid of lice? We can all imagine these poor Egyptians running around with torches trying to get rid of lice, perhaps even burning down their own houses in the process, and the stench of the burning lice filling the villages.

There are things that man can do, and there are things that man cannot do. Because God is the Lord of Hosts, it is God who presides over life and death, happiness and unhappiness, and blessings and curses. When this is the case, rather than placing confidence in ourselves and trying to stand against God, we must all think rationally and reach the logical conclusion to abandon our stubbornness. Among ourselves, we may insist on one's own way and try to prevail over others, but when dealing with the Messiah, this is no longer feasible.

We must think of what kind of person we really should be before God. We must seriously consider whether we should hold out against God, or whether our hearts should indeed be gentle and meek. And we must reach the definitive conclusion that we must all be meek before God. Before men, we may hold out in our stubbornness and at times face its consequences, but before God, our hearts must absolutely be meek.

"God, I have done wrong"—those who admit this are the ones who choose the right way. These are the people who can be saved from their accursed lives. For those who had left God because of their sins, the way to be embraced in God's arms and feed on His life-giving water is to be born again by the water and the Spirit. What can we ever expect from our lives, when such lives are spent fruitlessly in the wilderness of this world, floating around its empty and barren land without any purpose, only to return to a handful of dust?

The only way for us, who are to return to dust and are bound to be cast out into the lake of fire, to be saved is by believing in the gospel of the water and the Spirit and thus receive the remission of our sins. This is for the desperate and hopeless lives who were destined for eternal destruction for standing against God and for their sins to be miraculously revived again before God through His love of mercy, the love of salvation. We must, therefore, all be clothed in this salvation.

How can anyone, being a mere mortal, ever challenge God? When God tells us to bring such and such offerings, we must all obey His Word. Looking at the main passage above, where God tells us what offerings we need to bring to Him, we must all come to the realization, "Ah, so this is the kind of faith that God is asking us to bring to Him."

On the breastplate of the High Priest, twelve precious stones were to be placed. And beneath the breastplate of judgment, the Urim and the Thummim, which mean literally *the Lights* and *the Perfections,* had to be put in so that the High Priest could bear the right judgment over the children of Israel.

This refers to none other than the fact that only the servants of God can pass righteous judgment on their spiritual children of faith by shedding the light of the Holy Spirit dwelling in them and the Word of God.

We must all realize now that before God, the truth of blue, purple, and scarlet thread is the real truth and the real salvation. This truth of blue, purple, and scarlet thread is the true salvation that brings us to life, and apart from this, nothing else is constitutes our salvation. This is all based on the Word of God, clear and true.

All the Materials of the Tabernacle Are Related to Man's Salvation from Sin

Yet out of foolishness, people still stubbornly refuse to believe. What then would happen to them? They will never, ever be saved. Before God, we must cast away our foolishness also. And we must empty our hearts. We must cast aside our own thoughts and stubbornness before God, and instead obey His Word and give Him our hearts. We must never hold out against God, insisting on our own recalcitrant ways. We may do so before other people, but as Christians, we simply cannot do this, at least before God. And yet foolish people stand against God and are meek only before other men. This is what's wrong with them. We must throw ourselves flat on our faces before God and admit that what God has spoken to us are all right.

And we must believe and trust in the Word of blue, purple, and scarlet thread. Faith is trusting in God's Word. When we throw ourselves at God's feet, confess all our troubles before Him, and cling to Him asking for His help, God will certainly answer us. We must then accept what He has done for us with thanks. This is what faith is all about. In what absurdness and lunacy, then, could we ever show God something other than the blue, purple, and scarlet thread, bringing to Him fishing lines or metal chains? Bringing some useless thread before God and saying to Him, "This is my own faith. This is how I have believed so strongly. This is the firm faith that I have kept particularly,"—this simply is not faith, but making a fool out of oneself before God.

One must yield his/her stubbornness before the Messiah. Before God, in other words, one must bend his/her will. We must all recognize ourselves before God. We must recognize according to what God says to us and how He decides for us. None other than this is the correct faith of Christians. Obeying and believing according to the Word of God is the correct posture and heart of the faithful. This is what we must keep in mind before God.

Among ourselves, of course, we may boast of one's own achievements, compare each other, compete against one another, and challenge each other. Although this, too, is a useless practice measuring what are essentially the same before God, among the human beings this is something that we have little choice but be engaged in continuously.

Even puppies recognize who their masters are, and submit to their owners and obey them. Even dogs, in other words, obey their owners, recognize their voices, and follow only their masters. When dogs get rebuked by their owners, they recognize their wrongdoings, lower their heads in obedience, and try to return back to the good grace with their master by doing all kinds of cute little tricks. When even animals do this, and yet people continue to challenge God by taking the faith of their own thoughts. They continue, in other words, to cling to God even as they insist on their own ways and their own thoughts.

With His blue, purple, and scarlet thread, God has thus made all the sins of mankind disappear, and all that He has told us is to have the faith that believes in the works of our Lord. Yet people still remain recalcitrant and challenge God. *desobidisoal*

The Lord has told us to bring to Him all our sins, and by making them all disappear with the blue, purple, and scarlet thread, He has given us the remission of sin. When God has told us to bring Him the faith of the blue, purple, and scarlet thread, people still do not believe in this, and are defying their own Master. These people will be cursed.

When they bring to the Messiah not the faith that He wants from them but the faith that He does not want, He can only be angered. They keep bringing their stubbornness before God and say to Him, "I have kept my faith this far and this well. Commend me for what a job well-done!" Would God commend them just because they have kept their faith, when in fact this faith has been simply useless this whole time?

There may be times when stubbornness is appropriately required in our lives. But the stubbornness of wrong faith is completely useless before God. God used the blue, purple, and scarlet thread in making our sins disappear. The Bible does not say that He used only the purple thread, nor that He used only the scarlet thread, even far less that He used metal chains, just as there is no mention of using nylon thread. Inside the House of God, and within His law of salvation given to us, the Messiah has demanded from us the faith of the blue, purple, and scarlet thread.

Christians refer to those who believe in and follow Jesus Christ. We, too, then are also Christians. However, there are so many people who have not been born again despite believing in Jesus as their Savior, who have not received the remission of sin, and who do not have the faith of the blue, purple, and scarlet thread—these are merely nominal Christians destined to hell, because they believe according to their own ways. God will abandon these people, for they are only religionists, not true Christians.

At least before God, we must all be honest, and recognize ourselves as we really are. Every moment, every minute and second, we must confess that we were bound to hell because of our sins. Before the Messiah, we must all have the faith of the blue, purple, and scarlet thread. Believing so is the right thing to do. And whenever we confess, we must remind ourselves of what the Messiah has done for us, that He was baptized to deliver us from sin and was judged for our own sins with His crucifixion, and recognize our salvation every time. This is the faith that God demands from us.

We can never please God unless we do exactly as the Messiah wants us to do. Why? Because as He has become our eternal Savior through His blue, purple, and scarlet thread, we need to believe every moment in what God has done for us. As the faith of the blue, purple, and scarlet thread is true, we need it even more for the remission of our sins that we ourselves commit everyday.

Would God Be Pleased If We Were to Give Him the Products of Our Own Efforts?

If we were to give to God the things of the earth, we would not only be garnering the wrath of God over us, but we would also be committing a great sin by mounting a challenge against Him. Such faith is treasonous, for it stands against God. Nothing in this world, no matter how precious and expensive it may be, can ever please God. Bringing to God such materials things of this world is never the right faith that can be commended by God. No matter how good they may be in worldly terms, God does not accept such material things. We must have the faith that God really wants from us, and give Him this faith.

Our faith must be one that believes in the Word of God as it is, one that takes exactly the offerings that God has asked from us. All the while, with each passing moment, we must also recognize what God has done for us, and we must admit our own infirmities and insufficiencies as well. We must remember the abundant blessings that God has bestowed on us, and we must know exactly and believe in what He has done for us, that He has willingly met us.

We must cast away all faiths of mysticism, and we must only have the faith that believes in the Word spoken by God. The offerings of this faith are what we must give to God. Only when we give to God the offerings of the right faith will He be pleased, meet us, and accept our faith. And it is when we do so that God gives us all the blessings that He has set and prepared for us.

When we dwell on the Word, we must therefore contemplate, "What is the faith that God really wants from us? What kind of prayer is the prayer that He wants?" We then realize that the prayer that God wants from us is none other than the prayer within faith. Our Lord wants from us the prayers that are offered within the faith of the salvation of the blue, purple, and scarlet thread, within the faith that has accepted what God has given us. All that God wants from us is this thankful prayer within faith; He will never accept anything of our own making that we try to give Him or leave at His feet. We must all realize that we should never do this.

God is telling us, "No, no, that's not the faith that I want from you. I was baptized and crucified for you. I received baptism to make all your sins disappear. It is because I had to take your sins upon Myself before I was judged for these sins and died on the Cross. I am your Savior, but I am fundamentally your God also. I am the King of kings, but because I am also your God, I came to this earth and fulfilled everything. I want you to believe in Me truly, to recognize My authority in your hearts, and to confess wholeheartedly that I am your true God." It is with this intention that God has given us the blue, purple, and scarlet thread and the fine woven linen. And this is the faith that God demands from us.

We must really have this faith of the blue, purple, and scarlet thread. You might think to yourself, "Well, it's still quite livable. I'm still doing quite okay, and things are going just fine. If it's not broken, why fix it? Why do I have to believe exactly in this way? Whether I believe in this way or that way, aren't they all the same?" No, they are not the same! If you have some faith other than this one in your hearts, then you have absolutely not been saved. Because in such hearts sin is still found, you must turn around your hearts and return to the faith that truly believes in the gospel of the water and the Spirit.

The hearts of those who believe in the true gospel and of

those who do not are fundamentally different from each other. God knows this, and so does we, who have been born again. When you come to know yourselves, you must turn around. "God, I am indeed sinful. Please save me." When you thus turn around your hearts and seek after your salvation, God will meet you with His truth.

Our Lord Has Saved Us from All Our Sins

Our Lord was baptized and crucified for us. As written in Matthew 3, this is what the Lord has done for us. We believe in it. We thank Him for it. When Jesus was baptized, all our sins were passed onto Him. When He was crucified, it was because He took upon all our sins that He could carry these sins to the Cross. He was judged for not only our own sins, but all the sins of the entire world.

When our Lord tells us to bring to Him the offerings of building materials for the Tabernacle, or whenever He tells us anything, He always proceeds with a sequence. He always tells us, "Bring me blue, purple, and scarlet thread." The blue thread always comes first. And He follows this with His mentioning of the fine woven linen, telling us to believe in God's Word. Believing in the blood of the Cross first and then believing in Jesus' baptism may seem okay at first glance, but this is in fact wrong. It was because Jesus was first baptized that He could shed His blood on the Cross. I am saying to you again that it is never okay to first believe in the blood of the Cross and then in His baptism. God never allows such faith.

Coming to this earth in the flesh of a man, when our Lord turned 30, He was first baptized to take all our sins upon Himself. After having done so, He then carried these sins of the world to the Cross, was judged with His crucifixion, and then rose from the dead again, thereby becoming our Savior. As such, we must believe in what the Lord has done for us according to the order in which He fulfilled His works. This is how we must believe. Only then can our faith stand as whole, never to be confused, nor ever to be shaken. And when we spread the gospel to others, we must do so accordingly. We must believe, in other words, according to what would please God, according to how He has set for us.

What offerings of faith is God asking you to bring to Him? Is He not telling you to bring the faith of the blue, purple, and scarlet thread and the fine woven linen? Do you have this faith? Are you not, by any chance, believing in reverse order? "Whether I believe this way or that way doesn't matter. I still believe, and that's all there is to it. I believe in the scarlet thread first, and then in the blue thread, and then in the purple thread." If this is how you believe, then you must believe again. The Lord will never approve this reversed faith of yours.

Our Lord is the God of justice and the God of truth. As such, He does not approve wrong faith. Because faith cannot stand upright when its order is all mixed up, God cannot approve this faith even if He wants to. Just as we cannot try to lay the foundation after having finished building a house, it is because Jesus had taken upon our sins with His baptism that He could then be crucified.

We must therefore believe according to what the Lord has told us. This is the laying of the cornerstone for the right faith. Because God has saved us correctly, justly, and righteously, we cannot change His order on our own. If we believe in the blood of the Cross first and then in the baptism of Jesus, then this faith is simply wrong. And sin is still found in the hearts of those who believe so, for their sins were not washed away because of the reverse order of their faith. This is truly marvelous. None other than this is the amazing truth.

Before the Messiah, many of us used to believe only in Jesus' blood on the Cross. We believed, "Jesus took upon all my sins and bore all my judgement by shedding His blood on the Cross. We have therefore been wholly saved. Our salvation came from Christ who died for us on the Cross. Anyone who believes in this is now saved." We then realized the original meaning of Jesus' baptism. So on top of our first, wrong faith, we just added the faith of truth. What happened then? Our sins did not disappear in reality. Because this kind of faith is of merely intellectual and doctrinal one, it could not be the real and true faith of our hearts.

If your faith is like this, you must quickly turn around and change it. First of all, you have to admit explicitly that your faith has not been right. And then, you have to renew your foundation of faith at once. All that you have to do is change the order again. "Having come to this earth, when the Lord was baptized by John the Baptist at the Jordan River, He took upon all my sins. It is because Jesus was baptized that all the sins of the world were passed onto Him, and since all the sins of the world were thus passed onto Him, all my sins were also passed onto Jesus. And then, He shed His blood on the Cross to pay the wages of all my sins." This is how you should believe.

"Who cares whether I believe in this way or that way? All that matters is that I believe in these four ministries of the Lord. Why be so stubborn and insist on this order?" Do you, by any chance, still cling to this view? You must then take it to your heart this truth: Jesus died on the Cross only after being baptized. And this is the truth that you must believe in.

The Holy Spirit never approves injustice. God the Holy Spirit approves our faith only when we believe in what the

Messiah has done for us on this earth as they are. The Holy
Spirit does not say, "So you believe in all these four works of
Jesus. Amen. Whether you believe correctly or in a reverse
order, whether you believe in this way or that way, that's OK if
you just believe anyway. Amen. Alright, you are My child
then."

Jesus the Messiah came to this earth according to the will
of God the Father and did according to the Father's bidding.
This is how He lived His 33 years of life on this earth. Coming
to this earth, He completed His work of our salvation by being
baptized, crucified, and resurrected, and then ascended to
Heaven. And He has sent us the Holy Spirit.

God the Holy Spirit dwells in the hearts of those of us
who have received the remission of sin, and He approves the
faith of those who believe in what the Lord has done for them
as they are. This is why we can never believe according to our
own thoughts. Though you and I truly believe in Jesus, do you
not, by any chance, believe upside down on a reverse order? If
so, you must believe again correctly.

When you do so, the Holy Spirit works in your hearts.
Though we are full of shortcomings, the Holy Spirits holds our
hearts steady, is with us, and bestows us with His grace when
we come short before Him. The Holy Spirit gives us power. He
gives us strength. He comforts us. He blesses us. He promises
us a brilliant future. And to those of us who believe, He leads
us from faith to faith not to lose the qualification to enter His
eternal Kingdom.

This is what we need when we believe in what the Lord
has done for us, or when He tells us to bring to Him our
offerings—that is, we must believe that He has saved us with
the water and the Spirit. All the items inside the Tabernacle are
important because they all consistently tell us about the secret

of being born again of the water and the Spirit. Through so many things of the Tabernacles, in other words, God wants to tell us about one thing—the gospel of the water and the Spirit.

For Our Faith, Its Foundation Is Very Critical

If we build the house of faith without first laying the foundation of our faith firmly, the longer we believe in Jesus, the more sins we accumulate, the more prayers of repentance we must give, and the more hypocritical sinners we become. But when we believe in the gift of salvation, that our Lord has saved us with His blue, purple, and scarlet thread and fine woven linen, then we can all become the perfect children of God. Therefore, we must all believe in the truth of the blue, purple, and scarlet thread and the fine woven linen, and we must all thus become God's children.

Those whose foundation of faith is whole can always carry out their priesthood in the bright light, even when they themselves may have shortcomings. They can, in other words, fulfill all such tasks of priesthood as truly embracing all the people of this world into their bosoms, praying to God for their remission of sin, and serving this gospel before God.

In contrast, for those whose foundation of faith is not clear, the more time goes by, the more hypocritical they become. They become evil. They become more hypocritical religionists. As our Lord told us that we shall know a tree by its fruits, the fruits born by such people are all disgusting, filthy, and hypocritical. However, those of us who are born again are not hypocritical at all. They are all truthful. Though they have their own shortcomings, they are truly sincere. They recognize their own weaknesses and wrongdoings, and they always live in the midst of the bright light. Because our Lord was baptized and crucified to blot out all our sins, and because He has indeed thus made all our sins disappear, by believing in this truth we have received the remission of our sins. Because the foundation of our faith is solid, though we are insufficient, though we commit sins, and though we are weak, our lives are still bright, for our hearts are always sinless. Because of our shortcomings we may go astray at times, but because we are actually sinless, we do not go astray to lead others and ourselves to destruction. Though we are insufficient, we nevertheless walk on the path that pleases God, moving ahead step by step and serving the Gospel even more. This has been made all possible because Jesus has saved us perfectly.

If Jesus Christ, our Messiah, and our Savior had not thus saved us wholly with the four threads, we could never have been saved at all. It is because He has saved us that we are saved, and it is because of this that we believe, spread the gospel, and praise God with our faith. It is by our faith that we thank God, by our faith that we serve Him, and by our faith that we follow Him. This is who we have now become. We have, in other words, become the ones who please God with our faith. We have become the ones whose foundation of faith stands firmly.

Those whose foundation of faith is not properly laid must lay it again. This is why Hebrew 6:1-2 say, *"Therefore, leaving the discussion of the elementary principles of Christ, let us go on to perfection, not laying again the foundation of repentance from dead works and of faith toward God, of the doctrine of baptisms, of laying on of hands, of resurrection of the dead, and of eternal judgment."*

What does this passage tell us? It tell us to know and confirm clearly, and to firmly lay the foundation for such

questions as: "Why was Jesus baptized?"; "Is this baptism the antitype of the Old Testament's laying on of hands?"; "Would we live again?"; and, "What is the eternal judgment?" It tells us to have the whole faith and lay out its foundation firmly from the very beginning, so that we would neither be shaken nor be forced to lay our foundation again by these things. The faith that believes in the blue, purple, and scarlet thread and the fine woven linen is the whole faith that believes that our Lord has completed our salvation perfectly. We must stand firmly on this foundation of faith, and we must run from there. We must run the race of faith.

Some people interpret the above passage from Hebrew as saying that we cannot say again that our sins were passed onto Jesus through His baptism, and that the passage is telling us that we do not need to build the foundation of faith again. But would God have told us not to rebuild our foundation of faith if it had been built correctly in the first place? This passage tells us that those who do not have the correct foundation of faith should lay this foundation, and those who have the foundation of faith correctly should make it even more firm and solid, and run forward.

To save us, God commanded Moses to build the Tabernacle and to accept offerings from His people. To the people of Israel, He commanded them to bring to Him gold, silver, and bronze; blue, purple, and scarlet thread, fine linen, and goats' hair; ram skins dyed red, badger skins, and acacia wood. Just as laid out in these materials, our Lord has indeed given us the gift of salvation by delivering you and me from the sins of the world. In this way, God had actually told the Israelites to bring these offerings to Him, built the Tabernacle, set its sacrificial system, and forgave the sins of the Israelites who gave Him their sacrificial offerings in accordance to the

requirements of this sacrificial system.

Our Faith Is Made Whole by Believing in the Blue, Purple, and Scarlet Thread and the Fine Woven Linen That Foretold Us of the Perfect Fulfillment of Our Salvation by Jesus Christ

If we, unable to believe in the perfect truth fulfilled by Jesus Christ, do not lay the foundation of our faith firmly at once, our faith would be continuously shaken. Without the knowledge, realization, and faith in the fact that our Lord has saved us wholly, we will all end up trying to reach our salvation through our own efforts. Such faith is not whole, but it is mistaken.

Let's turn to Hebrews 10:26-31: *"For if we sin willfully after we have received the knowledge of the truth, there no longer remains a sacrifice for sins, but a certain fearful expectation of judgment, and fiery indignation which will devour the adversaries. Anyone who has rejected Moses' law dies without mercy on the testimony of two or three witnesses. Of how much worse punishment, do you suppose, will he be thought worthy who has trampled the Son of God underfoot, counted the blood of the covenant by which he was sanctified a common thing, and insulted the Spirit of grace? For we know Him who said, 'Vengeance is Mine, I will repay,' says the Lord. And again, 'The LORD will judge His people.' It is a fearful thing to fall into the hands of the living God."*

The passage tells us that if we sin willfully after we have received the knowledge of the truth, there no longer remains a sacrifice for sins, but only fearful judgment. Here, those who sin willfully after having received the knowledge of the truth

refer to those who do not believe in the gospel of the water and the Spirit even as they know it. We must believe in the truth that God has saved us with His blue, purple, and scarlet thread and fine woven linen, that He has saved us with gold, silver, and bronze, and that He made the roof of the Tabernacle with the coverings of blue, purple, and scarlet thread and fine woven linen, of goats' hair, of ram skins dyed red, and of badger skins. We must all know these things clearly and lay the foundation of our faith firmly.

Our Lord promised us that He would wholly save us, and when the time came, He was baptized to take our sins upon Himself, died on the Cross, rose from the dead again, and thereby has indeed saved us wholly. We have therefore been saved perfectly by believing in this Jesus Christ who laid the foundation of our salvation wholly.

But those who know this truth and yet refuse to believe it will all surely face God's fiery judgment when the day of their last judgment comes. Their bodies will not die but suffer forever. The Bible tells us that there will be only fiery indignation for them, and their suffering of hell will be so great that it describes it as being seasoned with fire (Mark 9:49). It tells us that there will be only a certain fearful expectation of judgment, and fiery indignation that will devour the adversaries.

When just failing to keep the Law leads to this fearful judgment, how greater would the judgment be for those who do not believe in their salvation given by the Son of God? This is why we must all believe in Jesus Christ as our Savior, in the Lord who came to this earth in the flesh of a man, who took all our sins upon Himself with His baptism, who carried these sins of the world to the Cross and bore all the condemnation of sins with His crucifixion, who rose from the dead again, and who now lives.

The Foundation of Our Faith Must Therefore Be Laid Firmly

Why did God tell Moses to build the Tabernacle? When we look at each and every item of all the materials used for the Tabernacle, we can see that they all manifest the truth that Jesus Christ came to this earth in the flesh of a man, took our sins upon Himself with His baptism received from John the Baptist, carried these sins of the world to the Cross and died on it, rose from the dead again, ascended to Heaven, and sits at the right hand of the throne of God the Father, and has now become our eternal God. From its gate to its pillar and their bronze sockets, all the items of the Tabernacle show us the truth of the gospel. The whole Old Testament, in other words, is telling us about the baptism of Jesus Christ, His sacrifice, His identity, and His works of salvation.

From the Old Testament to the New Testament, because Jesus Christ speaks to us of the gospel of the water and the Spirit—that is, the gospel of the blue, purple, and scarlet thread and the fine woven linen—those who believe in this truth always speak of the truth of the blue, purple, and scarlet thread and the fine woven linen whenever they get a chance. Because they are preached and heard so often, sometimes we may even forget how preciousness this truth is. But just how important is this truth? As if we were living King Solomon's reign when precious gold and silver became so abundant that they were treated like stones, because we hear this Word of truth everyday in God's Church, we might at times come to take this salvation for granted. But you have to remember this: this truth cannot be heard anywhere outside God's Church, and without this salvation no one can be saved, nor lay the foundation of faith solidly.

The faith with which you and I have been saved is the belief in the fact that our Lord has saved us wholly and laid the foundation of our faith firmly with the four threads of the blue, purple, and scarlet thread and the fine woven linen. Let me reiterate once more that we must all believe in this in our hearts. God promised us, and just as He promised, He came to this earth as the Seed of a woman (Genesis 3:15), took all our sins upon Himself with His baptism, bore all the condemnation of our sins on the Cross, rose from the dead again, and has thereby saved us perfectly. Because this is such a simple truth that is so easy to explain and understand, we can preach this gospel all over the world everyday. Of course, there are still many pitiful ones who do not know this truth. However, even more pitiful than those who do not know this truth are those who do not believe even as they remain in God's Church.

Even though you have truly received the remission of your sins, your thoughts may still be evil, but at least your hearts have become very meek. But the hypocrites who are not so, though they may try to paint themselves as meek outwardly, are so evil in their inner beings that they keep deceiving God and countless people everyday. You and I must lay the foundation of faith firmly. And on this salvation that our Lord has established for us so firmly, we must stand before God by believing in it.

Faith That Stands Firmly Like the Constituents of the Tabernacle

God told us to bring such offerings and to build His Tabernacle. You and I must all become the people of faith who believe that Jesus Christ came to this earth and has thus saved us spiritually. We must stand firmly before God by having the kind of faith that is like the building materials used for the Tabernacle. Do you believe? Do you really have this kind of faith? By God's Church, the gospel of the water and the Spirit is still being preached. Because this is the very foundation of the true faith, I cannot emphasize it enough.

So many churches and denominations of this world remain ignorant of the truth that Jesus accepted all sins onto Himself with His baptism, and instead believe only in the blood of the Cross. Even in these circumstances, our Lord has still allowed us to find the truth. The reason why Jesus was nailed and pierced on the Cross was because He had been baptized by John the Baptist at the Jordan River. It was because He had accepted all the sins of the world passed onto Him with His baptism that He was crucified and pierced on the Cross.

As such, the faith of those who claim to have received the remission of sin just by believing in the blood of the Cross alone is a false faith that would, no matter how devout they may be, all crumble down eventually. Regardless how tirelessly they preach to the crowds in a loud voice to believe in Jesus, their faith, which believes in the blood of the Cross alone, only offers the prayers of repentance, and cannot even solve their own problem of sin, is built on a flawed foundation that will simply collapse when the rain pours, the wind blows, and the flood comes.

I myself had not heard of the baptism of Jesus in any detail for well over 10 years since I started to believe in Jesus. However, Jesus met me with His Word of truth, and I could be born again of water and the Spirit. Now, I know that there are many people throughout the whole world who are seeking the truth but have not yet reached it. I want to speak to them all, so that they may hear the truth of the water and the Spirit, and so that they may receive the remission of their sins by believing it in their hearts.

Before you were born again, you, too, might have led your religious lives. At that time, you probably had not heard of the blue, purple, and scarlet thread and the fine woven linen. Not only that, you probably had not heard of the gospel of the water and the Spirit either, far less that our sins were passed onto Jesus when He was baptized.

It is critically important for Christians to know and believe in the truth of the blue, purple, and scarlet thread and the fine woven linen as it is. Only when the foundation of faith is laid with the blue, purple, and scarlet thread and the fine woven linen can we all stand firmly and solidly with our faith. If you have not believed so thus far, it is never too late—all that you have to do is believe so even now. Only when you thus believe can you be saved wholly, lay your foundation of faith firmly, and establish your faith on this foundation.

Those Who Are in God's Church Must Also Lay Their Foundation of Faith Firmly

Matthew 24:40 says, *"Then two men will be in the field: one will be taken and the other left."* When we have all been professing to believe in the same truth and serving the same gospel together in God's Church, what could be more tragic if some of us were left behind later on?

Because the Word of God is intellectual and polite, faith cannot be forced upon anyone by coercion. When you thus hear the Word of God preached to you politely, you must believe it with a fair mind, centering your mind on the fact that you are in fact hearing God's Word. When the people of Israel heard what Moses told them, they considered it not as his own words but the very Word of God. Likewise, when you are told about what the Word of God says, you need to check to see whether or not you do indeed believe according to this Word of God. You need to consider the Word with a cool head, and then believe in what it actually tells you.

The Bible commended the believers of Berea for their fair-minded attitude over the Word of God. The believers in Berea *"were more fair-minded than those in Thessalonica, in that they received the word with all readiness, and searched the Scriptures daily to find out whether these things were so"* *(Acts 17:11)*. In short, they believed rationally in His Word as they were taught.

True faith comes from the rational and fair-minded heart that searches the Word. Would it make any sense to be forced to believe against your will? Even if one were to force someone else to believe, this actually would be completely futile, for the one thus being forced would not necessarily believe in what he/she is told to believe. Before God, everything depends on what one believes on his/her free will. If someone does not believe when he/she has been told the same story over and over, then there is no other way but for this person to end up in hell.

Therefore, every sinner throughout this world deserves our pity, but if some of us do not believe in His Word as it is even as we are all under the same roof of God's Church, then they are even more pitiful. How could there be anyone more pitiful than those of us who end up in hell, even as they have remained physically in the same Church of God with us?

Jesus had twelve disciples, and among them only Judas did not believe that Jesus was the Messiah and the Savior. So Judas always called Jesus as a teacher. Peter, too, used to call

Jesus as a teacher at times, but He eventually came to believed otherwise and confessed, "Lord, You are Christ and the Son of God. You are the Son of God, the Savior who came to make my sins disappear. You are the God of salvation."

Peter's faith, in other words, was different from that of Judas. After Judas betrayed Jesus and sold Him out, he hung and killed himself. Although Judas had been with the other eleven disciples, in the end, he failed to recognize who Jesus Christ really was, and thus end up in hell. Peter, in contrast, was saved by recognizing Jesus Christ and believing in Him as his Savior, despite the fact that he was an impatient man of many shortcomings.

Likewise, salvation depends on whether one knows the truth and believes it in his/her heart or not. One cannot believe the truth when he/she does not know it. However, if people do not believe the truth even as they know it, they will face even greater punishments (Luke 12:48). This is why God is telling us that the foundation of our faith must be firm and upright.

How Is Our Faith?

Has the foundation of our faith been strengthened now? Is it firm? Do you believe that the Lord has definitively saved you? Through the water and the Spirit, our Lord has indeed saved us for sure. This is not something peculiar that only our denomination is teaching, but it is what God promised in the Old Testament and what Jesus has actually fulfilled in the New Testament—that is, this is how Christ has indeed saved us.

Jesus is the King of kings (the purple thread) who came to this earth in the flesh of a man, took the sins of the world upon Himself with His baptism (the blue thread), carried these sins

to the Cross and was crucified (the scarlet thread), rose from
the dead again, and has thereby saved us. He promised that He
would do so in the Old Testament, and He has saved us by
indeed fulfilling this promise in the New Testament. Do you
believe? None other than this is the laying of the solid
foundation of faith.

There are hundreds of millions of Christians throughout
the world, and yet for most of them, their foundation of faith
remains fragile. We can find out whether or not people have
the right faith just by browsing through the many Christian
books that are now available. The authors of these books tend
to be the leaders of Christian communities, and by reading their
books, we can find out whether or not they have the correct
knowledge of the truth. If even just one of these leaders is
ignorant of or does not believe in the truth even as he/she
knows it, then everyone following such a leader will all be
bound to hell. The sad reality is that hardly anyone at all knows
the truth, as few as one in a million. This is why the few of us
who know the truth have to spread the gospel faithfully
throughout the whole world.

God is working through us. You and I cannot avoid but
preach the gospel, for not proclaiming this gospel of the water
and the Spirit throughout the world is akin to committing a
great sin before God. In fact, if we do not truly follow and
serve this work in faith, then we would indeed be committing a
great sin before God. This is the sin of sending people to hell
even as we know we can stop it; it is simply an unforgivable
sin that people would end up in hell in their ignorance because
those of us who know the truth have kept their mouths closed.

If we do not fulfill the task assigned to us, these people
will protest to us, for it is our mandatory task. The Bible warns
us, saying, *"But if the watchman sees the sword coming and*

does not blow the trumpet, and the people are not warned, and the sword comes and takes any person from among them, he is taken away in his iniquity; but his blood I will require at the watchman's hand" (Ezekiel 33:6). We who have first known and first believed must carry out this task of the watchman.

I thank the Lord for giving us this gospel and for enabling us to know this truth. I thank Him even more when I realize that we are the chosen few in this world who know this truth and believe in this gospel. We have preached the gospel of the water and the Spirit to many pastors and laymen believers throughout the entire world, but everyday we have confirmed the fact that there was no one who actually knew and believed in this gospel before. Through us, the preachers of the gospel of the truth of the water and the Spirit have been emerging throughout the world. Like us, they, too, have the solid foundation of faith, and are spreading this solid faith.

If there are many such people who are spreading the gospel, we could perhaps breathe a little easier and rest a little in our preaching of the gospel, but, sadly, there are yet not so many people in this world who know and believe in this truth. Many have overestimated the achievements of the Reformation in the world's history. When we examine it in detail, we can find out that the reformists had misplaced the first button of the foundation of biblical faith during the Reformation, and that everything else that followed was also misplaced. Regardless of correcting these latter mistakes, with the first button still misplaced, it still remains flawed; as such, the history of Christianity must be rewritten.

I hope and pray that you would all stand before God on your solid foundation of faith, and that on this foundation of faith, you would live your lives for the sake of serving the true gospel. When you live for the gospel, your hearts will naturally be filled with joy. When one lives for the gospel, his/her heart is transformed into a spiritual one. And as the Holy Spirit fills your hearts and works in them, they will all be overflowing with joy.

But if you do not live for the gospel but pursue only the desires of your flesh even as you have received the remission of sin and known the gospel of the water and the Spirit, you will then end up living meaningless, empty lives.

I thank God for giving us this precious gospel, and for giving us our salvation freely. It is my prayer and hope that you would all examine your faith once more, and receive the gift of perfect salvation through the blue, purple, and scarlet thread and the fine woven linen. ⊠

SERMON

8

The Color of the Gate of The Tabernacle's Court

< Exodus 27:9-19 >

"You shall also make the court of the tabernacle. For the south side there shall be hangings for the court made of fine woven linen, one hundred cubits long for one side. And its twenty pillars and their twenty sockets shall be bronze. The hooks of the pillars and their bands shall be silver. Likewise along the length of the north side there shall be hangings one hundred cubits long, with its twenty pillars and their twenty sockets of bronze, and the hooks of the pillars and their bands of silver. And along the width of the court on the west side shall be hangings of fifty cubits, with their ten pillars and their ten sockets. The width of the court on the east side shall be fifty cubits. The hangings on one side of the gate shall be fifteen cubits, with their three pillars and their three sockets. And on the other side shall be hangings of fifteen cubits, with their three pillars and their three sockets. For the gate of the court there shall be a screen twenty cubits long, woven of blue, purple, and scarlet thread, and fine woven linen, made by a weaver. It shall have four pillars and four sockets. All the pillars around the court shall have bands of silver; their hooks shall be of silver and their sockets of bronze. The length of the court shall be one hundred cubits, the width fifty throughout, and the height five cubits, made of fine woven linen, and its sockets of bronze. All the utensils of the tabernacle for all its service, all its pegs, and all the pegs of

the court, shall be of bronze."

There are clear differences between the faith of the born-again and that of the nominal Christians: the former knows and believes that God has blotted out all our sins, and the latter believes in Jesus based on one's own thoughts, merely as a matter of religious practices. Yet those who believe in God only as a religious matter are prospering so much that those who are preaching the real truth are even disheartened to see these people of wrong faith spreading their false teachings and prospering. They are disheartened because they clearly know that so many Christians have been drawn into such false religions of deception and frauds.

I, too, were disheartened by this for a while. Because I was truly born again by encountering the truth, and truly thankful to God for using me as an instrument for His works, and because my heart yearned for the truth of God to be spread far and wide, when I saw so many people leading their religious lives deceived by lies, I could not but become deeply saddened.

Nevertheless, what is clear is that the Holy Spirit is in my heart, and that despite my shortcomings, my heart has no sin. In my heart, therefore, is found thankfulness, and I have no shame over the gospel that I believe in. When I preach this gospel to people throughout the whole world, if they hear this Word of truth and believe in it, they, too, can have no shame before both God and people, for when they believe in this truth, they all really become God's children.

You too can surely have the same blessings by faith. Even though you have not studied theology, if you just believe in the truth of this gospel of the water and the Spirit, you will receive the remission of your sins, become the children of God, and receive the Holy Spirit into your hearts. And with the Holy Spirit, you can also walk with the servants of God. This is the clear truth, and believing thus is the true faith.

Although I am living in a world that is filled with lies, because in my heart is this true faith, I have been able to keep preaching the gospel of truth until this very moment. Since I began to preach the Word on the topic of the Tabernacle, I came to know more clearly about the schemes of the liars, and thus I came to discern the truth from the false. This is the reason why I have been testifying this truth of the Tabernacle. It brings me an immense joy that with the spreading of the real truth through the Tabernacle, people are enabled to discern between the truth and the false.

In writing this book on the Tabernacle, the most difficult task for me was trying to deal with its terminology. I have devoted a great amount of attention to this issue, looking up the original texts, to make sure that the difficult glossaries associated with the Tabernacles would not result into any conveying of wrong information, nor to such mistaken reception by the readers. Despite my own understanding and knowledge of the Tabernacle, because the modalities of the Tabernacle and its hidden spiritual meanings had to be explained to those whose knowledge is very limited, I was somewhat concerned about the task, unsure of how precisely and definitively I could really explain the significance of the Tabernacle.

It would be nice, of course, if people could understand and believe as soon as they first hear it. But Rome was not built in a day; likewise, and as in all matters, the spreading of the truth and the true faith is not accomplished in a day, either, but it is achieved gradually, as we dig deeper into the core little by little.

I was therefore particularly concerned about digging too deep from the beginning, for not everyone would then be able to understand it, and this was one of the most formidable challenges that I faced in writing this book.

Nevertheless, with God's help, the book has finally come out without too much trouble. Needless to say, I am very happy and thankful for it. Through this book, and by discerning the truth from the false, I will reveal just how preciously, clearly, and undoubtedly today's believers of the gospel of the water and the Spirit have been saved, and how, in contrast, religious and vain the faith of the believers of the other gospels other than this gospel of the water and the Spirit really is. I am therefore thankful to God, above all, for saving me from my sins.

Today, there are many so-called evangelicals, who claim unconditionally that they are sinless just because they believe in Jesus. Their hearts are filled with all kinds of unfounded and delusional faith. While studying the Tabernacle, I have come to realize even more clearly just how vain and false their faith really is, and because of this realization, I thank God even more with all my heart for my salvation.

The Gate And the Fence of the Tabernacle's Court

From the main passage, we can find out the fact that the length of the rectangular court of the Tabernacle was 45 m and its width was 22.5 m, as a cubit is a unit of length equal to 0.45 meter; that the court of the Tabernacle was surrounded by 60 pillars on all sides, the height of each pillar was 2.25 m; that to its east was the gate, measuring 9 m in width; and that the rest of the entire fence (about 126 m out of 135 m) was surrounded by the hangings of white fine linen.

The gate of the court of the Tabernacle was woven with blue, purple, and scarlet thread and fine woven linen, and it measured 9 m in width with 2.25 m in height. These four different threads, in other words, were woven to make a screen measuring 9 m by 2.25 m. Blue thread was first woven in full length and width into the fine white linen, and then purple thread was woven 2.25 m high, and then scarlet thread was woven 2.25 m high, followed by the weaving of white thread, making a thick and sturdy screen, woven like a carpet, that was 2.25 m high. In this way, a screen woven to measure 2.25 m in height and 9 m in width was put up on four pillars of the court of the Tabernacle to its east.

To enter into the Tabernacle's court, as such, people had to pull the carpet-like screen up. Unlike most other gates, the gate of the Tabernacle was not of wood. Although its pillars were made of wood, the gate that was hung on these pillars was a screen woven of blue, purple, and scarlet thread and fine woven linen.

You might have been to a circus show on tour before, and seen how a circus tent is built. Its door is usually made with thick fabrics. The gate of the court of the Tabernacle was somewhat similar to this kind of door. As it was made of thick fabrics, it was not opened by pulling or pushing, as in hard doors, but it was pulled up instead to enter. This was the case not only for the gate of the Tabernacle's court, but also for the gates of the Holy Place and the Most Holy inside the Tabernacle.

Why did God tell the Israelites to make all three gates of the Tabernacle's court, the Holy Place, and the Most Holy by weaving them with blue, purple, and scarlet thread and fine woven linen? We need to find out clearly what the will of God was behind this command. The Book of Hebrews tells us that all the good things of the Old Testaments are the shadows of one real substance to come, that is, Jesus Christ (Hebrews 10:1).

Likewise, the gate of the court of the Tabernacle is intricately related to the baptism of Jesus Christ, His death on the Cross, and His own identity. As such, when we have trouble understanding the Old Testament, we can reach this understanding by looking at the New Testament. Without seeing the actual substance, it's hard to figure out its shadow, but when see what or who is casting the shadow, we can realize what it is all about. We must all realize clearly who the Savior of sinners that God has prepared from the Old Testament really is, know Him as the actual substance of the Tabernacle, and believe that His works have saved us from all our sins.

Who, then, is the real substance of the Tabernacle, the One who has become the Savior of sinners? It is none other than Jesus Christ. When we examine how Jesus Christ, our Savior, came to this earth and how He has saved us from our sins, we can then find out the sure truth that He has saved sinners through the blue, purple, and scarlet thread.

In understanding Jesus' salvation of sinners, knowing and believing in the truth manifested in the colors of the gate of the Tabernacle's court is the most important. When delving into the Tabernacle, the first thing we must realize is that the gate of its court was made of four threads. And when we solve the mystery of this gate, we can then come to a firm grasp of all the works of Jesus Christ. By looking at the screen gate woven of these four threads, we can also understand clearly just how we must know and believe in Jesus, and exactly what kind of faith is wrong faith.

The outer court of the Tabernacle actually reminds us of a sheepfold. Jesus, our Messiah, is in fact the door of the sheepfold of God, and has also become the good Shepherd (John 10:1-15). When we think of the pillars surrounding the court, we are actually reminded of the Messiah, who has become the door and the good Shepherd of His sheep, the born-again saints.

The Shepherd has actually put up posts around the sheepfold to protect His sheep and has made a door there, and through this door, He is guarding His sheep. Through this door the Shepherd has close fellowship with His sheep and protects them. As a matter of fact, all those who are not His sheep are not permitted to get in through this door. The Shepherd differentiates between sheep and wolves. This is why sheep need the Shepherd.

Yet it is possible that there are some among these sheep that are refusing to be led by the Shepherd. Such sheep may enter into the way of death, thinking that it is a beautiful and good way when it is, in fact, a treacherous and dangerous one, for they have not listened to the voice of the Shepherd and refused to be led by Him. These sheep can actually have their lives spared and be fed well by the Shepherd, and live their lives beautifully because of Him. Our Shepherd, in fact, is Jesus Christ, who has become our Messiah.

Jesus Christ Showed Us the Four Colors of the Gate of the Tabernacle

The screen that was put up as the gate of the Tabernacle was woven of blue, purple, and scarlet thread, and fine woven linen. This thread of four different colors was used to make the gate of the Tabernacle. They symbolized the four ministries that the Messiah, coming to this earth, would have to fulfill to save the lost sheep—that is, the spiritual Israelites all over the world—from their sins and to turn them into the sinless people of God.

If we actually know who our Messiah that came to us with His four ministries is, then, the unequivocal truth is that we have been washed of all our sins by this faith, have dedicated our remaining lives to preaching the gospel of the water and the Spirit, and will enter Heaven through this very faith. Therefore, everyone must in fact know the Word of the truth that the Messiah has come to us by the blue, purple, and scarlet thread and has saved us from all our sins.

Do you want to receive the remission of your sins by believing in the four ministries of the Messiah? Let us, then, learn about the Tabernacle. Those who know these four ministries will in fact become the righteous by receiving the remission of sin woven of blue, purple, and scarlet thread, and fine woven linen.

The people of Israel, looking at the gate of the Tabernacle woven of four different colors of thread, had to actually believe that the Messiah would indeed come in the future and fulfill these four ministries.

The Truth That Every Sinner Must Believe

Had we looked at the white linen hangings of the court of the Tabernacle, we would have recognized our need for the Savior by realizing just how holy God really is. Everyone who came to know God's holiness, in fact, could not help but admit, saying, "God, I recognize that I am bound to hell because of my sins, for I am just a big mass of sin." Looking at the white linen draping over the pillars of the court, because its cleanness and majesty would be so great, people would have recognized the sins found in their hearts and realized that they are completely unfit to live with God. Whenever those whose hearts are not straight try to go before God, their sins are always revealed. As such, people have been reluctant to go before God, for they are afraid that their sins would be revealed.

But when such sinful people realize that their Savior has solved their problem of sin with His blue and scarlet thread, they can confidently go before God with a great conviction of salvation and hope in their hearts.

The four-fold truth shown in the gate of the Tabernacle tells us that the Messiah came to this earth in the flesh of a man, took all the sins of the world upon Himself with His baptism received from John, and shed His blood on the Cross. Those who, through the gospel of the water and the Spirit, know exactly and believe in the truth of the four colors of the gate of the Tabernacle's court can then receive the eternal remission of sin. The baptism of Jesus and His crucifixion, the truth that Christ wholly saved us from all our sins with His baptism and His blood on the Cross, are salvation like the four colors of the gate of the Tabernacle's court.

The blue, purple, and scarlet thread, and the fine woven linen actually show us the Messiah's ministry that has saved sinners from all their sins. The truth of salvation that God has given to the mankind is revealed in these blue, purple, and scarlet thread, and the fine woven linen. Those who have sin in their hearts, in fact, are forgiven of all their sins by believing in the truth of salvation revealed in the gospel of the water and the Spirit.

Countless religions have sprung up in this world. All these worldly religions have come up with their own doctrines made up with their own thoughts, all making people try to reach holiness. But not even a single person has ever been washed of their sins through these worldly religions. The reason is because they had made up and believed in their own doctrines of salvation based on their own thoughts, without realizing that they are just filled with sin. Because everyone is a big mass of sin who can never become holy by him/herself, no matter how hard one tries to get rid of his/her fundamental nature of sin, no one can ever achieve this. This is why everyone absolutely needs the Savior who can deliver him/her from sins—that is, why everyone needs Jesus. You must realize that human beings have no true Savior apart from Jesus Christ.

Because the Law of God does not allow sinners to enter the House of God, we must know and believe that the Messiah has actually blotted out all our sins.

The gospel that has forgiven the sins of mankind once for all is none other than the gospel of the water and the Spirit. Placing one's faith in the worldly religions' doctrines will only lead him/her into great difficulties on account of his/her sins, for our Holy God condemns, without fail, every iniquity of sinners.

The truth revealed by the blue, purple, and blue thread and the fine woven linen was fulfilled by the gospel of the water and the Spirit in the age of the New Testament. Have you ever heard someone claiming that the gate of the court of the Tabernacle was made with only scarlet thread or only purple and scarlet tread? If so, you must now realize, from this moment on, that the gate of the Tabernacle was actually woven of blue, purple, and scarlet thread and fine woven linen. God clearly commanded the Israelites to make the gate of the Tabernacle's court with a screen woven of blue, purple, and scarlet thread, and fine woven linen made by a weaver.

Yet because many people have mistakenly thought that

the gate of the court of the Tabernacle was woven of only scarlet thread, they could not solve the mystery of the true four ministries of our Lord. This is why they had sin in their hearts even when they believed in Jesus. Realize now that that Christ took away all your sins through His ministries of blue, purple, and scarlet thread and of fine woven linen, and believe in this truth. The work of salvation fulfilled by these blue, purple, and scarlet thread and fine woven linen has indeed wholly saved you from all your sins. You must realize that Jesus took away all your sins with these four ministries. Setting your own standard of the remission of sin while remaining ignorant of this truth, in other words, is simply wrong.

Some people, even as they remain oblivious to what the meaning of the blue, purple, and scarlet thread used for the gate of the Tabernacle's court is, mistakenly claim that one can be saved unconditionally just by believing in Jesus as the Savior. In fact, when we ask the leaders of Christian communities about the four ministries of Jesus, we find out that many of them are ignorant of them. They say that they believe only in the ministry of the scarlet thread. If they believe in one more thing, they might say that they believe in the ministry of the purple thread also. However, our Lord actually completed all the tasks for the salvation of mankind with the blue, purple, and scarlet thread and the fine woven linen. As such, we must believe that our Lord carried out for us His four ministries of salvation. Whoever has a heart that desires to know the truth revealed in the blue, purple, and scarlet thread and the fine woven linen of the Tabernacle's gate can in fact know it and believe in it.

"How should I understand the true meaning of the blue, purple, and scarlet thread and the fine woven linen?" If you were to ask this question to someone in search of the truth of these thread and linen, you might be rebuked in return, "You must not try to know the Bible in too much depth and detail; it may bring harm to you," and your curiosity might be ignored. Disheartened, many people may then lose their curiosity of the blue, purple, and scarlet thread and the fine woven linen. And you would never meet the Messiah ever, who is revealed in detail through the gate.

Those who try to meet the Messiah without realizing the role of the blue, purple, and scarlet thread and of the fine woven linen are, as a matter of fact, only religionists who believe in Christianity as one of the worldly religions. To enter into the House of God, we must know properly the truth of the four ministries of God's salvation revealed in the blue, purple, and scarlet thread and the fine woven linen used for the gate of the Tabernacle's court. And those who have found this truth must realize that the Lord fulfilled them with the gospel of the water and the Spirit in the New Testament's time.

God commanded Moses to weave the gate of the Tabernacle's court with blue, purple, and scarlet thread, and with fine woven linen. What, then, is the spiritual meaning of this? Each color of the blue, purple, and scarlet thread and of the fine woven linen used for the gate of the Tabernacle's court is the work of Jesus that He did for us to make our sins disappear. These thread and linen therefore are intricately related to one another. As such, those who pay attention to and believe in the gospel of the water and the Spirit can believe in their eternal remission of sin as the four ministries of Jesus.

Despite this, not trying to know and ignoring the truth of salvation manifested in the colors of blue, purple, and scarlet are, therefore, the expression of one's complete indifference to the Messiah and the same as becoming the His enemy standing against Him. Many people, in fact, remain indifferent to the truth manifested in the blue, purple, and scarlet thread and the fine woven linen, and are turning Christianity into only one of the many worldly religions. If these people regard Jesus' four ministries with indifference, then this is the evidence that they are the fruits of the worldly religionists who stand against Christ. Fortunately, however, there is still hope for us, for in this world many people are still looking for the gospel of the water and the Spirit.

When people have the knowledge of the spiritual truth of the remission of sin revealed by the gate of the court of the Tabernacle, they can receive all the spiritual blessings of Heaven. Because this faith is actually the required faith that one must know and believe in to meet the Messiah, we must dwell on it not only once, but forever. If you truly are a Christian, you must pay attention to this truth.

Whoever wants to enter into the House of God must discover the truth manifested in the blue, purple, and scarlet thread and the fine woven linen, and praise God accordingly.

The Messiah Who Came as the Fulfiller of the Prophecies

God prophesied with His Word that the Messiah would be born through the body of a virgin. Isaiah 7:14 says, *"Therefore the Lord Himself will give you a sign: Behold, the virgin shall conceive and bear a Son, and shall call His name Immanuel."* Micah 5:2, on the other hand, states that the Messiah would be born in Bethlehem: *"But you, Bethlehem Ephrathah, Though you are little among the thousands of Judah, Yet out of you shall come forth to Me, The One to be Ruler in Israel, Whose goings forth are from of old, From everlasting."* The Messiah did indeed come to this earth exactly as prophesied by this Word of the Old Testament. He came to this earth in the flesh of a man as the fulfillment of the prophecies in accordance to the Word of God.

At which point in human history, then, did the Messiah come? When did Jesus Christ come to this earth? He came to this earth during the reign of the Roman Emperor Augustus (B.C. 27-A.D. 14). Jesus came to this earth to deliver you and me from all our sins and condemnation by receiving baptism from John and being crucified and bleeding on the Cross.

Jesus came as the Savior of mankind when Israel had been turned into a colony of the Roman Empire and when Augustus was reigning as its emperor. Because Israel was a Roman colony, it had to follow Rome's decrees. At this time, the Emperor Augustus had decreed everyone in the entire Roman Empire to return to his/her hometown and to register for a census. Following Augustus' decree, this census was immediately begun. Because the census sought to account for each and every person living in the Empire, including those living in Israel, all the Israelites had to also return to their hometowns. From this moment, Jesus Christ was already working in the history of mankind.

Look at the Fulfillment of the Word of the Old Testament!

At the time, in the land of Judea, the Messiah was already conceived in the womb of the Virgin Mary. This Mary was engaged to Joseph. Both Mary and Joseph were from the tribe of Judah, just as God promised that of the twelve tribes of Israel, kings would continue to be born only from the tribe of

Judah.

So when the Roman Emperor Augustus decreed for a census to take place, Mary, of the tribe of Judah, was already carrying a baby in her womb. When her time came near and she was about to give birth, because of the Emperor's decree, she had to go to Joseph's hometown and register for the census. Mary therefore headed to Bethlehem with Joseph even as she was expected to give birth at anytime. When Mary went into her birth pain, they had to find a room for her, but they could not find any in town. They therefore had to use whatever place that was available to them, even as they ended up in a stable. And Mary gave birth to her baby Jesus in the stable.

On A.D. 1, Jesus was born and placed in a manger. The Almighty God came to this earth in the flesh of a man. To the place where animals once stayed, the Savior of mankind came. This means that Jesus was born in this lowest place to become our Messiah, and all these things had been set and planned by God even before the creation. Though people might have known that Yahweh God moves the history of mankind, none could ever realize that God Himself would actually come to this earth to save them. God, therefore, made it possible for anyone to realize that He would save him/her by lowering Himself to be born unto this earth in the humble body of a man to deliver all human beings from their sins.

Why, then, was Jesus born, of all places, in Bethlehem? We may also wonder why He had to be born in a stable, and why, of all times, when Israel was subjugated by Rome as its colony? But we can soon find out that all these things came under His elaborate providence carefully drawn to deliver His people from their sins.

When Joseph and Mary registered for the census in their hometown, they had to provide evidence proving that they indeed were from this town, and document their exact identity. They could register for the census only when they could provide the necessary evidence to prove that their ancestors had indeed lived in Bethlehem for generations. So they had to disclose who their ancestors were and in whose houses they belonged, and record all such details of their family lineage on the census. As none of these could be invented or omitted, by historically recording the exact identities of Joseph and Mary, God made sure that the history of mankind would also testify to the birth of Jesus (Matthew 1:1-16, Luke 3:23-38). All these were God's works that He did to fulfill the prophecies of the Word of the Old Testament.

Micah 5:2 states, *"But you, Bethlehem Ephrathah, Though you are little among the thousands of Judah, Yet out of you shall come forth to Me, The One to be Ruler in Israel, Whose goings forth are from of old, From everlasting."* That the day of birth came and the Savior was born in the prophesied town of Bethlehem precisely by making Joseph and Mary arrive at the very town means that God did this work to fulfill the prophecies of His prophets. This is for sure God's planned achievement in order to blot out all the sins of mankind. That Jesus had to be born in the little town of Bethlehem was to fulfill the Old Testament's Word of Prophecy.

Hundreds of years before Jesus Christ was born in the small town of Bethlehem, God had already given His Word of prophecy through His prophet Micah, as quoted above (Micah 5:2). As well, the Prophet Isaiah had also prophesized about 700 years before the coming of our Lord how the Messiah would come to His people to become the Savior of sinners (Isaiah 53). As Jesus Christ was indeed born in Bethlehem exactly as God prophesied through the Prophet Micah, He always fulfills all His Word of prophecy.

This prophecy was fulfilled as a historical fact when Mary and Joseph went up to their ancestor's hometown to register for the census. God fulfilled His Word by making sure that the time for the baby to be born would come just when Mary arrives at Bethlehem, so that she would have no choice but to give birth in this town.

Here, we discover that our God is the God who speaks His Word of prophecy to us and fulfills all such Word accordingly. From this, we can find out that the "fine woven linen" used for the gate of the Tabernacle's court implies the fineness and wholeness of God's Word. God had elaborately planned the salvation of mankind even before the Creation, and He has fulfilled this without fail according to His Word of prophecy.

We can therefore realize that the Word of the Old Testament is surely the Word of God, and that the Word of the New Testament is also the Word of God. We can also realize, as well as believe, that God indeed rules over and moves all the history of the entire universe and this earth. We can find out, in other words, that just as God created the whole universe, He has shown us that He reigns over all peoples, all histories, and all conditions of everyone thoroughly. God therefore shows us that nothing can be achieved according to one's own will, no matter what it is, unless He allows it.

When the Baby Jesus was born unto and came to this world, He could not but be born in the resting place of animals, for there was no room in the inn. And He Himself was indeed born in the town of Bethlehem. We must realize that all these were the wonderful achievement of God's prophesied providence according to His faithfulness.

Therefore, we must believe that the One who moves the history of this universe is our God, the Savior who has delivered us from our sins. This truth is the Word of God that shows us that He rules over all, for God is the Lord of all.

It thus has now been proven that the birth of Jesus in the small town of Bethlehem was not an accidental incidence, nor something that was arbitrarily invented by manipulating the Word of the Bible. This is what God Himself said, and it is also what God Himself fulfilled through Jesus.

We must know this and believe in it. We must take it to our hearts and believe that the salvation of our Messiah is the truth that is fulfilled by the blue, purple, and scarlet thread and the fine woven linen. God has shown us that the remission of sin, too, is not something that is accidentally achieved, but it is achieved through the four ministries of Jesus prepared in God's providence.

This also shows, in addition, that Christianity is not just one of many worldly religions. The founder of a worldly religion is a mere mortal, but the founder of Christianity is our Savior Jesus, and God has shown us that the truth of Christianity starts from the fact that this Savior of ours is God Himself. God is testifying to us, in other words, that the Christianity that we believe in is not merely a worldly religion. Unlike all the other earthly religions, Christianity is established on all the grace given by God. As it is written in Romans 11:36, *"For of Him and through Him and to Him are all things, to whom be glory forever,"* He gave us His only begotten Son as our Savior, the gospel of the water and the Spirit for the remission of our sins, the indwelling of the Holy Spirit, and the Kingdom of Heaven. Therefore, we must all know and believe in our hearts that we should fear and obey God and His Word with all our hearts.

The birth of the Messiah on this earth was according to the plan of salvation determined by God the Father even before the creation. Our salvation had been perfectly planned within this. God has allowed us to clearly realize that this truth is the actual substance of the blue, purple, and scarlet thread and the fine woven linen. Therefore, we must recognize the salvation that has come to us through the gospel of the water and the Spirit as the remission of our sins, and believe so. It is through this faith that you and I could be saved from all our sins. We must believe that this truth of the four colors, too, is made whole by our faith in the gospel Word of the water and the Spirit.

Jesus Christ, the Savior Who Has Saved Us with His Blue, Purple, and Scarlet Thread and Fine Woven Linen

The works by which Jesus Christ saved sinners from their sins are four-fold: the blue thread (Jesus' baptism); the purple thread (Jesus as King of kings—God Himself, in other words); the scarlet thread (the blood of Jesus); and the fine woven linen (the completion of the salvation of all sinners from their sins through the elaborate Word of the Old and New Testaments). Jesus has become precisely the Savior with the blue thread, the purple thread, the scarlet thread, and the fine woven linen.

We must realize that unless we believe that Jesus, who came to us through the water and the Spirit, saved us from our sins with the blue thread (the baptism of Jesus), the purple thread (Jesus is God), the scarlet thread (the blood of Jesus), and the fine woven linen (Jesus who achieved salvation with the Word of the New and Old Testaments), we can never be delivered from our sins and the condemnation of these sins. Without thus saving us from our sins and condemnation, our Lord could not have become the perfect Savior.

We must realize spiritually the reason why the curtain of the gate of the Tabernacle's court was woven with blue, purple, and scarlet thread, and fine woven linen. The gate of the Tabernacle's court was made with these blue, purple, and scarlet thread and fine woven linen so that everyone could obviously recognize the gate and easily find it. Through this gate, God allowed anyone to enter into His shining House.

The Tabernacle itself is the shining House of God. No one who wished to enter the House of God could do so without realizing the truth of salvation manifested in the fence and the gate of the Tabernacle's court. God said that those who, ignoring the holiness of the white linen curtain draping the Tabernacle, do not enter into the Tabernacle by the gate, but climb over some other way, are all thieves and robbers. The gate of salvation refers to Jesus Christ (John 10).

When the Bible says that this gate is woven with blue, purple, and scarlet thread and fine woven linen, God is showing us clearly, through His true Word of the Old and New Testaments, that Jesus Christ came to this earth as the Son of God, was baptized by John, died on the Cross, rose from the dead again, and thereby has become our Messiah. We can thus find out the mystery of the blue, purple, and scarlet thread and the fine woven linen. We must believe that God has allowed us to believe that Jesus Christ is the Son of God who came to save us from the judgement of the sins of this world, and that He is the Savior who has now achieved the salvation of mankind through the Word of the Old and New Testaments.

We must be able to actually realize why the gate of the Tabernacle's court was woven with these blue, purple, and scarlet thread and fine woven linen. What does the blue thread tell us? And what do the purple thread, the scarlet thread, and the fine woven linen tell us? When we realize God's plan, we can also realize that the works of the blue, purple, and scarlet thread and of the fine woven linen are all God's plan of salvation for us and the truth of eternal life, and we can thereby enter into His Kingdom through our faith of the remission of sin.

When we say that we know and believe in the blue, purple, and scarlet thread, it means that we know well the reason why Jesus was baptized by John the Baptist and shed His blood on the Cross, who the Messiah is, all the mysteries of the sacrificial system of the Old Testament, and the gospel of the water and the Spirit of the New Testament. In short, the truth implied in the gate of the Tabernacle's court is essential to all the believers who earnestly seek the truth to be eternally saved.

It may seem that many people are well knowledgeable of the Tabernacle, but in fact, this is actually not the case. People are actually quite ignorant of what is meant by the blue, purple, and scarlet thread woven into the gate of the Tabernacle's court. As the mystery of these blue, purple, and scarlet thread and of the fine woven linen are difficult to understand, many people have a true desire to learn and believe in them. However, because this mystery cannot be understood just by anyone, many of them have ended up interpreting it erroneously based on their own opinions. Many religious leaders, in fact, have misinterpreted and misunderstood this truth in whatever way they felt like, only using it for their own religious ends. But God could no longer allow Christians to continue to be deceived by these liars. He thus had to explain clearly the meaning of the truth of the blue, purple, and scarlet thread and the fine woven linen used for the gate of the Tabernacle's court, and thereby save them from all their sins.

1 John 5:6-8 from the New Testament states, *"This is He who came by water and blood—Jesus Christ; not only by water,*

but by water and blood. And it is the Spirit who bears witness, because the Spirit is truth. For there are three that bear witness in heaven: the Father, the Word, and the Holy Spirit; and these three are one. And there are three that bear witness on earth: the Spirit, the water, and the blood; and these three agree as one." This passage explicitly states that our Lord came to this world in the flesh of a man, took upon our sins with His baptism, and saved us by shedding His blood. This is why the gate of the Tabernacle's court was all woven of the blue, purple, and scarlet thread and the fine woven linen.

First, what does the blue thread show us? It shows us a part of the truth on Jesus, who became the actual Messiah of sinners, coming to this earth and taking upon the sins of the world by receiving His baptism from John. In fact, this baptism that Jesus received from John at the Jordan River is the truth of Jesus taking upon all the sins of the world once for all. Jesus actually bore all the sins of the world on His shoulder by being baptized by John the Baptist, the representative of all mankind. Because the sins of all human beings were thus passed onto Christ's own head, those who believe in this truth have no sin in their hearts.

Second, what is the actual meaning of the purple thread woven into the gate of the Tabernacle's court? It tells us that Jesus is the actual King of kings. Jesus, in fact, did make the universe, is the Creator Himself, not a creation, and is the actual Messiah who came to this earth. He, the Messiah, actually came to this earth already in the likeness of a human flesh. And by bearing all the sins of the world on His own body through the baptism that He received from John, and with His sacrificing death and resurrection, Jesus has saved all His people, who have recognized, feared, and believed in their Messiah, from all their sins and their judgment of sin.

Jesus is in fact our absolute God and absolute Messiah. He is the absolute Savior. Because Jesus took all our sins of the world upon Himself with His baptism, by bleeding and dying on the Cross and resurrecting from His death, He not only cleansed away all our sins, but He also received the vicarious judgment of sin in our place.

The scarlet thread, thirdly, refers to the blood that Jesus shed on the Cross, and its meaning is that Christ has given new life those of us who believe. This truth of the scarlet thread tells us that Jesus Christ not only received the judgment of our own sins by taking the sins of the world on Himself with His baptism received from John, but He also gave new life to believers by bestowing the life-giving faith to those who had died to sin. To those who believe in His baptism and the blood that He shed, Jesus has indeed given new life.

What, then, does the fine woven linen mean? It manifests that with the New Testament, God fulfilled His promise of salvation written in the Old Testament. And it tells us that when Jesus took all the sins of the world upon Himself with His baptism and was judged for our sins on the Cross in the New Testament, He fulfilled the salvation that God had promised to the Israelites and us with His Word of covenant.

Yahweh God said in Isaiah 1:8, *"'Come now, and let us reason together,' Says the LORD, 'Though your sins are like scarlet, They shall be as white as snow; Though they are red like crimson, They shall be as wool.'"* Also, the Old Testament's sacrificial system governing how the sacrifices are offered in the Tabernacle, under which the sins of the people of Israel were passed onto the sacrificial lamb with the laying of hands, was the promise that God made to the Israelites and us. This was God's revelation of the promise that He would save all the people of the world from their daily sins and yearly sins through the Lamb of God in the future.

This was also the sign of the promised Messiah to come. So in the New Testament's time, when Jesus Christ took all the sins of the world upon Himself all at once by receiving His baptism according to the way of the Old Testament, it was the accomplishment of God's covenant. Having given us all His Word of promise, God has shown us that He has actually fulfilled them all, exactly as He had promised. The baptism that Jesus received manifests this truth, that the God of covenant has fulfilled all His covenants.

Jesus Christ Who Came by the Water, the Blood, and the Spirit

Why was Jesus baptized by John? The reason was to take upon Himself all the sins of mankind, and to receive the judgment of sin on our behalf. To make all the sins of the entire mankind disappear, and to become our true Savior, Jesus was baptized by John the Baptist, went to the Cross, and bled and died on it. By doing so He not only washed away all our sins, but He also received all the judgment of these sins in our stead, and has thereby become our eternal Savior. All our sins were passed onto Jesus when He was baptized by John, and He carried these sins of the world to the Cross. It is because Christ bore all our sins with His baptism, and because He carried these sins of the world to the Cross, He could be crucified, shed His blood, and die in our place.

Isaiah 53:5 says, *"But He was wounded for our transgressions, He was bruised for our iniquities; The chastisement for our peace was upon Him, And by His stripes we are healed."* Through our Lord's baptism, our original sins that were inherited to us from our common ancestor Adam and our own actual sins that we commit throughout our lives were all passed onto Him. And He was judged for all these sins. By thus coming to us by the water and the blood, our Lord has made all our sins disappear (1 John 5:5-8).

Who, then, is this Jesus Christ, our Savior and Messiah who took care of all our sins and made them all disappear? Genesis 1:1 states, *"In the beginning God created the heavens and the earth."* Who was this mighty God that created the universe with His Word? He was none other than the Messiah of sinners, He who came by the water of His baptism to save you and me from all the sins of the world, the One who came as the Savior who bled on the Cross to be judged for all the sins of the world. Through the water, the blood, and the Spirit, Jesus has delivered us from our sins and judgment. Our Lord came to us as our Savior to take upon all our sins and be judged of these sins in our place.

Jesus Christ, in fact, is the Son of God and God Himself, for the Messiah actually is our God. The name "Jesus" means "the Savior who will save His people from their sins" (Matthew 1:21). "Christ," *"Basileus"* in Greek on the other hand, means "King of kings." Jesus is the Creator who made the whole universe, the absolute ruler of all, the Savior of sinners, and the King of kings who judges Satan.

This absolute God actually created man after His own image. As we, His own creation, fell into sin and became doomed to destruction because of our weaknesses, this King of kings promised us to save us from our sins, and to fulfill this promise He came to us. And to make us the whole people of God and sinless, our Lord Himself came to us by the water, the blood, and the Spirit.

The Messiah, who is the Creator, actually came to this

earth in the flesh of a man to make all our sins disappear, and took all our sins upon Himself by receiving baptism from John at the Jordan River. And by dying on the Cross, He was judged for all our sins in our place. Because Jesus was in fact the very Messiah for us, because He is our Savior and the Lord of our life, we could earn new and eternal life by believing in Him. The Messiah therefore has indeed become our God. This is why the gate of the Tabernacle was woven of the blue, purple, and scarlet thread, for this was the mystery of the water and the Spirit that delivers us from all our sins and the judgment of our sins.

The truth that the Lord has indeed saved us from our sins is not vague. Our Lord did not promise us His salvation ambiguously, did not achieve it roughly, and cannot approve the faith of those who believe in Him arbitrarily, apart from His concrete truth that He has actually saved us through His water and blood. Our Lord therefore said to those who nominally believe in Him, *"Not everyone who says to Me, 'Lord, Lord,' shall enter the kingdom of heaven, but he who does the will of My Father in heaven" (Matthew 7:21).*

False teachers insist that they actually did make people receive the Holy Spirit in the name of Jesus, cast out demons in His name, and did many wonders in His name. But God has said to them in Matthew 7:23, *"I never knew you; depart from Me, you who practice lawlessness!"* This tells us that among Christians, there actually are many who still remain sinful, who would be judged for their sins on the Day of Judgment, and then be cast out to hell.

There are, in fact, many Christians who clearly confess, "Jesus is our Savior. Jesus has unequivocally saved us from all our sins." But despite making such claims, they actually do not even try to learn that the Messiah did indeed take upon their sins with His baptism, and that He did indeed bear their sins and the judgment of these sins by shedding His blood on the Cross. These people would all go before God while still remaining sinful, for they only believe nominally, as if they were merely practicing one of the many worldly religions.

As such, because they do not believe according to the truth that our Lord has said, *"You shall know the truth, and the truth shall make you free,"* they have not been admitted by the Lord. Whether people believe in Jesus or not, those who have sin in their hearts cannot enter the Kingdom of God, where no sin is found, for they are not qualified to enter it. They must, therefore, make sure that they can be qualified to enter Heaven only by believing in the truth of the blue, purple, and scarlet thread while on this earth. Making the gate of the Tabernacle's court by weaving its curtain with these blue, purple, and scarlet thread and fine woven linen was the providence of the Messiah. Those who are headed to hell because of sin must believe in this.

Because these people are ignorant of the truth, and because they believe in Jesus with their mistaken knowledge attained on their own, they still remain sinful. They still have sin because they, instead of believing according to the truth hidden in the materials of the Tabernacle, have thought of their Savior on their own and made their own doctrines of salvation based on these thoughts, believing that salvation comes through their own efforts by offering prayers of repentance to God and trying to reach their incremental sanctification.

There are many in this world who claim to believe in Jesus as their Savior, and yet do not actually believe in the baptism of Jesus and His blood. There are many in this world who, instead of actually believing in the blue, purple, and scarlet thread as their salvation, think that they can enter the

Holy Kingdom of God just by believing in the blood of Jesus, even if they still remain sinful.

The Matching of the Old and New Testaments

God tells us in Isaiah 34:16 that every Word of God has its matching pair. The Word of God, in other words, does all match up. God said to look and see for ourselves whether or not His Word of the Old Testament matches with His Word of the New Testament. What is written in the Old Testament has its corresponding Word in the New Testament. For example, whereas the Israelites passed their sins onto a sacrificial lamb with the laying on of hands in the Old Testament, in the New Testament this is matched by Jesus Christ being baptized to take upon all our sins of the world, and thus passing all our sins onto Himself.

Through His water and blood, Jesus came to this earth as the sacrificial offering and the Savior of sinners. Had He not taken upon the sins of the world by receiving His baptism, there would have been absolutely no need for Him to die on the Cross. Our Lord has clearly made all our sins disappear with the blue, purple, and scarlet thread. This, too, was promised by God with His Word, whereupon our Lord came to us through this Word and washed away our scarlet sins, turning them as white as snow.

Before realizing this truth, in fact, we were undoubtedly overflowing with endless sins. We therefore have nothing to boast of before God. Not only do we not have anything to boast of before God, but we have nothing at all to be confident of before Him. There is nothing, in other words, which would allow us to even pretend to be smart. Before God, all that we can say is, "Yes, You are right."

If God says, "You are a seed of iniquities, bound to hell."

"Yes, You are right; please save me."

"I have saved you in this way, through the water, the blood, and the Spirit."

"Yes, Lord! I believe!"

We can only say "yes" all the time. Standing before God, we cannot say to Him, "I did this and that; I served my church this well; I really believed in Jesus wholeheartedly; I defended my faith with a stubbornness that no one else can even imagine!"

How did the Lord actually make all our sins disappear? He has shown us that He made them disappear through the blue, purple, and scarlet thread, and through the Word of the Old and New Testaments. In the Old Testament, He made our sins disappear with the blue, purple, and scarlet thread, while In the New Testament, Jesus became our Savior by coming to this earth in the flesh of a man, taking all our sins upon Himself with His baptism received from John, and taking care of all our sins and the judgment of these sin by shedding His blood on the Cross.

By being baptized, our Lord took upon all the sins of the world all at once (Matthew 3:15). All our worldly sins were passed onto Jesus' shoulder. After thus taking upon all our sins of the world with His baptism, He carried these sins to the Cross, was crucified, shed His blood, died on the Cross, rose from the dead again, and thereby made all our sins truly disappear. Jesus Christ has thus become our certain Savior.

The righteousness of God that we have received is the righteousness acquired by believing in this Jesus Christ who came to this earth through the water, the blood, and the Spirit. This is the very salvation received from God, not something that we achieved on our own. There is nothing that we can brag about before God.

In fact, we are saved from all our sins by believing in Jesus Christ who has become our certain Savior. We who had been sinners, in other words, actually received the remission of sin by believing in the baptism of Jesus and the blood that He shed for us. Were Jesus' work of salvation to account for, say, around 70 percent of our salvation, and the remaining 30 percent to be accounted by our own efforts to not commit sin, for us to be gradually sanctified and for our salvation to be completed little by little, we would literally have to stay up all night praying fervently, spend every day offering our prayers of repentance, serving the community, or otherwise trying to do everything and anything possible!

But the Apostle Paul said in Romans, *"O wretched man that I am! Who will deliver me from this body of death? I thank God—through Jesus Christ our Lord! There is therefore now no condemnation to those who are in Christ Jesus" (Romans 7:24-8:1).* Just as Paul thus confessed, we also must believe in Jesus Christ like he did. The Scripture tells us that Jesus Christ has fully saved us from this body of death, 100 percent. Who, then, can possibly condemn us? No one can ever condemn us, for Jesus Christ has already saved us 100 percent, regardless of our own infirmities.

You and I, Too, Were All Spiritual Pharisees

Some of you may have known and believed in Jesus a little bit for a long time. You had believed in Jesus as your Savior, in other words, even before you met the gospel of the water and the Spirit. I myself also had been a Christian, without being born again, for ten years.

When we first believed in Jesus as our Savior, it was a rather refreshing experience. This start was so refreshing that we thought we would be saved unconditionally just by believing in Jesus as our Savor, even if we remained ignorant of the truth of the blue, purple, and scarlet thread.

When I first believed in Jesus, my heart was in fact filled with joy. So I rejoiced greatly when I first believed in Jesus, but after about five years, I came to look at myself, and I saw that I had been bound continuously by the sins that I had committed, and came to the recognition that I was still not free. Do you think I committed sins, or not committed any at all, in those five years of my early Christian life? Whether you know me or not, the answer is pretty clear: of course I did. During this time, when I did not know the truth, I was tormented every time I committed sin, and to get rid of this agony I had to offer prayers of repentance, at times even fasting for three days. The burden of my heart then seemed to lift up a little, allowing me to praise God, "♪Amazing grace! ♪How sweet the sound, that saved a wretch like me! ♪" But after this, of course, I would end up committing sin yet again. Because I had so many shortcomings and was full of blemishes, everyday I committed sin, even as I hated myself for doing so. Not once could I resolve all my problems of sin for good.

Under these circumstances, five more years went by, and when I thus had been a Christian for about ten years, suddenly, I was shocked to discover just how many sins I had committed over all those years. Looking at myself committing such great sins everyday, I was deeply saddened and utterly disheartened. And when I stood before the Law, I also discovered just how sinful I really was. It became more and more difficult for me stand before God, and I ended turning into a sinner who could not even claim, in good conscience, to know Jesus well and to believe in Him. So into my tenth year as a Christian, I could not but confess my sinfulness to myself.

When I first believed in Jesus, I actually thought that I was a fairly good Christian. But as time went by, I only realized more and more that I really had nothing to boast of before God. I recognized, "I am actually a Pharisee. Pharisees are not found just in the Bible, for I myself am a Pharisee of today!"

Pharisees are the kind the people who, in their pretentious holiness. Every Sunday on their way to the church with the Bible tucked at their sides, they shout out at their fellow Christians, "Good morning! Hallelujah!" And when they are worshipping, every time they hear someone speaking of the Cross, they end up crying. I myself, too, shed many tears, thinking of Jesus' blood. I thought this is what giving the true worship was all about. But while living in this world, everyone eventually discovers one's self, committing sin after sin. So people once again resort to giving the prayers of repentance. They might actually feel better for a while, but sooner or later, they would all run out of these prayers of repentance, for there are just way too many sins that they had committed. Some people even speak in tongues and see visions later on, but they are all useless. No matter what kind of attempt they might have tried, it was of no use for them to solve the problem of their sins in their hearts.

If they eventually realize that they are simply worthless beings before God and recognize that they are bound to hell because of their sins, even if this realization comes late, it would still be a fortunate outcome. In fact, the longer we have believed in Jesus, the more we realize just how awfully sinful we really have been. But the Pharisees are good at hiding this.

How does the Father inspire and edify you through the body of Christ?

◆ God works through other believers to keep you accountable, so you will not drift in your relationship with Him.

◆ God gives you opportunities to use your talents and bless others through the body of Christ.

◆ God provides the companionship, teaching, and support you need through other believers.

In Touch Ministries.

intouch.org | 800-789-1473

BOCMK

No Christian has ever been called to "go it alone" in his or her walk of faith.

LIFE PRINCIPLE 28

"He who walks with wise men will be wise, but the companion of fools will suffer harm."

PROVERBS 13:20

They are so good at hiding the sins of their hearts and playing the hypocrite that they are even approved by those around them for their piety.

The religionists of this world greatly respect each other. But regardless of how much respect and approval they get from others, when they stand before God, they are just a big mass of sin.

When we did not know the truth, we, too, used to offer our prayers of repentance diligently. But after a while, we get tired, and so we end up praying, "Lord, do whatever you want to do. I have so many sins. I've sinned yet again. Now it's become too embarrassing for me to even tell you about it." Though it's way too embarrassing, because we were told that God would be pleased whenever we confess our sins, and that He would forgive our sins with His righteousness and cleanse away from all unrighteousness, we continued to pray to Him, "Lord, I've sinned. Please forgive me, Lord!" And yet our sins, nonetheless, were still left in our hearts.

Whenever people bow their heads to pray to God, their conscience reminds them of their sins and eats away their hearts. Our conscience torments our hearts telling us, "With so many sins committed, how dare you to even pray to God?"

So, after a while, because we really had nothing more to say, we ended up just crying, "Lord, Lord!" More and more often, we found ourselves going up a mountain and shouting out the Lord's name. To avoid the embarrassment of drawing people's attention, we've climbed up a mountain late at night, entered in some cave there, and cried out the Lord's name. But this, too, was just having a fit by ourselves, and our sins thus still remained with us.

We also tried to placate our conscience, telling ourselves that we are no longer sinful, "God is so merciful that He has made my sins disappear. I've fasted and prayed for three days. What is more, I think, I haven't sinned that much. Wouldn't our merciful God then forgive me?"

But could we really deceive ourselves, even if we were to praise God for His mercifulness? How could we ever deceive our own hearts when we remained sinful before God? We could never do so! No matter how high we climbed up into leadership positions of our churches, and no matter how much we were commended by others, as long as we still continued to commit sin on our own, we could never be freed from these sins, and thus ended up as hypocrites at last.

Sinful desires continued to rise up in our hearts. Though we spoke of Jesus' blood on the Cross for countless times, though we shed many tears just by thinking of His blood of the Cross, and though we had been good Christians, we still remained sinful until we met the perfect gospel of the water and the Spirit. Despite living according to all the rituals of Christianity, we still had sin. This was the Pharisee's religion. There are still many people on this earth who have this kind of faith, and they are found even in our Christian communities.

All Our Sins Disappeared by Believing in the Gospel of the Water and the Spirit

Before knowing the gospel of the water and the Spirit, and before believing in this gospel, we all had sin in our hearts. Before we believed in this truth of the blue, purple, and scarlet thread and the fine woven linen, our conscience was sinful. In all honesty, we were all sinful before God, and we were all bound to hell because of our sins, for the Bible tells us that "the wages of sin is death." We were thus greatly tormented because of our sins. And we were bound to hell both physically and spiritually because of God's judgment on us for our sins.

We had converted many people to Christianity and had taught them. But we had worked while we were unable to cleanse away even our own conscience. We could not deny this before God. We recognized before God that our hearts are sinful and that we are bound to hell.

I had always had an unsolved question: "Why was our Lord baptized when He came to this earth?" I wanted to find out why Jesus had received baptism. Why, and for what purposes did Jesus have to be baptized? I could understand our own water baptism as the mark of our faith in Jesus, but I could not understand at all why Jesus had been baptized by John the Baptist. Why was He baptized? Why?

So I asked some leaders in Christian communities, "Reverend, I have a question. Do you mind if I ask?" They told me to go ahead, and so I asked them. "It's about the Bible. It is clear that Jesus did receive baptism from John in the New Testament. But, I'm not sure why He was baptized. Do you know why, Reverend?" They then smiled, saying to me, "You don't even know that? It's something that even our kids in the Sunday school know! It's found in the original Scriptural texts, and in the Bible dictionaries as well. Wasn't Jesus baptized to lead us by example, as a model, and to show us His humility?" So I said, "But Reverend, if the answer was so simple, even the kids in our Sunday school would indeed know it. I've examined it both in the original text and historically, but His baptism did not mean that. Wouldn't there have been a reason why Jesus really was baptized by John?"

I continued to ask. I began to search for the answer right after I became a Christian. I had no choice but to devote years in search of the answer to that question. I looked up all the scholarly works on this question. Even though I thus searched, asked, and investigated everything, nowhere could I find anything that explained Jesus' baptism clearly and definitively. I had struggled to find out the final answer until the Lord enlightened me on the gospel of the water and the Spirit manifested in the blue, purple, and scarlet thread and the fine woven linen.

While I was captured by the unsolved puzzle of the baptism of Jesus, I then came upon a chance to peruse Matthew 3:13-17: *"Then Jesus came from Galilee to John at the Jordan to be baptized by him. And John tried to prevent Him, saying, 'I need to be baptized by You, and are You coming to me?' But Jesus answered and said to him, 'Permit it to be so now, for thus it is fitting for us to fulfill all righteousness.' Then he allowed Him. When He had been baptized, Jesus came up immediately from the water; and behold, the heavens were opened to Him, and He saw the Spirit of God descending like a dove and alighting upon Him. And suddenly a voice came from heaven, saying, 'This is My beloved Son, in whom I am well pleased.'"*

Reading this Word, I finally realized, "So this is it! The reason why Jesus was baptized was because He was the sacrificial offering of the Old Testament! This is the truth of His salvation hidden in the blue, purple, and scarlet thread and the fine woven linen!"

John the Baptist was actually Elijah whom God had promised to send in the Old Testament. God said in Malachi 4:5 that He would send Elijah before the day of judgement, and Matthew 11:14 tells us that this Elijah whom He promised to send us is none other than John the Baptist. So I found out about Elijah, but I still was not sure why Jesus had to be baptized by John the Baptist. Then I went back to Matthew

3:13-17 and perused the passage again, *"'Permit it to be so now, for thus it is fitting for us to fulfill all righteousness.' ...When He had been baptized, Jesus came up immediately from the water... 'This is My beloved Son, in whom I am well pleased.'"* All my doubts were then dissolved. "To fulfill all righteousness," He did actually receive His baptism. Jesus did indeed fulfill this righteous work of saving all people through His baptism.

Baptism is the same as the Old Testament's laying on of hands, as when hands were laid on the heads of the sacrificial offerings in accordance to the sacrificial system of the Tabernacle. For sinners to bring forth these sacrificial offerings before the altar of burnt offering, to lay their hands on them and thereby confess their sins and pass them onto their sacrificial offering; for high priest to confess all the sins of the people of Israel and to pass them onto the sacrificial offerings for the Israelites and for themselves; and for Jesus to be baptized by John the Baptist in the New Testament's time—all these things match with one another. I finally realized that Jesus thus received His baptism (laying of hands) in order to take upon Himself all the sins of the world and to make everyone's sins disappear.

So I looked up the original Scriptural texts. I looked up how the phrase, *"for thus it is fitting for us to fulfill all righteousness,"* is written in Greek "Ἄφες ἄρτι, οὕτως γὰρ πρέπον ἐστὶν ἡμῖν πληρῶσαι πᾶσαν δικαιοσύνην." In this phrase, "for thus" and "righteousness" were written in Greek as "hutos (οὕτως)" and "dikaiosune (δικαιοσύνην)." The former means "like this," "appropriately," "only by this method," "the most fitting," or "with this method." And the latter means, "righteousness, justice or the virtue acceptable to God."

It told us that Jesus saved sinners from their sins. It told us that Jesus fulfilled the righteousness of God by being baptized and shedding His blood. It mean, in other words, that He took upon all our sins with His baptism. All our puzzles were thus solved, for we now realized the true meaning of what had caused us so much confusion and wandering. It is because Jesus took upon all our sins with His baptism that He went to the Cross and died on it as the judgement of these sins. This was the truth found in the gospel of the water and the Spirit.

We, the born-again, came to realize, in other words, that the baptism that Jesus received from John was the indispensable constituent of our salvation, and that He took upon the sins of the world onto Himself all at once with this baptism. You also have to realize the same truth in the gospel of the water and the Spirit. Only then your souls can be lighted.

We cannot, in fact, ever forget the day when Jesus received baptism from John. We cannot ever forget the day when we realized that all our sins were actually passed onto Jesus. We have seen the changes that occurred in our hearts with our realization of this truth. They spread throughout our hearts like waves fanning out in a lake. Piercing through the darkness, the bright light of dawn entered us, allowing us to know the truth of salvation.

The Baptism that Jesus Received Passed the Sins of the World onto Him

After reading Matthew 3:13-17, I could not utter a single word for a long time. Though I was in fact sinful, Jesus received His baptism, and said, "*Permit it to be so now, for thus it is fitting for us to fulfill all righteousness.*" Therefore, the reason why He had to shed His blood on the Cross (the scarlet thread) was Jesus' baptism (the blue thread). This Jesus was God Himself (the purple tread). And with the Word of the Old and New Testaments (the fine woven linen), He has taught us the real truth of salvation. Jesus, in other words, took upon all our sins.

"Do we, then, still have sin or not? When Jesus was baptized by John the Baptist, everyone's sins were passed onto Him. Were our own sins passed onto Him as well? Were the sins of the world passed onto Him at that time? Are the sins that we already had when we were still in our mothers' wombs worldly sins or not? What about the sins that we committed when we were just a year old? Are they not also the sins of the world? What about the sins that we committed in our childhood? Do they not also belong to the sins of the world?"

We have to ask ourselves these questions to make sure that we are on the right footing. Like this, faith is all about making sure that we are standing on the right ground with the Word of God. The sins that we committed in our childhood are indeed the sins of the world, as the sins that we committed in our teens are also worldly sins. All the sins that we commit in our lifetime, not to mention in our adulthood, are the sins of the world. All such sins of the world were passed onto Jesus already. Were they not? Of course they were! It is written that our Lord took upon not only our sins, but all the sins of each and every human being. So we realized, "All our sins were indeed passed onto Jesus. Do we then still have sin? No, we no longer have any sin left in us!"

It is because Jesus was actually baptized by John that John the Baptist testified, *"Behold! The Lamb of God who takes away the sin of the world!" (John 1:29)* Jesus took away all the sins of every person who ever lived and will ever live, from the very beginning of mankind to its end. All the sins that anyone ever committed throughout the entire life, and even the sins of everyone's children, were all taken away by Jesus. No matter how long this world lasts, whether for thousands of years or even billions of years, our Lord took upon the sins of all its people with His baptism, carried these sins on His shoulder to the Cross, was crucified, and thereby received all the judgement of sin for our sake—this is what we realized.

As we, the born-again, actually realized that Jesus rose from the dead again and became our Savior because of this, and as we believed so, all our questions were answered.

With the baptism that He thus received and by shedding His blood on the Cross, our Lord took care of all our sins. This is why the Bible speaks of the blue, purple, and scarlet thread and the fine woven linen on the gate of the Tabernacle's court, and why it tells us in 1 John 5:4-6 that Jesus came to us not only of the water, but of the water and the blood. We thus came to realize, "So this is why the Bible tells us that our Savior Jesus fulfilled all God's righteousness by receiving His baptism. This is the truth! However, Christian leaders didn't teach us this truth because they were all ignorant of it!"

We become sinless only when God's truth of the blue, purple, and scarlet thread and fine woven linen tells us that we are sinless. No one can approve the salvation of another soul. It is of no use to gain the good word of others. How could what people say to us—that we are pretty good Christians, or even grading us A^+ Christians—ever constitute our salvation from sin? We become sinless not when people approve us, but only when the Word of God tells us Christ made all our sins disappear with the blue, purple, and scarlet thread and the fine woven linen.

The Word of God tells us that Jesus made not only my sins disappear, but also your sins. It tells us that because Jesus

Christ the Messiah has made all the sins of all the people disappear, we would all receive the remission of sin if we would only believe. This is how we could enter into the gate of the Tabernacle's court, by receiving the remission of sin through the water and the Spirit.

What Is the Perfect Faith?

The gate of the Tabernacle's court was woven with blue, purple, and scarlet thread, and with fine woven linen. Everyone must have this perfect faith that believes that our Lord came to this earth and thus saved us from all our sins. When we believe that the Lord was born unto this earth in the flesh of a man, was baptized by John, died on the Cross, rose from the dead, and thereby became our Savior, we can all become God's children. Though our deeds fall short, and though our flesh is worthless, by believing in the blue, purple, and scarlet thread and the fine woven linen in our hearts, we have become sinless. Therefore, to become the righteous is only possible through faith. By believing in the salvation manifested through the blue, purple, and scarlet thread and the fine woven linen, we have been clothed in God's righteousness. By believing in the gospel of the water and the Spirit, in short, we have become God's children.

Some of you still may not understand fully. If so, all that you have to do is just continue on perusing this book or attend God's church. So far we have discussed only the general aspects of the Tabernacle, but once you begin to read the detailed explanations, you will all be able to reach the complete understanding of the Tabernacle. It is so easy that even a child can readily comprehend.

If people were to base their faith on their rough knowledge of Jesus, they would never be saved from their sins, no matter how long they believe in Jesus, for a thousand or ten thousand years to come. They would still have sin everyday. They would then cry everyday, for they cannot be escape from the curse of their sins. When things start go okay for them, these people think that God is helping them. But when things go bad even slightly, they wonder, "Is it because I didn't give tithe? Or is it because I missed church last Sunday? I've sinned and failed to serve God properly, and I think He is actually punishing me for them." In this way, they end up dying locked up in the Law, for the Scripture tells us that "the law brings about wrath" (Romans 4:15).

To really have the kind of faith that is whole, we must know correctly and believe in the four ministries of Jesus Christ who came to us through the blue, purple, and scarlet thread and the fine woven linen. We must realize the truth given by Jesus Christ. Only when we have a clear understanding of this four-fold truth and believe in it, we can have faith that is whole before God, and we can truly become His perfect children. Because we have become sinless by believing in these four ministries of Jesus, we are always the sinless righteous, even without our own struggle to free ourselves from the bondage of sin; we are the sinless people of faith, even without exerting our own willpower; and we are the perfect children of God whose sins were all washed away as white as snow, even without our own good deeds or trying.

Like a baby playing and resting in peace under the watchful eyes of the parents, by believing in this truth, we in fact have peace and tranquility in our hearts before the merciful eyes of God the Father. Even though your deeds may be insufficient, all that you have to do is believe in the Lord's works, for the more insufficient you are, the more you would feel the love of our Lord.

Are you clamoring to receive the remission of your sins, still unable to have the faith that believes in the blue, purple, and scarlet thread and the fine woven linen? Now those who know this truth do not have to clamor to receive the remission of sin, but just believe quietly. The ones who have become the children of God by faith are those who truly know and believe in Jesus Christ, He who came to us through the water, the blood, and the Spirit. They serve God not with their superficial acts, but they love and serve Him with their faith first. Because we believe, God grants us His audience and walks with us. Because we believe in Him, He helps us. And because we believe in Jesus who has saved us with the baptism and the blood in which we place our faith, we have become God's servants who serve His righteous works.

We must now all realize the truth that God made the gate of our salvation in the Tabernacle's outer court, weaving it with the blue, purple, and scarlet thread and the fine woven linen, in order to give us the salvation of the definitive remission of sin. The Scripture tells us that Jesus came to us through the water, the blood, and the Spirit, and that He has saved us from our sins with the blue, purple, and scarlet thread and the fine woven linen of the gate of the Tabernacle's court in the Old Testament. Our Lord has become the gate of our salvation from sin. We must believe, and believe yet again, in these four works of the Messiah who has actually and factually delivered us from all our sins.

The Baptism that Jesus Received from John Is the Real Substance of the Blue Thread Manifested in the Gate of the Court of the Tabernacle

Let's turn to Matthew 3:13-17 again: *"Then Jesus came from Galilee to John at the Jordan to be baptized by him. And John tried to prevent Him, saying, 'I need to be baptized by You, and are You coming to me?' But Jesus answered and said to him, 'Permit it to be so now, for thus it is fitting for us to fulfill all righteousness.' Then he allowed Him. When He had been baptized, Jesus came up immediately from the water; and behold, the heavens were opened to Him, and He saw the Spirit of God descending like a dove and alighting upon Him. And suddenly a voice came from heaven, saying, 'This is My beloved Son, in whom I am well pleased.'"* At this time, when Jesus was baptized, it had been 30 years since He was born of the Virgin Mary. The word "then" here refers to the time when both John the Baptist and Jesus had turned 30.

John the Baptist, born 6 months prior to Jesus, was the representative of this earth's mankind who were giving them the baptism of repentance (Matthew 3:11, 11:11). When Jesus turned 30, He came to this John, who was baptizing people at the Jordan River, to be baptized. But John the Baptist tried to prevent Him, saying, *"I need to be baptized by You, and are You coming to me?"* Jesus then replied, *"Permit it to be so now, for thus it is fitting for us to fulfill all righteousness."* John then allowed, and Jesus was baptized by him. The Scripture also records that when Jesus was thus baptized, heaven was opened to Him, and a voice came from it, saying, *"This is My beloved Son, in whom I am well pleased."*

In Matthew 3:15 here, Jesus tells us the reason why He was baptized by John. This truth refers to the blue thread of the

Tabernacle's court: *"Permit it to be so now, for thus it is fitting for us to fulfill all righteousness."* The purpose of the baptism of Jesus received from John was to forgive the iniquities of sinners through His works manifested in the Tabernacle's blue, purple, and scarlet thread—"for thus it [was] fitting for [them] to fulfill all righteousness."

That Jesus Christ would take everyone's sins upon Himself by being baptized by John the Baptist was the righteous love of God and the fulfillment of His work of salvation of all sinners. As John 3:16 says, *"For God so loved the world that He gave His only begotten Son, that whoever believes in Him should not perish but have everlasting life."* Jesus was baptized to save us from the sins of the world, so that we may not be condemned because of our sins. This is why Jesus took all the righteousness of God and all the sins of mankind upon Himself by being baptized by John, for thus it was fitting for them to fulfill all righteousness.

What is "all the righteousness of God?" The passage above tells us that the reason why Jesus was baptized by John the Baptist was to fulfill all the righteousness of the Father.

Here, we need to find out exactly what all the righteousness of God really is. "All righteousness" refers to the fact that Jesus Christ, by being baptized by John, took all the sins of mankind upon Himself. With His baptism, He took all the sins of the world upon Himself, all at once. As the purpose of His birth was to blot out all the sins of the world at once, the baptism that Jesus received from John was clearly righteous. To fulfill all the righteousness of God meant to fulfill the righteous works that make all the sins of the world disappear—that is, it was to fulfill salvation.

The baptism of Jesus was the indispensable method by which God would deliver us from our sins. God set in the Old

Testament that to blot out our sins, He would raise John the Baptist as the representative of mankind, make Him baptize His Son Jesus Christ, and thereby pass all our sins onto His Son. None other than this was the work of God's mercy. Because God has loved us so much, God made Jesus be baptized by John to turn us into His own children and to complete the righteous work of blotting out our sins. This is why God said, when Jesus had been baptized and came up from the water, *"This is My beloved Son, in whom I am well pleased."* God the Father, in other words, said, "With His baptism, My Son has taken all your sins upon Himself."

Jesus Christ, in other words, came to this earth, and through this method of being baptized by John, He bore all our sins all at once, in the most appropriately way, and thus became the sacrificial offering to make our sins disappear.

It was because the Son of God was baptized for our sake, and because He thus accepted all our sins onto Himself, that He carried these sins to the Cross, was crucified and shed His precious blood, and thereby became the Savior of all of us. Jesus has saved us who believe, in other words, by being baptized for our sins, sacrificing Himself with His blood on the Cross, and rising from the dead again. And after rising from the dead and completing His works of salvation, He now sits on the right hand of the throne of God, and when His time comes, He will most surely return. This truth is the gospel of the water and the Spirit and the core of salvation.

On the gate of the court of the Tabernacle, Exodus 27:16 records, *"For the gate of the court there shall be a screen twenty cubits long, woven of blue, purple, and scarlet thread, and fine woven linen, made by a weaver."* So the gate of the court of the Tabernacle was woven of these blue, purple, and scarlet thread and fine woven linen. This tells us the truth that we enter the Kingdom of Heaven by believing in the gift of salvation.

The **blue thread** woven into the gate of the Tabernacle's court refers to the fact that all our sins were passed onto Jesus when He came to this earth and was baptized.

The **purple thread** tells us that Jesus Christ, who was baptized for our sins, was fundamentally the Creator Himself who made the whole universe and everything in it, the Lord of you and me. Purple is the color of kings (John 19:2-3), and therefore it tells us that Jesus Christ is the King of kings and the Lord of all. The word "Christ" means "the anointed," and only kings, priests, or prophets could be anointed. As such, although Jesus Christ came to this earth in the flesh of a man, His true identity was actually the King of kings. Jesus, in other words, was the Lord and the Creator who made the whole universe. Jesus was the Almighty God Himself and the only begotten Son of God the Father.

The **scarlet thread** woven into the gate of the Tabernacle refers to the sacrifice that this King of kings made when, after coming to this earth in the flesh of a man and taking our sins upon Himself with His baptism, He was crucified and shed His blood on the Cross. Jesus Christ paid the wages of our sins on our behalf, by being baptized, shedding His precious blood, and thus sacrificing Himself for our sake. The scarlet thread manifests the sacrifice of the blood of Jesus Christ.

Lastly, the **fine woven linen** refers to God's intricate Word of the Old and New Testaments. The Bible tells us of our salvation through the Word of the Old and New Testaments. From the Old Testament, God promised that He would come to us as the Savior of sinners, and in the New Testament, just as He had promised, Jesus Christ, God Himself, did indeed come to this earth, was baptized, and shed His blood on the Cross—

all give Himself up as the sacrifice for our sins.

With the blue thread, God manifested the Word that Jesus Christ came to this earth to save us from our sins and took these sins of ours upon Himself with His baptism; and with the purple thread, He manifested that this One who was baptized was in fact God Himself. And with the scarlet thread, God manifested that He has saved you and me from our sins by coming to this earth as our Savior, being baptized, carrying the sins of the world to the Cross, and shedding His precious blood.

That this salvation came by the Word of God promised from the Old Testament, on the other hand, was manifested with the fine woven linen. This is why the gate of the court of the Tabernacle was woven with these blue, purple, and scarlet thread and fine woven linen. When we look at the gate of the Tabernacle's court, this gate manifests and shows us clearly just how God has saved us from our sins and made us His people; as such, we must all believe in the spiritual meaning of the four threads used for the gate of the court of the Tabernacle.

Speaking of the colors of the gate of the Tabernacle's court, the Bible first mentions its blue thread. We usually think in the order of purple, blue, and scarlet thread, but the Bible actually lists in the order of blue, purple, and scarlet thread. This shows us the importance of the blue thread. While Jesus Christ indeed came to this earth as our Savior, had He not been baptized by John, we would not have been able to be cleansed of our sins. This is why Jesus, to save us from the sins of the world, was baptized by John and crucified, all in obedience to the will of the Father.

Jesus is the Lord of the universe who created all things, and He is our God. He is God Himself who has made us be born unto this earth, who has given us new life, and who rules over our lives. For Him to save us from our sins, He had to be baptized by the representative of all mankind and thereby take all our sins upon Himself. It is by being baptized by John, in other words, that Jesus Christ has become our true Savior.

It was to deliver us from our sins that Jesus Christ came to this earth, and it was to take all our sins upon Himself that He was baptized. Were it not for His baptism in the first place, Christ would never have been able to be crucified. This is why the gate of the court of the Tabernacle is showing us clearly just how exactly Jesus Christ has saved us from our sins—that is, the precise method of His salvation.

The colors of the gate of the court of the Tabernacle tell us that Jesus Christ would come to this earth, take all the sins of mankind upon Himself with His baptism received from John, and be crucified—that He, in other words, would take care of all our sins by Himself. When Jesus was baptized, the door of Heaven was opened, and God the Father spoke, *"This is My beloved Son, in whom I am well pleased."* Jesus Christ is our Messiah and Savior, but He is also the Son of God, the very God the Creator who made the whole universe with His own Word. As being the Holy God, Jesus could bore all our sins by being baptized in order for Him to become our true Savior.

Jesus Christ who created the whole universe and rules over it has shown us the clear salvation from our sins. It is because Jesus Christ, to blot out our sins, came to this earth, took all such sins upon Himself with His baptism and died on the Cross that you and I have been truly saved. Jesus Christ is the Creator who rules over our life and death, who created the whole universe, and who brought our forefathers and the entire mankind out onto this earth. He was the very substance of the blue, purple, and scarlet thread and the fine woven linen.

God Himself came to this earth as the sacrificial offering of sinners. Jesus who has saved us was this God, the Almighty and the God of mercy. It is because Jesus Christ took all sins upon Himself with His baptism that He fulfilled all the righteousness of God, and this is why He carried the sins of the world to the Cross, was crucified and shed His precious blood. Just as it is manifested in the gate of the court of the Tabernacle, Jesus Christ became our own sacrificial offering to blot out all our sins.

This is why not only the gate of the Tabernacle's court, but also the gate of the Holy Place, the gate of the Most Holy, and even its covering of the House of God were all woven with blue, purple, and scarlet thread and fine woven linen. It is because Jesus Christ was baptized for your sake that you and I are washed of all our sins by believing in it. Jesus was baptized to fulfill all righteousness, and this righteousness was accomplished by taking the sins of all people upon Himself through His baptism. What we must do, therefore, is to realize that all our owns sins were also passed on Jesus at that time, and believe so.

However, there are so many Christians who believe in Him arbitrarily and recklessly. They are too stubborn to abandon their own religious faith of lawlessness, challenging God from the very beginning. We have to believe in Him according to the way of salvation He has given us. Jesus said, *"I am the way, the truth, and the life" (John 14:6)*. He is telling us, "I am the way. I am the way that leads you to Heaven. I am the Shepherd, the way and the truth. I am indeed the life that saves you." By saving us from our sins, Jesus Christ has become the Lord of new life to us.

When We Believe in Jesus, How Should We Understand and Believe in Him?

We can be saved from all our sins only by believing in the exact way that He came to this earth and has saved us. The word "faith" includes such meanings as "to rely on," "to hold on to," and "to entrust." Seniors often rely on their children when they grow too old, as they find it too difficult to live by themselves. Likewise, the reason why we live by entrusting ourselves to God is because we simply cannot make our sins disappear on our own. Even if we try not to sin ourselves, we still end up living our lives always sinning. It is because we cannot free ourselves from our sins that we believe in God and place our trust in Jesus Christ our Savior by believing in what He has done for us.

This is why when we believe in Jesus and seek our salvation, we must first know what kind of faith is the right faith. Over 2,000 years ago, Jesus came to this earth to save you and me—indeed, each and every human being of this world—from our sins. Turning 30, He then was baptized by John the Baptist and thereby took all the sins of the world upon Himself. We must all believe in this fact. We must believe that when Jesus accepted not only your and my sins but all the sins of the world onto Himself with His baptism, every sin, of the past, the present, and even the future, was all taken up by Jesus Christ already.

However, many people are still ignoring this fact that not only all the sins of the world but also all their own sins were passed onto Jesus when He was baptized, and continue to believe only in the blood of the Cross. That's why none of them can easily discern which faith is the right one, even though they all see that all the gates of the Tabernacle were woven of blue, purple, and scarlet thread and fine woven linen.

When Jesus Christ came to this earth to save us, He did not save us in a slapdash fashion. It is because He actually took all our sins upon Himself with His baptism and bore all the condemnation of our sins with His crucifixion that you and I have been wholly saved. This is how Jesus Christ has saved the entire mankind. This is why our Lord said, *"The one who comes to Me I will by no means cast out" (John 6:37).*

When we say that we believe in Jesus, we do not believe only in His character, nor only in His omnipotence. Rather, we are saved by believing that Christ, despite the fact that He is God, came to this earth, took all your and my sins upon Himself with His baptism, and was sacrificed on the Cross for our sake. When we look at the salvation manifested in the Tabernacle, it becomes crystal-clear to us just what exactly is the right faith that we must have when we profess to believe in Jesus.

Today, there are many people who believe only in the blood of the Cross, incessantly chanting, *"♫ Would you be free from the burden of sin? ♪ There's power in the blood, power in the blood ♫,"* and blindly shouting out, in their own eagerness, "Lord! I believe!" No matter how ardently they believe in Jesus, they can never be freed from their sins just by believing in the blood of the Cross alone.

Because we are such that we can never be freed from our sins throughout our entire lives, we absolutely need the Savior, and this Savior is none other than Jesus Christ. Jesus Christ who came to deliver you and me is the Savior, the King of kings, the Creator who made the whole universe and everything in it, and the Lord of our lives. He came to this earth, took our sins upon Himself with His baptism, and cleansed us of our sins by dying on the Cross. We are saved, in other words, by believing in Jesus Christ, who bore all the condemnation of our sins with His baptism and Cross, as our Savior. This is what the gate of the court of the Tabernacle is clearly and definitively showing us.

People Who Believe in Jesus Only Religiously

In these days, people claim that they can be saved just by believing in the blood of the Cross alone. Making such empty claims is nothing more than a display of their religious faith. These people say, "When I gave my prayers of repentance to God, the Holy Spirit spoke to me in my heart, 'My child, I have forgiven your sins.' How thankful I was when I heard His voice!" They make such claims saying that such beliefs are their testimony of faith.

But our salvation does not come by our own emotional feelings. Rather, we are saved through the entire dimensions of our personality: knowledge, emotion, and will. We must be saved, in other words, by first knowing just how God our Savior has saved us, and then believing in it. But what about religions? What are they? Religions are nothing more than man-made institutions built on people's own thoughts.

Long ago, in my family, my mother was the chef. I used to be her assistant, following her all around the kitchen, asking what help she needed—sort of like Jacob from the Bible. When my mother was busy in the kitchen preparing the meal, I was busy setting the table in the dinning room. My mother and I used to make a fantastic combination. Getting up in the morning, we got the fire going, prepared the table, and after the meal, brushed the kitchen floor with a broom. All the morning's chores were finished with this broom.

This was not a peculiar scene in Korea those days. But the more interest thing was that this very broom that was used to clean the kitchen floor would all of a sudden turn into a god that would ostensibly give us anything we ask for. There were, in other words, people who actually prayed to this worn-out broom. Such absurdities were frequent in our lives; not only this, but whenever there was some misfortune in the family or the neighborhood, we used to call in a shaman to perform witchcraft. Because people at the time held pantheistic beliefs and believed that gods were everywhere, not only this broom that was used to brush the ground could turn into a god, but also ancestral tablets on which their forefathers' names were written, a large rock up in the hill, or practically everything else seen by their eyes could turn into a god.

Nowadays, with the passing time, people have gradually come out of this kind of ignorance, but at that time, it was a frequent happening that just about anything would turn into a god. So one of the most brisk businesses of the time was none other than witchcraft. I remember seeing witches reciting incomprehensible spells while performing witchcraft. I used to mimic the witch's way of chanting a spell, saying, "Abracadabra Abracadabra, may the daylight come, may the daylight come, everything is mine when the daylight comes. The pumpkin barrel was broken because of the lack of devotion. Abracadabra Abracadabra." I had no idea, of course, what they meant.

When such witchcraft was performed in one of the neighborhood's houses, everyone from the whole village used to gather together to see it. The highlight of such an occasion came when bills were stuffed into the head of a dead pig, smiling without a clue. How many bills were stuffed used to determine the witch's spells and her potency. This witchcraft would continue throughout the whole night until the daylight breaks.

Among my acquaintances of old, there was someone who claimed to be possessed by a virgin ghost. He used to claim that he could drive away pretty much all demons, because he was possessed by a virgin ghost—virgin ghosts presumably held more power than others. He said that if he ends up facing a more powerful demon, he himself could be strangled rather than driving out this demon, but he nevertheless claimed that he could drive out all the garden-variety demons. He was none other than a sorcerer.

He spent his usual times ordinarily, just like anyone else. But whenever someone asked him to perform his exorcism, he changed his clothes in a sorcerer's outfit and performed his spectacular show. It is because people's hearts are occupied by such superstitious minds that they follow this kind of primitive religions that have nothing to do with the Word of God and end up believing in all kinds of crazy and shameful things.

People, in other words, have made up their own religions. As in the above story, they have invented their gods on their own. Because people have this kind of instinct, even as Christians, when they are told that Jesus was crucified for them, they can also be easily overwhelmed by their own emotions over this, and end up obsessing over and blindly believing in Him. And when they are told that Jesus is the Son of God and the Creator who made the whole universe, they just love it, and once again believe unconditionally. They also love to hear, *"I am the way, the truth, and the life. No one comes to the Father except through Me,"* and, yet again, believe in it unconditionally without any real understanding. Because no Word of God is erroneous, even when they hear the good Word for the first time, all that they say is that they just love Jesus.

But Jesus will come to judge these people whose hearts still remain sinful despite professing their faith in Jesus. He will also come to take away those who believe in the gospel of the water and the Spirit. Most of the people who are ignorant of the truth of the gospel of the water and the Spirit and believe in Jesus only based on their own thoughts will eventually realize, in about 10 years since the beginning of their religious lives, that they are really sinners unable to live according to the Law of God.

I, too, used to believe in Jesus arbitrarily. I used to sing praises all the time, simply overjoyed to have encountered Christ. But after knowing Jesus, I came to know the Law, and after knowing the Law, I came to know my sins. After knowing my sins, I then came to realize that there would be eternal judgment of sin, and, as a result, the suffering of sin followed.

To solve this suffering of sin, I therefore offered my sincere prayers of repentance. However, such faith was just like the superstitious beliefs with which people prayed to all things to be blessed. Because my heart was so troubled after I came to know the Law written in the Word of God and realized my sins, I thought I had to give my prayers of repentance, and such prayers of repentance did bring me some emotional relief. But sin still remained in my conscience, and discovering that my soul was still in the bondage of sin, I continued to suffer.

In this way, it was not because I had been bound by my sins that I came to believe in and love Jesus, but it was because I had believed in Jesus that I came to realize my sins, and it was after I thus realized my sins that suffering came to me. "I must have believed in Jesus too early," I even thought, and ended up even regretting that I came to know and believe in Jesus so early in my youth. Yet I could not simply stop believing in Jesus. And so to break away from this bondage of sin, I gave my prayers of repentance, but to no avail, for these prayers did little to solve the problem fundamentally.

Ordinary people are not aware of what sins they have committed even as they are committing them, but when they start attending church, they hear about the Law and come to realize their sins, and therefore become locked in their sins. They then first try to solve the problem of their sins by giving their emotional prayers of repentance, but the more time passes by, the more they realize that they are bound in their sins and they must be forgiven of them.

No matter how much they pray their prayers of repentance, the more they pray, the more they realize that their sins, far from disappearing, become even more clearly revealed and remind them even more of their presence. From this point and on, such people's religious lives turn tortuously painful and they continue to suffer. They wonder, "I felt so good when I first believed, but why do I feel so much worse now than 5, 10 years have passed by? Why am I more troubled?" They realize that even their conviction of salvation, which had been held so firmly when they first believed, is no longer there. Thinking that they became sinful after believing in Jesus, they resort to fitting all kinds of doctrines to their beliefs, and end up become such religionists.

It is because these people are ignorant of the truth that Jesus has saved them from their sins with His blue, purple, and scarlet thread and fine woven linen that they ultimately end up becoming mere religionists. Though they profess to believe in Jesus, they are still troubled, for their hearts have no peace. Such people cannot even resort to changing to a different god, for even if they try, they know already that believing in anything other than God Himself is committing idolatry. Because they know clearly that only Jesus is the Son of God, that He alone is God Himself, and that only He is their Savior, they cannot even believe in a different god. And yet because they do not know the truth, they live in suffering, always troubled by their sins.

This is why they must know and believe in the Jesus Christ that came through the blue, purple, and scarlet thread and the fine woven linen. These Christians who ended up turning into religionists also know that Jesus is the King, that He shed His blood on the Cross, and that the Word of the Bible is the Word of God.

What they do not know, however, is that Jesus took not only their sins but also all the sins of the world upon Himself with His baptism, and this ignorance is the reason why they are living as sinners even as they profess their faith, and why they will all end up going to the place reserved for sinners. Because such Christian religionists have no idea just how exactly Jesus took care of their sins, they believe in their own emotions whenever they spring up. As a result, the actual reality does not coincide with what they believe, like a blind trying to make out an elephant by touching its parts. This is why they are completely oblivious to what is wrong with their faith, and this is why then up in confusion once again.

What Would Happen to Us If We Do Not Believe in the Truth of the Blue Thread?

What would happen if we were to believe in Jesus as our Savior while leaving the blue thread out of the gate of the Tabernacle's court? When God commanded to build the gate of the Tabernacle's court by weaving it with blue, purple, and scarlet thread and fine woven linen, what would He have said had Moses instead told the Israelites to build the gate with just purple and scarlet thread and fine woven linen, and had the Israelite indeed completed the gate in this way? Would God have approved it as the gate of His Tabernacle? He would have never approved it as such. Because God told the Israelites to build the gate of the Tabernacle with four threads of different colors, if it was not built accordingly, it could never be called as the gate of the Tabernacle. Not a single one of the four threads can ever be left out.

The gate of the Tabernacle's court had to be woven of blue, purple, and scarlet thread and fine woven linen. Because Jesus, God Himself, came to this earth as our Savior in the flesh of a man, took all the sins of the world upon His own body, died on the Cross, rose from the dead, and has thereby washed away our sins as white as snow, it is by trusting and believing in this Jesus Christ that we have been delivered from our sins. The colors of the gate of the Tabernacle tell us how we have to believe in Jesus to be saved from our sins. Those who believe in the truth manifested in the gate of the Tabernacle have all been saved from their sins. They have all received the remission of their sins, as white as snow. Jesus Christ has washed away your and my sins, turning us as white as snow. Jesus Christ has become the actual Savior of you and me.

This is the very truth manifested in the gate of the Tabernacle. Yet there are many people today who do not believe in the implication of the blue thread, even as they profess to believe in the purple and scarlet thread and the fine woven linen.

To do preliminary research for this book, I once went to a Christian bookstore. There I found some books on the Tabernacle written by some of the most famous Christian leaders. However, some did not even address the gate of the Tabernacle's court, while others made such unfounded assertion as the following: "What do the blue, purple, and scarlet thread and the fine woven linen of the Tabernacle's court tell us? Blue is the color of the sky, and it therefore tells us that Jesus is God. Scarlet refers to the precious blood that Jesus shed on the Cross when He came to this earth. Purple tells us that He is King."

This kind of interpretation is way off the mark. That Jesus is God is told to us through the purple thread. When God has already told us through the purple thread that Jesus is the King of kings and the Lord of lords, why would He repeat this with the blue thread again? It is because these people do not know the mystery of the blue thread that they have failed to interpret it properly.

Because they know only the blood of the Cross, they place a great emphasis on the scarlet thread. When we see their drawings of the gate of the Tabernacle, we see that it is dominated by white and red colors. When the four colors of blue, purple, and scarlet thread and fine woven linen must be clearly shown in the gate of the Tabernacle's court, their drawings only show scarlet and white thread, with some purple thread, but no blue thread at all.

There are so many people in this world now who speak of such untenable faith without even realizing the truth of the blue thread. There are so many in today's time who claim that they can be saved just by believing in Jesus' blood on the Cross alone, even as they do not even realize that Jesus took our sins of the world upon Himself with His baptism all at once to bear our condemnation. Such people's hearts always remain sinful. For today, tomorrow, and beyond—in fact, until they die— such people remain tormented as they cannot be freed from their sinfulness. So some people confess, "I am a sinner before God until I die." But is this really the right faith, that they would remain as sinners until their death, even as they believe in Jesus?

After believing in Jesus, when exactly do we become righteous then? Is Heaven not a place reserved for those who have become sinless by believing in Jesus' baptism and blood? Heaven is indeed a place for the righteous, not for the sinful. Only the righteous who have been definitely saved from their sins and who have become sinless can enter Heaven.

Those who declare themselves to be sinners until death even as they believe in Jesus have no conviction of their salvation no matter how many times they have confessed their faith in Him, because they are ignorant of the blue, purple, and scarlet thread and the fine woven linen. Even as they believe in Jesus and pray to Him, they have no conviction that their prayers would be answered. Though they believe in Jesus, they are neither helped nor loved by Him. They might feel loved while they show their devotion, but when they slacken off their devotion, they feel as if they have been abandoned by God, as if they are hated by Him. They think that God loves them and blesses them only when they give their offerings and devotion to Him, and that He no longer loves them when they fail to give Him their offerings. When they encounter some hard times, they think that God hates them, unable to understand why they must go through such hard times, and ultimately end up blaming Him for their misery and no longer believe in Him.

In the end, the trust between such people and God gets broken. Because their faith is a product of their own thoughts and emotions, it is very arbitrary, precarious, and wrong. When we go to God, we must cast aside our emotions. When we to go God, we must go only with our faith that clearly believes in the truth that Jesus Christ has saved us, who were bound to hell because of our sins, with His baptism and blood. Before the Word of God and the Word of the Law, before the gospel of the water and the Spirit, and with our consciences also, we must clearly recognize that we were the ones who could not but be doomed to hell without exception. Only when we know, learn, believe, and trust in what sinful beings we really are and how God has saved us from our sins can we all realize that Jesus Christ has already become our true Savior.

Only by True Faith Can We Receive the Gift of Salvation

Therefore, you and I must realize that we are saved from our sins by believing in the blue, purple, and scarlet thread and the fine woven linen, not by doing virtuous deeds of our own. And we must know and believe that to save us from our sins, Jesus Christ came to us clearly in this four-fold truth. He promised in the Old Testament to come as the Messiah, and just as this promise, He did indeed come to this earth, and with His baptism, took our sins and the sins of the entire mankind upon Himself all at once. He then carried these sins of the world to the Cross, was crucified, shed His precious blood, and died after uttering, *"It is finished!" (John 19:30)* Rising from the dead again in three days, He testified for 40 more days and ascended to the right hand of the throne of God, promising to return. We must believe these.

"I have saved you definitely with My ministries of the blue, purple, and scarlet thread and the fine woven linen. And I will come back to take away those who believe in this truth of salvation. I will also give them the right to become God's children. For those who believe in this truth in their hearts, I will cleanse their sins and make them white as snow, I will give them the Holy Spirit, and I will make them My own children." This is what our Lord has told us.

We must believe in this Word. Our Lord has already fulfilled these promises, and He is actually working in the lives of those on this earth. He protects those who believe in this truth and bears witness for them. This is how we have been saved through our Lord's works of baptism and blood, dwell in the grace, protection and love of God, and live the life of the righteous. It is because He has saved us that we have been delivered from our sins by believing.

When this book on the Tabernacle is translated into all the languages of the whole world, I am sure that people of the entire world would be saved from their sins through their faith in the truth. Those who claim that the remission of sin comes only by the blood of Jesus will no longer be able to make such claims, but they will instead come to realize just how false their claims had been. They will no longer be able to hold on to something false and claim that this is salvation. They will never be able to say that they can be saved just by believing in the blood of Jesus alone.

In the gate of the Tabernacle's court is found the gospel of the water and the Spirit, the clear Word of salvation of the blue, purple, and scarlet thread and the fine woven linen. Because this is the Word of God promised and prophesied from the Old Testament, and because God has kept this promise in the New Testament by fulfilling salvation from all sins with His baptism and crucifixion, if we just believe in this gift of salvation in joy and thankfulness, we can all receive the eternal remission of sin.

This is the Word that is so easy and perfect, but it also is the truth that cannot be understood even with all the knowledge of the entire universe, if you do not have the pure faith in His Word. That's why we must believe in His Word as it is. Because it is such a precious truth that we cannot afford to be remain ignorant of, you and I must most certainly believe in the gospel of the water and the Spirit. By teaching us the truth of the blue, purple, and scarlet thread and the fine woven linen manifested in the Tabernacle freely and easily, God has allowed us to have this priceless gift of salvation with our faith.

You and I alike, who believe in this truth, we all give our thanks to God for His love of truth. Yet there are many who remain ignorant of the real truth of the blue, purple, and scarlet thread and are teaching and leading people to their false ways. To them also, we want to spread this truth. To those whose hearts are tormented by their ignorance of the truth, we preach this gospel of the truth of the water and the Spirit, wanting them to be freed from their sins and enter into the door of salvation. When we preach the truth of the Tabernacle, those who believe in it will be saved, but those who do not believe will be condemned of their sins. If we have decided to believe in Jesus, we must believe in Him knowing the truth of the blue, purple, and scarlet thread.

No one knows the truth of the blue, purple, and scarlet thread from the beginning. God told us, *"And you shall know the truth, and the truth shall make you free" (John 8:32)*. What is the truth? The truth is the true gospel (Ephesians 1:13), that is, the gospel of the water and the Spirit manifested in the blue, purple, and scarlet thread. Knowing the blue, purple, and scarlet thread properly and believing in them is the correct faith in the truth.

Why did God say that the truth will make us free? How have you been saved from your sins? By believing in the blue, purple, and scarlet thread, have you been not only saved from all your sins, but are your hearts also dwelt by the Holy Spirit? From both your hearts and consciences, have your sins clearly disappeared? Do you really believe and can you really confess from the depth of your hearts that God is indeed your Father? Because God recognizes only those who are sinless as His children, He approves only the faith of those who know and believe in the blue, purple, and scarlet thread and the fine woven linen weaved into the gate of the court of the Tabernacle. Sinners are not God's children; only the born-again who believe in the gospel of the water and the Spirit, the only gospel that God has given us, are the children of God the Father.

Though we face many difficulties, hardships, and sufferings while living in this world, because God dwells with us, we are happy. Though we are insufficient, we are living our blessed lives, believing in the righteousness of God and preaching throughout the whole world the gospel of the blue, purple, and scarlet thread, the gospel that bestows us the righteousness of God.

I am thankful to God, above all, for the blue, purple, and scarlet thread. When I first believed in Jesus, regardless of how devotedly I believed, my heart had still remained sinful, and I was greatly tormented because of this. No matter how sincerely I had professed to believe in Jesus, sin was clearly present in my conscience. One can find out whether he/she is sinful or not before God by looking at his/her own conscience. In other words, those who still have sins written in their consciences are those who still have not been able to receive their remission of sin. If their consciences have even the smallest of all sins, this is the evidence that they have not received the remission of sin.

However, when I could not know the truth that would

solve all the problems of my sins, even the tiniest of all, and when all kinds of questions and wonderings arose in my heart as a result, God met me through His Word of the blue, purple, and scarlet thread.

This Word was found in the passage from the Gospel of Matthew that we have read previously. While reading Matthew 3:13-17, I came upon the passage, *"Permit it to be so now, for thus it is fitting for us to fulfill all righteousness" (Matthew 3:15)*. I then realized and believed that when Jesus was baptized and came up from the water, God testified His righteousness, and all righteousness was fulfilled as all sins were blotted out through this baptism of Jesus.

When Jesus Christ was baptized by John, all my sins were clearly passed onto Him, and at once they were all solved on the Cross. The very moment I realized and believed in the reason why Jesus was baptized, all the problems and questions about my unsolved sins were answered, as all my sins were at once cut off from me. I was so thankful for this truth of the remission of sin, for the fact that I received this remission of sin by knowing and believing in the gospel of the water and the Spirit, the true Word of God.

The Lord came to me through His written Word, and I received the remission of my sins through this Word of the water and the Spirit, by believing in it in my heart. From then on, through the Word of the Old and New Testaments, I have been testifying the gospel of the blue, purple, and scarlet thread to many people, and even now, I am continuing to spread all these truths and mysteries of salvation. The true gospel is not something made of the human beings' own thoughts, doctrines, or emotional experiences.

With the blue, purple, and scarlet thread and the fine woven linen, our Lord has blotted out our sins. Through the blue, purple, and scarlet thread, everyone throughout the entire world will come to realize the truth of salvation clearly and to recognize that this truth is none other than the gospel of the water and the Spirit. This is also the truth that is absolutely needed in this end times. Countless people will come to believe in this truth.

Today's era is an era where the righteousness of people is all breaking apart and their evilness is running rampant. When surrounding conditions deteriorate, people spill out all the evilness that were fundamentally lodged in them. Yet despite this, our Lord has saved you and me from our sins through the gospel of the blue, purple, and scarlet thread. How thankful and priceless is this blessing? I thank our Lord for this clear salvation, for I am overflowing with joy and happiness.

The world is now heading toward the end times foretold by God, and has already entered into this era. In times like this, when there are fewer and fewer people who serve God devotedly, and when even the faith of the believers are weakened, if you try to devote yourself to something other than the truth of the water and the Spirit, you will only end up with wounds in your hearts. When believing in God, if you do not believe in the gospel of the blue, purple, and scarlet thread, you will only be disappointed, for it would neither leave anything meaningful in your hearts nor produce any tangible fruits.

Because the truth of the gospel of the four colors of the Tabernacle—of the blue, purple, and scarlet thread and the fine woven linen—is the clear truth, it is the only, best gospel for this dark world. That we live our lives having received the remission of our sins by knowing and believing in the truth manifested in the Tabernacle is a priceless blessing, a precious gift, and great happiness for us.

Because those who know and believe in the truth of the

blue, purple, and scarlet thread and the fine woven linen manifested in the gate of the Tabernacle are serving the truth, not the false, a great joy is found in their hearts forever.

Do you also know and believe in this truth revealed in the gate of the court of the Tabernacle? You must know it, and you must believe in it. ✉

SERMON

9

The Faith Manifested in The Altar of Burnt Offering

< Exodus 27:1-8 >

"You shall make an altar of acacia wood, five cubits long and five cubits wide—the altar shall be square—and its height shall be three cubits. You shall make its horns on its four corners; its horns shall be of one piece with it. And you shall overlay it with bronze. Also you shall make its pans to receive its ashes, and its shovels and its basins and its forks and its firepans; you shall make all its utensils of bronze. You shall make a grate for it, a network of bronze; and on the network you shall make four bronze rings at its four corners. You shall put it under the rim of the altar beneath, that the network may be midway up the altar. And you shall make poles for the altar, poles of acacia wood, and overlay them with bronze. The poles shall be put in the rings, and the poles shall be on the two sides of the altar to bear it. You shall make it hollow with boards; as it was shown you on the mountain, so shall they make it."

I would like to discuss the faith manifested in the altar of burnt offering. When the people of Israel broke any of the 613 articles of the Law of God and the commandments that they had to keep in their everyday life, and when they recognized their sins, they gave to God their unblemished offerings according to the sacrificial system set by Him. The place where they gave these offerings is the altar of burnt offering. The people of Israel, in other words, received their remission of sin by laying their hands on the head of the unblemished sacrificial animal, cutting its throat and drawing its blood, putting this blood on the horns of the altar of burnt offering and pouring the rest on the ground, and burning the flesh of this sacrifice on the altar.

What Is the Spiritual Meaning of the Altar of Burnt Offering?

The altar of burnt offering, measuring 2.25 m in both length and width and 1.35 m in height, was made of acacia wood and overlaid by bronze. Whenever the Israelites looked at this altar of burnt offering, they came to recognize that they were the ones who had been locked in their judgment and unable to avoid their condemnation. And just as the sacrificial animal was put to death, they also realized that they, too, had to die because of their sins. But they also came to believe that the Messiah would come to this earth and blot out their sins by being condemned and put to death like the sacrificial offering because of their sins.

The altar of burnt offering was a shadow of Jesus Christ our Savior. As the unblemished animals were sacrificed with the laying on of hands and the shedding of its blood, Jesus Christ came to us as the Son of God and bore the condemnation of all our sins. Just as the sacrificial offerings of the Old Testament had to accept all sins through the laying on of hands and shed their blood, He accepted all the sins of the world passed onto Him by being baptized by John, and bore the condemnation of these sins by shedding His blood on the Cross.

In this way, the altar of burnt offering shows us that Jesus

Christ took all our sins upon Himself with His baptism, died on the Cross, rose form the dead again, and has thereby saved us.

To Be Forgiven of Their Sins, the Israelites Had to Give Their Sacrificial Offerings at the Altar of Burnt Offering

When we look at chapter 4 of the Book of Leviticus, we see that whenever the anointed priests, the whole congregation of Israel, a ruler, or any of the common people sinned, they received their remission of sin by bringing a sacrificial offering to God, putting their hands on its head, killing it, drawing its blood, and taking it to the altar of burnt offering and offering it to God.

As a matter of fact, as this altar of burnt offering was where the Israelites gave their sin offerings everyday, not a day went by when it was not busy. The Israelites who wanted to get rid of their sins prepared an unblemished animal and gave it to God on the altar of burnt offering as their sacrificial offering. Sinners passed all their sins onto the sacrificial animal by putting their hands on its head, and, as the judgment of these sins, drew its blood by cutting its throat. Priests then put this blood of the sacrificial offering on the horns of the altar of burnt offering, and burnt its flesh and fat on the altar. This is how the people of Israel received their remission of sin.

Regardless of who it was that sinned, whether it was a leader of the people of Israel, the High Priest, ordinary priests, the whole congregation, or any of the common people, they had to receive their remission of sin by bringing a sacrificial animal, such as a bull, goat, or ram, and giving it to God as the sacrificial offering.

Sinners or their representatives had to put their hands on the head of the sacrifice, kill it, put its blood on the horns of the altar of burnt offering, pour the rest of the blood on the ground, and thereby burn the fat of their sacrificial offering that would forgive them of their sins. Therefore, many had to bring their sacrificial animals to the altar of burnt offering, lay their hands on the head of the offerings, draw their blood and give it to the priests.

When offerings were given at the altar of burnt offering, these sacrificial offerings had to be unblemished. And when sinners gave offerings to God, they had to make sure to bring unblemished animals before God, and only by laying their hands on the heads of these unblemished sacrificial offerings were their sinned passed onto them. As such, nothing could be left out when giving the sacrificial offering.

Normally, the person who sinned had to put his own hands on the head of his sacrificial animal, but when the whole congregation of Israel sinned, its representative elders laid their hands on the sacrificial offering (Leviticus 4:15). Of course, the sacrificial animal on whose head hands were laid had to be killed by cutting its throat and drawing its blood. And lastly, it had to be burnt on the altar.

The smoke of burning flesh, fat, and wood therefore always filled the place around the altar of burnt offering, and its horns and the ground underneath it were all soaked with the blood of sacrificial animals. The altar of burnt offering was the place of the remission of sin where sacrificial offerings were given to God to cleanse away the sins of the people of Israel.

This altar of burnt offering, where smoke never ceased to rise, was a square measuring 2.25 m in both length and width, it was 1.35 m in height. A grate of bronze network was placed at its middle, and smoke incessantly rose from the offerings that were burnt by the fire of wood on its grate. Like this, the place where the offerings were burnt and given to God was the altar of burnt offering.

The Utensils of the Altar of Burnt Offering Were All Made of Bronze

The utensils of the altar of burnt offering used to remove and put away ashes were all made of bronze. The altar of burnt offering itself was made by overlaying bronze on acacia wood, and so the altar and its utensils were all made of bronze.

This bronze of the altar of burnt offering has a definite spiritual meaning. Bronze refers to the judgment of sin before God. As such, the altar of burnt offering is a place that shows us clearly that the sinful are most certainly judged of their sins. God will surely condemn people for their sins without fail. The place where the sacrificial offerings were vicariously judged for the sake of sinners by being burnt was this altar of burnt offering, and the altar itself and all its utensils were made of bronze; as such, these things tell us that every sin most certainly entails its judgment.

The altar shows us that because of their sins, people are bound to be condemned and put to death, but by bringing their sacrificial animal to the altar of burnt offering and giving it to God, they can be washed of their sins, receive the remission of sin, and thereby live again. Here, the offerings that were sacrificed on the altar of burnt offerings all tells us that the baptism of Jesus Christ and His bloodshed has forgiven the sins of believers. So this faith that gave the sacrificial offering at the altar of burnt offering is continued on into the New Testament's time as the faith in the baptism and blood of Jesus

Christ.

When we believe in Jesus Christ as our Savior, we must give to God our faith that believes in the baptism of Jesus and His blood as our remission of sin. In the Old Testament, this faith is traced to the faith that opens and enters into the gate of the court of the Tabernacle woven of blue, purple, and scarlet thread and fine woven linen.

All the Offerings That Were Sacrificed at the Altar of Burnt Offering Symbolize Jesus Christ

What did Jesus Christ do when He came to this earth? We were sinful; we had sinned against God and broke His Law and commandments. But to blot out all theses sins of ours, Jesus Christ was baptized by John and took the sins of the world upon Himself, and thereby shed His blood on the Cross. Just as the sacrificial offering bore the sins of the Israelites passed onto it with the laying on of hands, and was thereby killed and burnt at the altar of burnt offering, because Jesus Christ came to this earth as the unblemished sacrificial offering, and was baptized, He could then shed His blood of sacrifice on the Cross and die on it in our place. By being nailed on both his hands and feet and shedding His blood, our Lord bore the condemnation of all sins for us, instead of us being condemned for our sins. Thus, He has saved us from all our sins and condemnation.

What did Jesus Christ, who has become the true substance of this altar of burnt offering, do when He came to this earth? Jesus Christ has saved us by taking all our sins upon Himself with His baptism, being crucified and dying on the Cross, and rising from the dead again. Our Lord came to this earth, completed our certain salvation, and then ascended to the Kingdom of Heaven.

We Who Cannot Help But Sin Everyday

There is also another meaning of the altar of burnt offering, which is "ascending." As a matter of fact, you and I sin everyday. Therefore, we have to always give our sacrificial offering to God, and because of this, the smoke of the condemnation of our sins is always ascending to God. Is there any day at all when you do not sin but live perfectly? The sacrificial offerings of the people of Israel were given continuously until the priests were too exhausted from giving these offerings that forgave the countless of sins of the Israelites and could no longer carry them out. Because the people of Israel broke the Law and sinned against God everyday, they had to give their sacrificial offerings everyday.

Moses, representing Israel, declared the 613 articles of the Law and commandments of God to the Israelites: *"If you will indeed obey My voice and keep My covenant, then you shall be a special treasure to Me above all people; for all the earth is Mine. And you shall be to Me a kingdom of priests and a holy nation" (Exodus 19:5-6).*

The people of Israel then promised, *"All that the LORD has spoken we will do" (Exodus 19:8).* So the people of Israel wanted to recognize and believe in this God who appeared before Moses and spoke to them through him as their true God, and they wanted this God to protect them. By keeping all that God spoke to them, they also wanted to become not only a special treasure to Him, but also a kingdom of priests and a holy nation that belonged to God. As such, they tried to keep all the commandments of God that He had given them.

Did God already know that the Israelites would sin? Of course He did. This is why God called Moses to the Mountain Sinai, showed him the Tabernacle in vision, explained its format in detail, told him to build it, and made him build it accordingly. And He also established the sacrificial system by which offerings were to be given in this Tabernacle.

When the people of Israel sought to give a sin offering to God, they had to bring an unblemished bull, sheep, goat, turtledove, or pigeon; and save a few exceptions, they had to make sure to pass their sins onto their sacrificial offering by putting their hands on its head (Leviticus 1:1-3). And then draw its blood by cutting the throat and give this blood to the priests. Their priests then took this blood, put it on the horns of the altar of burnt offering, poured the rest of the blood on the ground, cut the sacrificial offering into pieces, put these pieces on the altar, and offered them to God by burning them.

This is how the Israelites could be forgiven of their sins. When the offering was burnt, they had to burn not only its flesh, but they had to also strip and burn all its fat from the entrails and the liver. In this way, God forgave the sins of the Israelites.

The Only Way to Receive the Remission of All Sins

When we look at ourselves, we can all actually realize that we cannot help but sin all the time. We live our lives always sinning. We commit countless sins for various reasons, whether it is because we are weak, have too many blemishes, are too greedy, or have too much power. Even among those who believe in Jesus as their Savior, there is no one who does not sin.

The only way for us, who always sin like this even as we believe in God, to be washed of all these sins and be saved is to believe in the baptism of Jesus Christ. He is God Himself who came by water and blood (1 John 5:6); He came to this earth as the sacrificial offering of the altar of burnt offering through the blue, purple, and scarlet thread and the fine woven linen. When this Jesus took our sins upon Himself by being baptized and paid the wages of our sins by shedding His blood on the Cross and dying on it, how could we not receive the remission of sin through faith? Because of the salvation of our Messiah Jesus Christ, through faith you and I could receive our remission of sin all at once.

Although we indeed sin always, because of the salvation of the baptism and the blood that Jesus Christ fulfilled when He came to this earth, we could be freed from all our sins. Our Lord took our sins upon Himself with His baptism, carried the sins of the world to the Cross and was crucified, and has thereby delivered us from our sins wholly. By being baptized for our sins, bearing the condemnation of all our sins with His crucifixion, and rising again from the dead, He has wholly saved us who believe in this truth. Though we could not avoid but be condemned for our sins, because of the love of salvation and mercy that Jesus has given us through the blue, purple, and scarlet thread, you and I have been saved through faith. God, in other words, has saved us from our sins. It is by believing in Him that we have been delivered from all our sins. This is what the altar of burnt offering is showing us.

You may think that inside the Tabernacle everything was beautiful, but if you had actually entered into its court, you would encounter an unexpected and disgusting scene. The bronze altar of burnt offering, shaped as a rectangular, would be threatening to spew out smoke and fire at anytime. The bronze altar would be waiting for sinners, its ground would be soaked in blood, and anyone would realize that this was the place of the condemnation of sin. As this place was where the sacrificial offerings were given everyday, you would be overwhelmed by the stench of burning flesh and wood.

Beneath the altar of burnt offering, blood would be flowing like a river. Whenever the Israelites sinned, they brought their sacrificial animal to the Tabernacle, passed their sins onto it by putting their hands, cut its throat, drew its blood, and gave this blood to the priests. The priest then put this blood on the horns of the altar of burnt offering and poured the rest on the ground.

They then cut the offering into pieces, and along with its kidneys and fat, put its flesh on the grate and burnt them. When blood is drawn, it is quite fluid at first, flowing in red. But after some time, it coagulates and becomes rather sticky. If you had actually entered into the Tabernacle, you would have seen this horrifying blood.

Whenever the people of Israel broke God's commandments, through the altar of burnt offering, they recognized that they were to die like their sacrificial offerings on the altar. Why? Because God made His covenant with them with blood. "If you keep My Law, you will become My people and the kingdom of priests, but if you fail to keep it, you must die like these sacrificial offerings are put to death." This is how God established His covenant with blood. As such, the people of Israelites accepted it as a given fact that if they sin and break the Law, they had to shed their blood.

As a matter of fact, not only the Israelites, but those who believes in God must also all give the blood of sacrifice for their sins. It shows us that anyone who sins before God and therefore has a sin in his/her heart, regardless of how small or great it is, must face the condemnation of this sin as a result. Although the law of judgment—that the wages of sin is death—applies to everyone before God, there are not so many people who actually are afraid of God's judgment and thus try to commit themselves to God's law of salvation manifested in His sacrificial system.

The altar of burnt offering tells us that according to the law that set the wages of sin as death, Jesus Christ has saved us from our sins and condemnation through the blue, purple, and scarlet thread and the fine woven linen manifested in the gate of the court of the Tabernacle. For us, who always sin and must be condemned for our sins, Christ came to this earth in the flesh of a man, took all the sins of us the mankind onto His own body by being baptized by John, carried these sins of the world to the Cross, was crucified and shed His blood on it, bore great sufferings and pain, sacrificed Himself, and has thereby saved you and me from all our sins.

It is because Christ sacrificed His own body and has thereby saved us that you and I could be delivered from all our sins by faith. For the sake of those who could not avoid but die because of their sins, in other words, Jesus Christ took all their sins upon Himself with His baptism, was crucified to death, rose again from the dead, and has thereby save them from all their sins and condemnation.

When we look at this altar of burnt offering, we come to have this faith. Seeing that the sacrificial offering was given all the time at the altar, we can realize and believe that even though it is we who have to die because of our daily sins, God did not turn us into His sacrificial offerings, but instead our Lord Himself came to this earth and fulfilled our salvation. By being baptized, shedding His blood on the Cross, and rising from the dead again, Jesus has saved us.

This is why God the Father accepted the sacrificial offering of the Israelites and forgave all their sins, instead of condemning them for sinning. By making the people of Israel pass their sins onto their sacrificial animal by putting their hands on its head, and by making them kill it and offer its blood, flesh, and fat to Him, God forgave the sins of the Israelites. Through this sacrificial offering, He has also washed us of all our sins. None other than this was the mercy of God and His love.

God Has Not Dealt with Us Only by the Law

If God were to judge you and me, and all the people of Israel just according to His Law, how many would still remain alive on this earth? If God measures and judges us by His Law alone, none of us would live even for a day. The vast majority of us would last not even for 24 hours, but die in just a few minutes. Some of us might die in just an hour while others might last for 10 hours, but the difference is insignificant— either way, we would all be bound to die. People would not be able to live as long as they do now, reaching 60, 70, 80, and even beyond. In no time, everyone would be condemned.

Think of what happened this morning. Your son is still struggling to get out of the bed, having stayed up all night partying. Your wife is trying to wake him up. A shouting match ensues, with your son yelling at his mother for waking him up, and your wife yelling at your son for shouting at her— and thus begins the morning battle. In the end, both the mother and the son here end up sinning before God, and neither of them would last even for today, for they would both be condemned for this sin.

But God has not dealt with us only by His righteous Law. *"He has not dealt with us according to our sins, nor punished us according to our iniquities" (Psalm 103:10).*

Far from judging us by the righteous Law, God instead prepared the sacrificial offering that would take our place, to fulfill this righteous Law. By making us pass our sins onto this offering of sacrifice by laying our hands on it, and by making us give Him the blood of this offering instead of our own life, God has accepted the life of the sacrificial offering instead of our own life, and has forgiven all the sins of mankind, including ours and those of the Israelites, has saved us from them all, and has made us live again. And by saving the believers from their sins, God has made them His own people. This is how God made the people of Israel into the priests of the Kingdom of God.

The sacrificial offering here refers to none other than Jesus Christ. Because of our sins, Jesus Christ became this sacrificial offering, and to save us who had faced the condemnation of sin, He took all our sins upon Himself with baptism, shed His blood and died on the Cross. To save us from our sins, the only begotten Son of God came to this earth in the flesh of a man and became the sacrificial offering through His baptism, all in obedience to the Father's will. By taking the sins of mankind upon Himself with His baptism received from John, by carrying these sins of the world to the Cross, being crucified, shedding His blood, and thereby sacrificing Himself, and by dying and rising from the dead again, Jesus has saved you and me wholly.

When we hear the Word of salvation telling us that Jesus, in our place, was baptized, crucified, and rose again from the dead in three days, our hearts are greatly inspired. Because He who was sinless received, instead of us, the baptism that passed all sins onto Him, and as the wages of these sins, He bore all kinds of persecution, oppression, pain, suffering, and ultimately death, all of which should have been ours in the first place. When Christ has thereby saved us from our sins, nothing could be more malicious than not believing in this truth.

We Must Believe in the Salvation Fulfilled through the Blue, Purple, and Scarlet Thread

When Jesus Christ bore our sins and the condemnation of these sins through His baptism for us, and when He has saved you and me from our sins by sacrificing Himself in our place, we must all have the kind of faith that says, "Thank You, Lord!" Though many people are easily inspired by touching love stories, life stories, or just about any kind of heartfelt stories, when it comes to their hearts toward God's unconditional love, they are as cold as ice. When the grace of our Lord is so great that He was baptized and died on the Cross for our sake, there are still beastly people who cannot realize this grace and do not thank Him for it at all.

Jesus Christ, the Son of God, came to this earth and became the sacrificial offering for us. He accepted all our sins onto His own body with His baptism and sacrificed Himself by giving up His body on the Cross. He was slapped, stripped naked, persecuted and oppressed, all for us. This is how He has saved us. It is by believing in this truth that we have become God's children. This is the greatest inspiration of all, the great grace of God that words cannot express. When this is how Christ has saved us, it saddens me deeply to see that many people still do not believe and thank Him even after hearing it.

It is because Jesus came to this earth, received His

baptism, and sacrificed Himself that you and I have been saved from all our sins. Therefore, Isaiah 53:5 says, *"But He was wounded for our transgressions, He was bruised for our iniquities; The chastisement for our peace was upon Him, And by His stripes we are healed."*

We sin throughout our entire lives. To save us, who could not avoid but be condemned, from all our sins, condemnation, destruction and curses, our Lord left the throne of the Kingdom of Heaven behind, and came all the way down to this earth. He bowed His head before John and was baptized, carried these sins to the Cross and suffered greatly, shed all the blood of His heart to the ground, rose from the dead again, became the sacrificial offering for us, and has become the true God of our salvation.

Do you think about this fact and keep it in deep in your hearts? When you hear the Word, it is only proper that you should believe and be greatly inspired in your hearts that Jesus Christ indeed came to this earth in the flesh of a man, and that He was baptized, crucified to death, and resurrected to save His people from their sins. If we realize that we had all been bound to hell, we can realize deep in our hearts just how greatly inspiring and thankful this salvation is. Though we had wanted to believe in God and become His people, there was no way for us to achieve this. But for you and me, who truly sought after our remission of sin, He has met us with the Word of truth that Christ came to this earth, was baptized, died on the Cross, and rose from the dead again in three days.

Were it no this sacrifice of Jesus, how could we ever have received our salvation? We could never have! Were it not for baptism of Jesus and the blood of the Cross, and were it not for the salvation of the blue, purple, and scarlet thread and the fine woven linen manifested in the Tabernacle, salvation would have been only a midnight summer dream for us. Were it not for His sacrifice, we could never have been freed from our sins and avoided their punishment, but would be cast into the eternal fire of hell and suffer forever. Yet Christ has saved us by sacrificing Himself for our sake, just like the sacrificial offering of the Old Testament.

The Salvation of the Blue, Purple, and Scarlet Thread Fulfilled in the New Testament

My beloved readers, you must never forget the truth of the blue, purple, and scarlet thread and the fine woven linen used for the Tabernacle. The fine woven linen is the Word of the Old and New Testaments, the Word that God promised from long ago that He Himself would come to us as our own Savior, and in accordance to this promise, Jesus Christ came to this earth. The blue thread tells us that Christ, coming to this earth, took all our sins upon Himself through His baptism. He was baptized, in other words, according to the promise that He would save us from our sins and deliver us from our condemnation. To take our sins and the sins of everyone in this world upon Himself, He was baptized by John, and did indeed bear all the sins of the world. We must never forget this, for if we forget that Jesus came as our sacrificial offering and took all our sins upon Himself through His baptism, there would be no salvation.

More often than not, we live in this world attaching a great self-importance to ourselves. People's hearts are such that although they cannot tolerate hearing someone else boasting, they themselves love to boast nevertheless. But there came a certain time when I started to boast of not myself, but of someone else, and this was when I became grateful to Jesus for saving me through the blue, purple, and scarlet thread and the fine woven linen. In other words, I came to boast of Jesus. Now, I tell and boast as often as I can that Jesus came to this earth; that to blot out our sins, He took all our sins upon Himself by being baptized; that Jesus could be crucified on account of His baptism; and that this is how the Lord has saved us. I do not fail to boast of this truth, to preach it, and to give all glory to God.

Yet there are way too many people who, though professing to believe in Jesus, preach the Word while leaving out His baptism, or only boast themselves by borrowing His name. There was a false minister who used to claim that he only spent $300 a month for his living. As if it were a great accomplishment, he used boast that he can get by with only $300 a month, and that he doesn't have to take any money when he is traveling because his followers pay for all his expenses. But is the believers' money somehow not money? Does this money not count for anything, while only his own money matters? This Christian leader claimed that all that had to do was just pray whenever he needed something. "God, cover my travel expenses! I believe You, Lord!" With this prayer, some saint popped out and gave him a load of cash, he testified. Looking at such people who say these things as if they were something to boast of, what kind of thoughts come to your minds?

Matthew 3:13-17 state, *"Then Jesus came from Galilee to John at the Jordan to be baptized by him. And John tried to prevent Him, saying, 'I need to be baptized by You, and are You coming to me?' But Jesus answered and said to him, 'Permit it to be so now, for thus it is fitting for us to fulfill all righteousness.' Then he allowed Him. When He had been baptized, Jesus came up immediately from the water; and behold, the heavens were opened to Him, and He saw the Spirit of God descending like a dove and alighting upon Him. And suddenly a voice came from heaven, saying, 'This is My beloved Son, in whom I am well pleased.'"* This passage describes what happened when Jesus was baptized. When Jesus was baptized by John the Baptist at the Jordan River and came out of the water, the gate of Heaven was opened and the voice of God the Father was heard: *"This is My beloved Son, in whom I am well pleased."* John the Baptist was stunned at that time.

John the Baptist was astonished twice at this Jordan River. He was first stunned when he saw that Jesus came to him and wanted to be baptized by him, and he was stunned again after baptizing Jesus when the gate of Heaven was opened and heard the voice of God the Father saying, *"This is My beloved Son, in whom I am well pleased."*

What is the reason for Jesus to be baptized by John the Baptist? Matthew 3:15 here gives us the answer. Let's read verses 15 and 16 again: *"But Jesus answered and said to him, 'Permit it to be so now, for thus it is fitting for us to fulfill all righteousness.' Then he allowed Him. When He had been baptized, Jesus came up immediately from the water; and behold, the heavens were opened to Him, and He saw the Spirit of God descending like a dove and alighting upon Him."*

Matthew 3:15 tells us the reason why Jesus was baptized by John the Baptist. Even though Jesus was the High Priest of the Kingdom of Heaven and the only begotten Son of God, He nevertheless came to this earth to save us, His people, from our sins. In other words, Jesus came to this earth as the sacrificial offering that pays the wages of our sins by taking these sins upon Himself and being sacrificed in our place. This is why

Jesus sought to be baptized by John.

But why was Jesus baptized by none other than John the Baptist? Because John the Baptist was the representative of mankind, for he was the greatest of all those born of women. Matthew 11:11 says, *"Among those born of women there has not risen one greater than John the Baptist."* John the Baptist was the servant of God prophesied from the Old Testament's time in the Book of Malachi: *"Behold, I will send you Elijah the prophet Before the coming of the great and dreadful day of the LORD" (Malachi 4:5).* John the Baptist was this very Elijah whom God had promised to send.

Why did God call John the Baptist as Elijah? Elijah was a prophet who turned the hearts of Israelites back to God. At that time, the people of Israel were worshipping Baal as their God, but Elijah showed them clearly who the real God was, whether it was Baal or Jehovah God. He was the prophet who, with his faith and through the sacrificial offering, demonstrated to the people of Israel who really was the living God, and thereby led them, who had been worshipping idols, back to the true God. This is why at the end of the Old Testament, God promised, "I will send you Elijah." Because all the human beings, who were made in the image of God, were on the wrong path of idolatry and demon-worship, God said that He would send them His servant who would lead them back to God. The one who would thus come is John the Baptist.

Matthew 11:13-14 state, *"For all the prophets and the law prophesied until John. And if you are willing to receive it, he is Elijah who is to come."* This Elijah who is to come is none other than John the Baptist. In verse 11-12, it is written, *"Assuredly, I say to you, among those born of women there has not risen one greater than John the Baptist; but he who is least in the kingdom of heaven is greater than he. And from the days of John the Baptist until now the kingdom of heaven suffers violence, and the violent take it by force."*

So when it says here that *"among those born of women there has not rise one greater than John the Baptist,"* it means that God raised John the Baptist as the representative of all mankind. God made John the Baptist be born unto this earth six months before the birth of Jesus. And God prepared him as the last prophet and priest of the Old Testament. Therefore, as the High Priest of the earth, John the Baptist baptized Jesus Christ and thereby passed all the sins of mankind onto Him. In other words, the reason why John the Baptist baptized Jesus was to pass all the sins of the world onto Him. The reason why Jesus Christ was baptized by John the Baptist was to take all the sins of mankind upon Himself through His baptism.

This is why Jesus said in Matthew 3:15, *"Permit it to be so now, for thus it is fitting for us to fulfill all righteousness."* Because all righteousness could be fulfilled only when Jesus received His baptism from John the Baptist to accept all the sins of the world, Jesus said that it was fitting.

Our Lord Has Thus Saved Sinners with This Method

This baptism that Jesus received from John is the same as the Old Testament's laying on of hands. It was, in other words, the laying on of hands that was done before the altar of burnt offering in the Old Testament's time to pass one's sins onto the sacrificial offering. By coming to this earth and being baptized, Jesus Christ fulfilled the promise of the laying on of hands— the promise made whenever the daily offerings were given where sinners passed their sins onto their sacrificial offering by putting their hands on its head, and whenever the yearly offering was given on the 10th day of the seventh month, the day of great atonement, through which the High Priest passed the year's worth of sins of all the Israelites onto the offering of sacrifice by putting his hands on its head.

Like the Old Testament's laying on of hands, because Jesus accepted all the sins of the world onto Himself by being baptized, He washed away all these sins, and because He took all these sins of mankind upon Himself, He bore the condemnation of these sins in our place and was sacrificed. This is how Jesus Christ could become the true God of our salvation.

As such, we must truly admit that because of our sins, we could not avoid but face our certain death and be condemned. We must know this and feel it. And we must realize that Jesus Christ our Savior has saved us by coming to this earth and being sacrificed for our sake—that is, through His works of salvation with His baptism, crucifixion, and resurrection, Jesus Christ has washed us of all our sins and saved us wholly from our sins. We must also believe that Jesus has given us the gift of salvation, that He has fulfilled our salvation and has given us this completed salvation as His gift for us. Jesus has fulfilled all righteousness, so that if one were to only believe, and if one were to only accept, he/she would surely be saved.

To make us realize this, the gate of the court of the Tabernacle was woven of blue, purple, and scarlet thread and fine woven linen. This is also the reason why we would first see the altar of burnt offering if we open and enter into this gate of the court of the Tabernacle. The offerings that were given at the altar of burnt offerings were also the foreshadow of the method of salvation through which Jesus Christ has saved us. The offerings that were sacrificed on the altar of burnt offering had to accept the iniquities of sinners onto themselves through the laying on of hands and bleed to death in the sinners' place. The blood of the sacrificial offerings was then put on the horns of the altar, and the rest was sprinkled on the ground. Then, they offered the flesh and fat of the animals on the altar as the burnt offerings. These were the method by which the sacrificial offerings were given to God. All these features of the sacrificial offerings are exactly the same as the method by which Jesus Christ has become our Savior. Through the sacrificial offerings, in other words, God has shown us that Jesus Christ would come to this earth and save us in this way.

Without fail, sinners' hands had to be put on the sacrificial animals given at the altar of burnt offering. This is why the Tabernacle is telling us of the gospel of the water and the Spirit. Coming to this earth, Jesus Christ was baptized to take the sins of mankind upon Himself. Baptism is the antitype of salvation that Christ received to become the sacrificial offering for all the sinners of the world before God the Father.

Through this Tabernacle, we can now have clear faith. Just as the sacrificial offering accepted the sins of the people of Israel on the Day of Atonement through the laying on of the High Priest's hands, and just as it had to be sacrificed in their place because their sins had now been all passed onto it (Leviticus 16), Jesus Christ came to this earth to take our sins upon Himself and to become our own sacrificial offering for these sins, did indeed become our sacrificial offering, and has thereby saved us from all our sins and condemnation. We can now wholly believe in this salvation of love. It is by believing in this truth that we can thank and repay our debt to God for this salvation of love that He has given us.

No matter how knowledgeable of the Tabernacle one might be, if he/she does not believe, then all this knowledge is useless. As such, we must realize, as well as believe, just how important the baptism of Jesus Christ really is. The Tabernacle had three gates, all of which were woven of blue, purple, and scarlet thread and fine woven linen. People may express each gate of the Tabernacle differently because of their ignorance.

In its ordering of threads, the first to be woven was blue thread, followed by the order of purple thread, scarlet thread, and fine woven linen. Only by making the gate in this way can it properly be described as the real gate of the Tabernacle, for this is exactly how God commanded the Israelites to build it in the Old Testament's time.

There was a reason why the gates had to be made in this way. Regardless of how Jesus Christ was born unto this earth as the Savior of mankind in the flesh of man and through the body of the Virgin Mary, if He had not been baptized to take our sins upon Himself in the first place, He could not have become our true Savior. If He had not been baptized, He could not be crucified and die on the Cross, either. As such, the blue thread had to be woven first, and its relative importance was also critical.

Whom Must We Believe in?

Therefore, we must believe in Jesus Christ who has saved us from our sins. We can be truly born again only when we believe in the salvation that this Son of God, Jesus Christ our Savior, has given us. When we believe in the Son of God as the God of our salvation, and when we believe in the truth that He came to this earth, took our sins upon Himself all at once by being baptized for us, and bore our condemnation on the Cross, we can then all receive our true salvation.

Because Jesus Christ could not take our sins upon Himself in any other way but through His baptism, only by bearing our sins by this exact method could He go to the Cross, shed His blood and die on it. No matter how He is the Son of God and how He came to this earth as our Savior, if He had not taken our sins upon Himself through His baptism, our salvation could never be found in this world.

Therefore, it is essential for you to confirm the biblical evidences in detail to be in full conviction that your sins have been blotted out already.

Let's assume for a moment that you owe a considerable debt. Then someone says to you, "Don't worry; I'll pay it off for you. No need to worry; I'll solve this problem." Whenever you meet him, this guy keeps telling us, "Didn't I tell you not to worry? I told you that I'd take care of it!" Let's further assume that this person even gets angry, asking why you don't believe him. Even if this person tells you everyday, "I paid it all off; just trust me," when he did not actually pay your debt off, would you really be freed from this debt just by believing him? Of course not!

No matter how confidently he tells you, "If you trust me, all your debt is resolved," if he did not actually pay it off, then your debt remains as it is, and this person is only deceiving you. So you ask him again and again, "So did you pay off my debt?" He then tells you repeatedly, "Why are you so doubtful? Just trust me unconditionally! I told you that I paid off all your debt. All that you have to do is just believe me, and yet you are so suspicious! Don't be like this!" So, let's assume again, you trusted him with all your heart. But no matter how much you believed him, if he did not actually pay off your debt, then his words are all lies.

This Is How the Faith of Today's Christians Are

Today's Christians say, "Jesus has saved you by shedding His precious blood on the Cross. He bore all the condemnation of sin there. This is how He has saved you." Many pastors preach like this to their congregations. When someone among the congregation rises and tells them, "But I am still sinful," they say, "That's because you have little faith. Just believe! None other than your disbelief is your sin!" "I too really want to believe, sir. But I don't know why I can't believe." "I don't know why I'm still sinful even though I believe. I really believe." "You don't have enough faith. You need to believe more. Climb up a mountain and try fasting. Believe while skipping your meals." "Can't I just believe while not skipping meals?" "No, you have to try believing while you fast."

Many of today's pastors tell you to believe, yet they do not solve the problem of your sins, and they only rebuke you for not believing. On your part, you try to believe and yet it's too hard to believe, or you truly believe blindly but the problem of your sins still remains. What's wrong here? What can explain this? People cannot have true and strong faith because they do not know that Jesus Christ took all their sins upon Himself by being baptized. It is because they believe in delusions with which they cannot solve the problem of their sins no matter how much they believe.

Does faith come just by believing unconditionally without any definite evidence? Of course not! Whole faith comes all at once only when you know how the problem of sin was really solved and believe in it. "Though I had doubted You, it is far too clear that You have already solved the problem of my sins. No matter how much I try not to believe, I cannot help but believe in Your salvation, for this salvation is so certain. Thank

You for solving my problem." Though we may doubt at first, in other words, because the evidence of our salvation is so certain that we can no longer doubt anymore. As the mark of our salvation and its evidence, Jesus has shown us His receipt called the gospel of the water and the Spirit. "I have paid off your debt for you in this way." Only when we look at this receipt that shows that all our debts have been paid off can the truth faith come to us.

We cannot believe even as we profess to believe in God, say that Jesus Christ, God Himself, is our Savior, and claim to believe in the Savior, when we do not have the evidence of how He has saved us and how our sins were blotted out. In other words, we can't have firm conviction unless we have seen the receipt showing the full payment of the wages of our sins. People who believe without seeing this receipt may appear to have a strong feeling of faith at first, but their faith is, in fact, simply blind. It is no more than a fanatical faith.

Do You Consider a Fanatical Faith as a Good Faith?

How would you like if a pastor with a fanatical faith demanded the same fanaticism from others also? "Believe! Receive the fire! Fire, fire, fire! The Holy Spirit that is like the fire, fill us with the fire! I believe that the Lord will bless you all! I believe that He will make you all rich! I believe that He will bless you! I believe that He will heal you!" When such a pastor puts up this kind of show, the audience's ears start ringing and their hearts start jumping. Channeled through a sound system of the highest quality, when he starts shouting, "Fire, fire, fire," the audience's hearts start jumping at the majestic sound of his voice. They are then overwhelmed emotionally, as if a strong faith had really come to them, and wail, "Come, Lord Jesus! O, come, the Holy Spirit!"

At about this time, the pastor then incites the audience's emotion even more by saying, "Let us pray. I believe that the Holy Spirit is now descending and filling us all." The band's playing of inspiring hymns soon follows this, and people raise their hands up high, going wild with enthusiasm, and their emotional outbursts reach the climax. Right on cue, this is when the pastor says, "Let us give our offerings. In particular, this evening, God wants to receive a special offering from you. Let us all give this special offering to God."

Overwhelmed by their emotions, people then end up emptying their pockets. This false pastor has already prepared an immense pulpit that is large enough to pile up all the money collected, and put dozens of butterfly nets (collection bowls) at its front. When the band starts playing hymns and people's hearts are overwhelmed by their excitement, he then sends off the butterfly collectors (volunteers passing the collection bowls) amid the audience.

By lying that more offerings mean more blessings, and by incite people's emotions, such false pastors induce people to shed their tears and open their wallets. It is to make them hand over their money without even realizing by depriving them of their reason and perception and overwhelming them with their emotions instead. This is neither based on the Word of God, nor any kind of a sermon, but a fanatical and blind act that verges on a fraud. Like this, the pastors whose faith is fanatical incite people's emotions to reach their own ulterior objectives.

If we know that our Lord took our sins upon Himself through His baptism, and if we believe in this Jesus Christ as our Savior, then we are not shaken, but remain at peace. The only thing that inspires us quietly is that Jesus shouldered our sins with His baptism and was crucified to death. When we think about this, that Jesus, God Himself, took our sins upon Himself with His baptism and died to pay the wages of these sins, we become immensely thankful, and our hearts are filled by a great joy. However, this tranquil inspiration in our hearts is far greater than anything else in this world; neither any romantic confession of love, nor any gift of the most precious diamond of this world can ever inspire us more than this.

In contrast, the emotionally oriented inspiration of the fanatics does not last that long. Though they may dwell in this inspiration for a while, when they sin everyday and are disgraced by such sins, they cannot but hide their faces out of shame. "When Jesus bore our condemnation and died on the Cross for us, why do I still sin everyday?" So they lose their face and can no longer be inspired as time passes by; what's more, out of shame, they cannot even go to God.

This is why God has shown us the altar of burnt offering. The offering of sacrifice that was given on this altar of burnt offering according to the sacrificial system was none other than Jesus Christ our Savior. As such, the altar of burnt offering manifests that Jesus came to this earth and has in fact saved us all at once through the blue, purple, and scarlet thread and the fine woven linen. God has made us see this altar of burnt offering, and He wants us to be saved by believing in it.

What Is It That We Must Do in This Era?

There are many things that we the born-again must do in this era. First of all, we have to preach the gospel of the water and the Spirit all over the world. We must spread the truth to those who remain ignorant of this truth of the blue, purple, and scarlet thread and the fine woven linen, and we must thereby help them to be saved from the condemnation of fire in hell. Why? Because there are many people who are following Jesus without even realizing and believing in the gospel of the water and the Spirit manifested in the Tabernacle.

To spread this truth to them, there are still many things for us to do. We have to publish our books that are sent throughout the whole world; from translating, proofreading, and editing to make these books to securing the necessary funds to print them and send them to countries all over the world, there indeed are many works that need to be done.

So when we look at our fellow workers and ministers, we see just how busy they all are. Because all the saints and workers of God's Church are so busy in this way, they are going through some tough time physically. It is said that marathon runners reach a certain point in their 42.175 km course when they become so exhausted that they are not even sure if they are running or doing something else entirely different. In short, extreme exhaustion would make them mentally vacuous. Perhaps we now have also reached this point in our run for the gospel. Living our lives for the gospel is like running a long distance toward our goal without stopping, as the marathon runners do. Because our running for the gospel must go on until the Day of our Lord's coming, we all face hardship.

But because our Lord is in us, because we have the gospel of the water and the Spirit, because our faith believes that the Lord has saved us with the blue, purple, and scarlet thread and the fine woven linen, and because we believe in the most certain truth, we can all receive new strength. It is because Jesus has given us the gift of salvation that you and I have received this gift. So our hardships of the flesh cannot trouble us. On the contrary, the more difficult it gets, the more strength the righteous find. I truly thank the Lord.

Spiritually, in our hearts, in our thoughts, and throughout our actual surroundings, we can feel the new strength that our Lord has given us, and that He is with us. Because we can feel that He is helping us and holding us, and that He is with us, we give even more thanks to Him. So, the Apostle Paul also said, *"I can do all things through Christ who strengthens me" (Philippians 4:13)*. We therefore confess everyday that we cannot do anything at all if the Lord does not empower us. Not only was Jesus Christ baptized for us, but He was also sacrificed for us by being crucified, faced His own death, rose from the dead again, and has thereby become our true Savior. Whenever we look at the altar of burnt offering, we come to remind ourselves of this truth.

The altar of burnt offering was made of acacia wood, and it was overlaid in and out with thick bronze. Its height was about 1.35 m, and its grate, a network of bronze, was placed near its middle, at about 68 cm in height. The flesh of offerings were put on this grate and burnt.

Whenever we look at the altar of burnt offering, we must be able to see ourselves as we are. We must also be able to see that Jesus Christ took our sins upon Himself by being baptized in His flesh, and that He bore all the condemnation of our sins by shedding His blood on the Cross. You and I truly could not avoid but die before God because of our sins and condemnation. Because of our sins and condemnation, you and I could not avoid but die and be cursed forever. But because of Jesus Christ, who came to this earth as the eternal offering of atonement, was baptized, and died, all for us, like the sacrificial offering of the Old Testament, we have been saved.

A sacrificial animal may look cute and cuddly when alive, but how gruesome would it be when it bleeds to death, with its throat cut open, after it accepts sins through the laying on of hands? That we, who deserved to die in this gruesome way, have escaped our condemnation is truly a great blessing. This blessing has been possible because the Lord has given us the gift of the salvation. Just as manifested in the blue, purple, and scarlet thread and the fine woven linen, Jesus Christ came to this earth in the flesh of a man, has saved you and me through His baptism and the blood of the Cross, and has thereby given us the true gift of salvation. God has thus given you and me the gift of salvation—do you believe this in your hearts? Do you believe in this gift of salvation, the love of Jesus? We must all have this faith.

When we look at the altar of burnt offering, we must realize that Jesus Christ has saved us this way. He was sacrificed like this to give us the gift of salvation. As hands were laid on the sacrificial offering, and as this sacrificial offering bled to death, Jesus has given us our salvation by suffering in this manner. This is how He has saved us from our sins. We must realize this, believe in our hearts before God, and give thanks to Him with all our hearts.

God wants us to receive through faith the gift and love of salvation that He has given us. He wants us to believe in our hearts in the salvation of the baptism and the blood of the Cross that He fulfilled by coming through the water and the Spirit. It is my hope that you would all believe in the love of our Lord in your hearts and truly accept into them His gift of salvation. Do you truly accept it into your hearts?

Who Was Sacrificed in This Way for You?

I once saw a witnessing leaflet that said, "Who will die for you? Whom did you meet today that comforted you? Jesus Christ was sacrificed for you. Is your heart not comforted by this?" Who will really bear your sins by being baptized and die on the Cross in your place to blot out your sins? Who will shed all his/her blood and die to bestow his/her love on you? Who will ever be willing to face this sacrifice for you? Is it your relatives? Your children? Your parents?

None of them! It is God Himself who made you. To save you from your sins, this God came to this earth in the flesh of a man, was baptized to take your sins upon Himself, was crucified and shed His blood to bear the condemnation of your sins, has become your true Savior, rose from the dead again, is living even as now, and has given you His salvation and love as a gift. Do you truly want to accept this salvation of love into your hearts? Do you really believe in your hearts?

Whoever believes will receive the Lord, and whoever receives Him will be saved. Receiving Him means to accept the salvation and love that Christ has given for us. It is by believing in our hearts in this love, this remission of sins, this bearing of sins, and this condemnation of sins, that we are saved. This is the faith that receives the gift of salvation.

Everything of the Tabernacle manifests Jesus Christ. God does not demand any sacrifice from us. All that He asks from us is that we believe in the gift of salvation that He has given us in our hearts. "To give you the gift of salvation, I came to this earth. Like the sacrificial offering of the Old Testament, I accepted all your sins passed onto Me through the laying on of hands, and like this offering of sacrifice, I bore the gruesome condemnation of your sins for you. This is how I have saved you." This is what God is telling us through the Tabernacle.

No matter how God has thus saved us, has loved us this much, and has given us the gift of perfect salvation in this way, if we do not believe, everything is useless. The salt in your cabinet must first be put into your soup for it taste salty; likewise, if you and I do not believe in our hearts, even His perfect salvation turns completely useless. If we do not thank in our hearts for the gospel of the water and the Spirit and accept it into our own hearts, the sacrifice of Jesus becomes worthless.

Salvation can be yours only when you know just what sacrifice and love Jesus, God the Savior, has given you, accept them into your hearts and thank Him for them. If you do not accept Christ's gift of perfect salvation into your hearts but only understand it in your heads, then it is completely useless.

All You Have to Do Is Just Grab the Truth

It does not matter how much your soup is boiling on the stove; if you only think to yourself that you are going to put in the salt and yet do not actually do so, your soup can never be salty. You can be saved only when you accept into your hearts and believe that our Lord has saved you from your sins by being baptized and sacrificed for us, just like the sacrificial offering that was sacrificed on the altar of burnt offering. When God is giving you the gift of salvation, just accept it in thankfulness. When our Lord is telling us that he has saved us wholly, the right thing for us to do is to simply believe so.

Is the love of God that He has given you only half-hearted? Of course not! The love of our Lord is perfect. Our Lord, in other words, has saved you and me completely and perfectly. Because He took our sins upon Himself perfectly with His baptism and died on the Cross for sure, we cannot have any doubt about this love. He has saved us this perfectly and given us the gift of salvation. We must all accept this gift of salvation that God has given us.

Let's assume for a moment that I am holding a very valuable jewelry made of most precious gems. If I give it to you as a gift, all that you have to do is just accept it instinctively. Is this not the case? How simple and easy is it for you to make it yours? To make this jewelry yours, all that you have to do is just reach out and grab it. That's it.

If you would just open your hearts and pass all your sins onto Jesus through His baptism, you can all easily receive the remission of your sins and fill your empty hearts with the truth. This is how the Lord said that He would give us salvation as a free gift. Salvation can be yours just by reaching out and grabbing it.

We have received our salvation as a gift, without paying a single cent for it. And because God is the One who is pleased to give this gift to whoever wants to receive, blessed are those who have received it in thankfulness. Those who accept the love of God in joy are clothed in His love, and they are the ones who love this giver, for by accepting it, they have pleased His heart. Accepting this gift is the right thing to do. It is only when you accept the gift of perfect salvation that God has given you that this true gift of salvation can be yours. If you do not accept it into your hearts, then the gift of salvation can never be yours, no matter how hard your try.

I, too, have received this gift of salvation. "Ah! The Lord was baptized in this way for me. By being thus baptized, He bore the condemnation of all my sins. He was baptized ultimately for my own sake. Thank You, Lord!" This is what I came to believe. I am, therefore, now sinless. I have received the perfect remission of sin. If you, too, would also like to receive this remission of sin and be saved, accept it right now.

I have thought about this gift of salvation all the time from then on. Even now, when I think about it again, I realize that there is nothing else I can do but to thank the Lord for my salvation. Because this love of salvation is in my heart, I can never forget it. When I first received my remission of sin by accepting and believing in the gospel of the water and the Spirit, the truth manifested in the blue, purple, and scarlet thread and the fine woven linen, I was infinitely grateful to God. And even now, after several years have passed by, I still have this same thankful heart, and am renewed everyday.

Jesus surely came to this earth to save me, was baptized to take all my sins upon Himself, and died on the Cross to bear the condemnation of my sins. When I realized that all these things were done for me, I immediately accepted them and made them mine. I realize all the time that this was the best thing that I have ever done in my entire life, the wisest and smarted act of all. I therefore believe that the Lord truly loves me and cares for me, and I also believe and confess that He did all these things because He loved me. "Lord, I give all my thanks to You. Just as You have loved me, I also love You." Confessing thus is a great joy for the born-again.

Our Lord's love is forever unchanging. Just as His love for us does not change forever, our love for Him cannot change forever, either. At times, when we suffer and face hardships, our hearts might turn astray and we might even wish to forget and betray this love. But even when we are overwhelmed by our pain and our consciousness fails us, and even when all that we can think of is our own pain, God still holds us faithfully so that our hearts would never forget His love.

God loves us forever. That our Lord came to this earth as a creation for our sake was because He loved us to His own death. Now, I entreat you to believe in this love of God for yourselves. And accept it into your hearts. Do you believe now?

I thank the Lord for saving us perfectly from our sins with this love. ✉

SERMON

10

The Faith Manifested in The Laver

< Exodus 30:17-21 >

"Then the LORD spoke to Moses, saying: 'You shall also make a laver of bronze, with its base also of bronze, for washing. You shall put it between the tabernacle of meeting and the altar. And you shall put water in it, for Aaron and his sons shall wash their hands and their feet in water from it. When they go into the tabernacle of meeting, or when they come near the altar to minister, to burn an offering made by fire to the LORD, they shall wash with water, lest they die. So they shall wash their hands and their feet, lest they die. And it shall be a statute forever to them—to him and his descendants throughout their generations.'"

The Laver in the Court of the Tabernacle

Material: Made of bronze, it was always filled with water.

Spiritual meaning: Bronze means the judgment of all the sins of mankind. To bear the condemnation of all the sins of mankind, Jesus took the sins of the world upon Himself by being baptized by John. As such, the meaning of the laver is that we can be washed of all our sins by believing that all these sins of ours were passed onto Jesus with His baptism.

The priests that served in the Tabernacle also washed their hands and feet at the laver before entering the Tabernacle and thereby avoided their death. Bronze refers to the judgment of all sins, and the laver's water refers to the baptism that Jesus received from John and through which He took the sins of the world upon Himself. In other words, the laver tells us that Jesus accepted all sins passed onto Him and bore the condemnation of these sins. The water in the laver means, in the Old Testament, the blue thread of the Tabernacle, and in the New Testament, the baptism that Jesus received from John (Matthew 3:15, 1 Peter 3:21).

So the laver refers to the baptism of Jesus, and it is the place where we confirm our faith in the fact that Jesus bore all our sins, including our actual sins, and washed them away all at once through the baptism that He received from John the Baptist over 2,000 years ago.

There are the righteous in this world who have been born again by believing in the gospel of the water and the Spirit. They are the ones who have received the remission of their sins by believing that all their sins were forgiven by the works of Jesus manifested in the blue, purple, and scarlet thread and the fine woven linen. However, because even the righteous who have received the remission of sin are insufficient in their flesh, they cannot help but sin everyday, and such sins are called actual sins. The place where the righteous who have received their remission of sin comes to solve the problem of their actual sins is none other than this laver. Whenever the righteous commits actual sins, they come to the laver in the court of the Tabernacle and wash their hands and feet, and they can thereby confirm the fact that Jesus has already forgiven all their actual sins also by believing in the written Word of God.

In the Bible, water at times is used to refer to the Word of God also, but the most important meaning of water is the baptism of Jesus. Ephesians 5:26 says, *"that He might sanctify and cleanse her with the washing of water by the word,"* and

John 15:3 says, *"You are already clean because of the word which I have spoken to you."* The laver enables the holy saints who have received the remission of their sins to possess the evidence that the Lord has forgiven all their sins with water no matter how insufficient their flesh might be.

1 Peter 3:21 and 22 state, *"There is also an antitype which now saves us—baptism (not the removal of the filth of the flesh, but the answer of a good conscience toward God), through the resurrection of Jesus Christ, who has gone into heaven and is at the right hand of God, angels and authorities and powers having been made subject to Him."* Just before these verses, Peter explains the spiritual meaning of the water of Noah's days. Even though Noah had warned sinners, the souls imprisoned by sin in other words, of the flood that would cleanse away all the filth of the first world, only eight were saved through water. The water of the flood at that time perished all those who had never believed in God's Word. And now, Peter extracts from the incident of flood that Jesus' baptism is the antitype of this water. As such, the laver is the place where we confirm our salvation once again before God both when and after we are saved.

The saints who have been saved from their sins by faith are clothed in God's grace by believing in the water of the laver (the baptism of Jesus), bronze (God's judgment of all sins), and that Jesus has delivered them from their sins. Even if we are so full of weaknesses and shortcomings that we can hardly even recognize ourselves as the righteous, we can surely confirm that we are wholly righteous by recommitting our faith in the baptism of Jesus (the bearing of sins, water) and His bloodshed on the Cross (the condemnation of sins, bronze). Because we believe in the Word of God that has already saved us all from all our sins and the condemnation of these sins, we can always become the righteous who are sinless.

The Word of God in which we believe tells us that Jesus took our sins upon Himself through His baptism received from John, shed His blood on the Cross to bear all the condemnation of sins in our place, and has thereby saved us wholly from our sins. God placed the laver in the court of the Tabernacle so that we would confirm with our faith that we are, no matter what the circumstances might be, the ones who have been saved perfectly from all our sins.

Have You Been Delivered Eternally from All Your Actual Sins?

During the Last Supper, after sharing the Passover bread and drinks with His disciples, Jesus, before dying on the Cross, wanted to wash Peter's and other disciples' feet with water. Because Jesus had already taken all the sins of His disciples through His baptism received from John, He wanted to teach them the truth of the laver. Jesus told them that after being baptized, He, as the Passover Lamb, would pay the wages (death) of sin by being hung on a tree. As such, the twelve disciples of Jesus, though they remained insufficient after believing in Him, never again became sinners.

Likewise, the fact that Jesus washed their feet confirmed them what the Word of truth witnessed—that Jesus has already washed away all their sins of the world. This is how the disciples could always preach to the people of the world that Jesus is the Savior and spread the gospel of the water and the Spirit that He had already fulfilled (Hebrews 10:1-20). The laver thus allows the righteous who have been saved from all their sins by believing in the truth to remember the baptism of

Jesus. It also gives them the conviction of salvation that God Himself has delivered them.

The Bible Does Not Record the Size the Laver

While the size of everything else in the Tabernacle is recorded, the size of the laver is not. This shows us the fact that Jesus the Son of God took our sins upon' Himself with His baptism is infinitely great. It also tells us that the love of Jesus who has saved us from our sins and condemnation is unlimited. The laver manifests the great love of God that is immeasurable. Human beings are bound to continue to sin as long as they live. But by taking all the sins of the world upon Himself through His baptism received from John, and by being crucified and shedding His blood on the Cross, Jesus has blotted out all our sins forever.

The laver was made by melting the bronze mirrors of the women who served in the Tabernacle (Exodus 38:8). This means that the Word of God shines the light of salvation on sinners and takes away their darkness. We must realize that God has made the laver so that He Himself could wash away our sins. This Word of truth has shone the light on the sins of people hidden in the depth of their hearts, washed away their sins forever, and has given them the remission of sins, and has thereby turned them into the righteous. In other words, the laver plays the role of clearly testifying the truth that Jesus Christ has saved us the sinners wholly with the Word of God.

The Laver Was Also Made of Bronze

Do you know what the significance of the bronze that was used to make the laver is? Bronze refers to none other than the condemnation of sin that we were to face. To be more precise, it tells us that Jesus carried all our sins to the Cross with His baptism and was condemned in our place. It was we who were actually supposed to be condemned for our sins, but through the water of the laver, we can confirm once again that all our sins have been washed away clean. Those who believe in this become the ones who have been judged through their faith, and therefore they no longer face any more judgment.

The laver filled with water is telling us, "Through the blue, purple, and scarlet thread and the fine woven linen, Jesus has already cleansed away your sins and has wholly saved you from your sins. He has made you clean." The laver, in other words, is the proof positive for the righteous who have received the remission of sin that they have been washed of their sins and saved.

The altar of burnt offering means the judgment of sin, while the laver, related to the blue thread among the materials of the Tabernacle, tells us that Jesus took our sins upon Himself with His baptism in the New Testament.

We can enter into the Holy Place only when we open and enter the gate of the court of the Tabernacle, pass by the altar of burnt offering, and then pass by the following laver. Those who can enter into the Tabernacle where God dwells are only those who have clearly gone through the altar of burnt offering and the laver by faith. Only those who have received the remission of sin by believing in the truth of the laver in the outer court of the Tabernacle can enter into the Holy Place.

When someone tries to enter the Holy Place by his/her

own strength, fire will come out of the Holy Place and devour this person. Even Aaron's sons were no exception to this, and some of them, in fact, actually died as a result (Leviticus 10:1-2). Those who are ignorant of God's righteous bearing of sins and judgment and ignore this truth will be put to death because of their sins. People who try to enter into the Kingdom of God by believing according to their own thoughts instead of believing in His exceedingly elaborate salvation from sin will most certainly face the judgment of fire for their sins. Because of the inevitable judgment of sin, all that awaits them as a consequence is only hell.

Jesus completed our salvation from sin with the blue, purple, and scarlet thread and the fine woven linen so that we would be able to enter into the Holy Place. It is by believing in this truth that we are wholly saved from all our sins. God had set His plan to save the mankind from sin even before the creation, and let us know His will in detail through the truth of the blue thread (the baptism of Jesus), the scarlet thread (the death of Jesus on the Cross), and the purple thread (God became a man) in the Bible. And according to this plan, He has indeed saved all sinners from their sins and iniquities through the works of Jesus manifested in these blue, purple, and scarlet thread.

1 John 5:4 says, *"This is the victory that has overcome the world—our faith,"* and this is followed by verse 10, which says, *"He who believes in the Son of God has the witness in himself."* What is this witness of salvation? The gospel of truth that has given us our salvation through the water, the blood, and the Spirit is the witness of our faith in the Son of God (1 John 5:6-8). In other words, only the gospel of the water and the Spirit in which we believe is the evidence that God has washed us of our sins and made us His own people. The only

way for us to be saved from all sins, enter into the Holy Place, feed on the bread of life given by God, and live in His grace is to believe in none other than this gospel of the water and the Spirit. By believing in the gospel of the water and the Spirit that cleanses away our sins, we must now be saved and live our lives of faith by uniting with God's Church.

It is by the truth of the gospel of the water and the Spirit that we can feed on the Word of God in His Church, be united with it, and live as the righteous whose prayers are heard by God. When we believe in this truth, we can become the righteous who have the faith of the blue, purple, and scarlet thread, and who live clothed in the grace of God before His presence. The life of faith that can be lived only by the people of God comes solely by believing in the water, the blood, and the Spirit. We can be saved from all our sins by believing with our hearts in the baptism of Jesus, His bloodshed and death, and that Jesus is God Himself. The faith that has enabled you to live in God's Church is the faith in the blue, purple, and scarlet thread and the fine woven linen.

Nowadays, many people are saying, "All that we have to do is just believe in Jesus; why bother with all these complexities? Let's not waste our time with useless talks and just believe in whatever way we think is fitting." To such people, we may only seem to be troublemakers in Christianity, but what is absolutely clear is that if one believes in Jesus without having received the remission of sin, he/she must face eternal condemnation. Not believing wholly in the gospel of the water, the blood and the Spirit is a false and flawed faith. It is, in fact, not believing in Jesus as the Savior.

If I, to win the favor of some stranger, were to insist blindly to this stranger, "I believe in you," would this person be convinced, "This guy really must really believe me," and be happy about it? On the contrary, he would probably say, "Do you know me? I don't think I know you." If I say to him again, "But I still believe in you anyway," and look at him with earnest eyes trying to making him feel better, would he then be happy about it? It's far more likely that he will only see me as a sycophant with no backbone, who is just trying to read his mind and curry his favor.

Neither is God pleased by people who just believe in Him blindly. When we say, "I believe in God. I believe in Jesus to be the Savior of sinners," then we must profess our faith in Him after knowing and believing how Jesus has taken care of the iniquities of sinners. If we believe thoughtlessly or blindly, as if we have no character at all, then we can never be saved. We are saved only when we believe by first knowing clearly how Jesus has made our sins disappear. When we say that we believe in someone, we place our true confidence in this person because we know him/her well enough and consider this person to be believable. Placing confidence in someone whom we do not know well can only mean that we are either lying, or we are fools primed for betrayal. As such, when we profess to believe in Jesus, we must know exactly how Jesus has made all our sins disappear. Only then can we not be abandoned by our Lord at the last moment and enter Heaven as the born-again children of God.

The true faith that can lead us to Heaven is the faith in the blue, purple, and scarlet thread. In other words, the real faith is believing in the gospel of the water and the Spirit that has saved us through the water (the baptism of Jesus), the blood (the death of Jesus), and the Holy Spirit (Jesus is God). We must know just how great is the grace of our Lord that has saved us, and believe in it, for believing in this truth will lead us to our salvation.

Whether one's faith is whole or not is determined just by whether or not this person knows the truth. You can believe in Jesus as your Savior only when you believe in the gospel of the water and the Spirit with your hearts. And this faith in Jesus as our Savior, who has given us the remission of sin through the gospel of the water and the Spirit, is the true faith that has saved us from all our sins.

The Laver Is the Affirmation of Salvation That Has Forgiven Our Sins

The laver was filled by water. It was placed right in front of the Holy Place. The laver is the place where we remind ourselves that we have received the remission of sin, and affirm its reception by faith. It is the affirmation of the fact that God has cleansed away all the sins of believers. Just as the priests serving in the Holy Place washed their hands and feet at the laver whenever they got soiled, those who have received the remission of sin, whenever they sin, also wash away such sins by reminding themselves and affirming once again, through the Word of God, that Jesus also has already blotted out these sins that soiled them and atoned for them as well by being condemned vicariously.

We get defiled because we cannot help but continue to sin as we live in this world. With what should we cleanse away all these sins that defile us then? We wash them away by believing that Jesus Christ, the King of kings, came to this earth over 2,000 years ago in the flesh of a man to save sinners, took their sins upon Himself through His baptism, shed His blood on the Cross, and has thereby forgiven sinners of all their sins. We can receive the remission of sin and wash away our actual sins as well only when we believe in the truth that Jesus took all sins upon Himself by being baptized. We can be cleansed of our actual sins as well, in other words, only when we believe in this truth that God has already washed away all our sins through the blue, purple, and scarlet thread.

We Must Have the Faith That Knows and Believes in the Truth of the Laver

Without faith in the laver, we can never enter into the Holy Place where God dwells. Our deeds cannot always be perfect. Because we have shortcomings, we sin at times. But the salvation that God has given us is perfect nonetheless, for the Word of God is perfect. Because God has washed away our shortcomings with His perfect salvation, we can boldly enter into the Holy Place by faith. Those who do not go through the laver can never enter the Holy Place. We are made eligible to enter into the Holy Place by our faith in the truth that Jesus came to this earth 2,000 years ago and blotted out all the sins of the world with the gospel of the water, the blood and the Spirit prophesied through the blue, purple, and scarlet thread. Without believing that the Lord has already blotted out all our sins and made us sinless, we cannot enter into the Holy Place.

As we cannot enter into the Sanctuary of God without believing in the blue, purple, and scarlet thread, if we do not believe in the gospel of the water and the Spirit, nor can we enjoy the blessing of going forth to the throne of the grace of God by believing in His Word in His Church, of praying to Him and receiving His grace, and of living with His servants and saints. We can live our lives in God's Church with our fellow believers, hearing and believing in His Word and praying to Him, only when we believe that God has already saved us from all our sins through the blue, purple, and scarlet thread.

The laver is the final confirmation of our salvation from sin. God placed the laver right in front of the Holy Place and filled it with water in order to give the affirmation of faith to those who believe in the gospel of the remission of sin. This laver cleanses the defiled consciences of the righteous who believe.

Let's read 1 John 2:1-2. *"My little children, these things I write to you, so that you may not sin. And if anyone sins, we have an Advocate with the Father, Jesus Christ the righteous. And He Himself is the propitiation for our sins, and not for ours only but also for the whole world."* Amen.

If we sin, we have an Advocate with the Father, Jesus Christ the righteous. Jesus washes the defiled hearts of the righteous clean with water. The day before He was crucified, during the Last Supper Jesus gathered His disciples together, poured water into a basin, and started to wash their feet. "When I was baptized, I bore all yours sins, including even the sins that you will commit later, and I will be condemned on the Cross in your place. I took even your future sins upon Myself as well, and I blotted them out. I have become your Savior."

It was to tell this that Jesus washed the disciples' feet during the Last Supper of the Passover. To Peter who refused to have his feet washed by Jesus, He said, *"What I am doing you do not understand now, but you will know after this" (John 13:7).* Jesus wanted to become the perfect Savior of those who truly believe in the gospel of the water and the Spirit. For those who believe in the blue, purple, and scarlet thread, Jesus has become their eternal Savior.

The Use of the Laver

The laver was used to wash away all the filthiness of the priests when they worked in the Tabernacle giving offerings to God. It was needed to wash away the grimes that the priests got from killing the sacrificial offering, drawing its blood, and cutting it to pieces to give to God the offering that would atone for the sins of the people of Israel. When the priests got soiled while giving offerings, they had to be washed with water, and the laver was the place where all this filthiness was cleansed away.

Whenever we sin, whether spiritually or in our flesh, and whenever we become defiled by breaking God's commandments, we must wash away all our filthiness with this laver's water. The priests, whenever their bodies touched anything unclean or dirty, had to wash the soiled parts of their bodies with water, whether they wanted to or not.

Like this, whenever all those who believe in God come into contact with something dirty or unclean, the water of the laver is used to wash away all such filthiness. In short, the laver's water was given to be used for washing away filthiness of the born-again. As such, the laver contains God's mercy. The meaning of the laver is not an optional item that we can choose to either believe or not, but it is the necessary item absolutely essential to those who believe in Jesus.

God set the size for all other items in the Tabernacle, specifying how many cubits they should be in height, length and width. But He did not specify the size of the laver. This is a characteristic particular only to the laver. This manifests the endless love that the Messiah has bestowed on us, who commit actual sins everyday. In this love of the Messiah was found His baptism, a form of the laying on of hands that washes away all our sins. As a lot of water had to be used when priests got soiled while performing their duties, the laver must always have been filled by water. So the size of the laver depended on this need. Because the laver was made of bronze, whenever the priests got washed with its water, they came to think of the judgment of sin.

The priests who were serving in the Tabernacle had to wash away all the uncleanness of their hands and their feet with the laver's water. If bronze manifests the judgment of God, then water manifests the washing of sin. Hebrew 10:22 says, *"our bodies washed with pure water,"* and Titus 3:5 says, *"the washing of regeneration and renewing of the Holy Spirit."* Like these passages, the Word of the New Testaments also tells us much about washing away filthiness with the water of baptism.

If the priests washed away their filthiness accrued in their lives with the water of the laver, we, the born-again Christians of today, can wash away all our actual sins committed in our lives by believing in the baptism of Jesus. The water of the laver of the Old Testament shows us that the Messiah came to this earth and has washed away all the sins of the world with the baptism that He received from John.

Through the Bible, God tells us that not only the sins committed by the people of Israel but the actual sins committed by all the people of the entire human history were all passed onto Jesus with the baptism that He received from John. When Jesus was baptized by John, He said in Matthew 3:15, *"Permit it to be so now, for thus it is fitting for us to fulfill all righteousness."* By receiving His baptism, the same form of the laying on of hands, from John, the representative of mankind, Jesus accepted all the sins of mankind onto His own body.

Therefore, by believing in the fact that all our sins were passed onto Jesus the Messiah through His baptism, we can all be washed of all the filthy sins of our hearts. Because we already passed all our sins onto Jesus by believing in this truth, all that we have to do is just believe that the Son of God carried the sins of the world to the Cross, was crucified and shed His blood, became the perfect sacrificial offering for all mankind, and has thereby delivered us from all our sins. Do you believe this in your hearts? Those who truly believe that the Messiah became our own sacrificial offering are eternally saved.

The Problem of Actual Sins Can Also Be Solved by Believing in the Baptism of Jesus

Does the Bible tell us how we can wash away all our actual sins? As the priests washed away their filthinesses with the water of the laver in the Old Testament, in the New Testament, we can receive the remission of our actual sins by believing that Jesus has fulfilled the righteousness of God by taking the sins of the world upon Himself through His baptism received from John. In the end, all sins are washed away by believing in the truth.

When the people of Israel gave the sin offering to God, they brought to the Tabernacle an unblemished sacrificial animal like a sheep or goat, confessed their sins and passed them all onto the offering by putting their hands on its head, and killed this offering of sacrifice that accepted their sins. They then cut its throat and drew its blood, putting the blood on the horns of the altar of burnt offering and pouring the rest on the ground (Leviticus 4). Even a year's worth of their sins were all remitted at once by faith through the sin offering of the

Day of Atonement (Leviticus 16). In the end, we receive our remission of sin with the same method as the sin offering of the Old Testament—that is, by believing in the baptism of the Messiah who came to blot out our sins and in the blood of the Cross.

The Old Testaments' laying on of hands is the same as the baptism that Jesus received in the New Testament. Our Messiah took care of and washed away all our sins by being baptized by John and crucified. When it is by the works of the baptism of the Messiah and His blood on the Cross that God has saved us perfectly from all our sins, what more is there for us to do to be forgiven of our sins? What we must remember and believe is that even when we sin daily in our lives because of our weaknesses, all these sins have also been washed away by Jesus Christ who came of the water and the blood. Even though we believe in God, because of our shortcomings, we still fall into our weaknesses and trespasses. But our God, who knows all this, has saved us by sending the Messiah to this earth, making Him take the sins of mankind upon Himself through His baptism, and sacrificing Him.

By placing the altar of burnt offering and the laver in the court of the Tabernacle, God has allowed us to wash away all our actual sins committed daily before we enter into the Sanctuary, the House of God. But this does not mean that we are supposed to wash away our actual sins with the daily prayers of repentance. On the contrary, it is our faith in the baptism of the Messiah and His blood on the Cross that cleanses away all our sins. God has set that when the righteous make mistakes and commit sins and wrongdoings after believing in Jesus, they should be washed of all such sins by believing in the baptism that the Messiah, the Lord of the laver, received.

Many people are prone to regard Jesus' bearing of sins and His being judged for all the sins as the same thing, tying them together blindly into a single bundle. But because we commits actual sins on a daily basis from our weaknesses, the washing of sin and the judgment of sin must be separated into two. The baptism that Jesus received from John and His death on the Cross were to bear all our sins upon Himself, to be judged for these sins, and to save us from them perfectly. In this faith, we can thus receive the judgment of our sins all at once. As such, the problem of our actual sins committed daily must be solved by believing in the baptism of the Messiah. It is by uniting these two components, the baptism and the Cross, that the single, perfect salvation is completed. This is the truth of the perfect remission of sin. Insofar as the solution to the problem of our sins is concerned, we must think of and believe in it by separating Jesus' baptism and the Cross from each other.

When the priests killed sacrificial animals in the Tabernacle, they were soiled by grimes and splashing blood. We can't even begin to imagine just how filthy they got. The priests had to wash away all this filthiness, but if there had been no water in the laver of the court of the Tabernacle, they would not have been able to do so. No matter if it was the High Priest or a common priest who had been forgiven of a year's worth of sins, without washing away the filthiness on him right away with the water of the laver, this person could not help but live with the filth still on him.

Even if the High Priest had all kind of filth on him, because there was the laver in the court of the Tabernacle, he could always be cleansed. Even if a priest were forgiven of a years' worth of sins entirely, it was still by thus washing away the daily sins that this person was cleansed. God set that the priests who gave offerings to Him had to be thus washed of all their filthiness at the laver. We can then realize why God put the laver in the court of the Tabernacle. We can also know why this laver was placed between the altar of burnt offering and the Sanctuary.

Why Do We Need the Laver?

The truth implied in the laver is revealed in John 13. During the Passover, after having the Last Supper with His disciples, Jesus began to wash their feet, starting with Peter. When Jesus tried to wash his feet, He asked Peter to put out his feet so that He could wash them. However, Peter declined, saying, "I should be washing Your feet; how can You, Lord, wash my feet?"

Peter declined because he thought that it just was not fitting for a teacher to wash his own disciples' feet. "How can I dare to ask my teacher to wash my feet? I can't."

Peter kept declining Jesus' service. What Jesus then spoke to Peter here is of deep import.

"What I am doing you do not understand now, but you will know after this" (John 13:7). This is what Jesus meant: "You cannot understand now why I have to wash your feet. But this will surely be the key to solving the problem of your actual sins. You will commits many actual sins from now on, but I have already taken even your actual sins of the future upon Myself, and because of these sins, I must now shed My blood on the Cross. You must therefore know and believe that I am the Messiah who took care of even your actual sins of the future."

In Peter's mind, it just looked simply unethical for the

Messiah to wash his feet, and this is why he declined to be washed. But Jesus told Peter, "You will know after this," and washed his feet.

"Only when I wash your feet can you have relations with Me. You do not understand now why I am washing your feet. But after I am crucified and ascend to the Kingdom of Heaven, you will know why I washed your feet. Because I am your Messiah, I already bore even your future sins with My baptism, and by becoming the sacrificial offering for your sins, I have become your Savior."

As our Lord said, Peter did not understand any of this at the time, but after the resurrection of the Lord, he came to realize it. Truly, this was the event that blotted out even his actual sins.

"Because I cannot but commit actual sins in the world, the Lord washed my feet so that I would believe that Jesus the Messiah took even these actual sins upon Himself with His baptism from John the Baptist! The baptism of the Messiah took care of even these actual sins of the future! Jesus took all these sins upon Himself with His baptism, carried the sins of the world to the Cross, and bore the condemnation of all sins by being crucified! And by rising from the dead again, He has truly and wholly saved us from all our sins!"

Only on a later time, after he even betrayed the Lord three times, did Peter come to realize this and believe in it. This is why he said in 1 Peter 3:21, *"There is also an antitype which now saves us—baptism (not the removal of the filth of the flesh, but the answer of a good conscience toward God), through the resurrection of Jesus Christ."* Here, the word 'antitype' means "one that is foreshadowed by or identified with an earlier symbol or type, such as a figure in the New Testament who has a counterpart in the Old Testament." So, the preceding context clearly declares that the baptism of Jesus is the very antitype of the 'water' in the Old Testament.

In the Old Testament, when the sin offering of the Day of Atonement was given to God to receive the remission of a year's worth of sins, the High Priest, representing the people of Israel, had to lay his hands on the sacrificial offering and confess the sins that the Israelites had committed in order to pass their sins onto the offering. This method of the laying on of hands was the same format as the baptism of Jesus. In the Old Testament, the sacrificial offering had to bleed to death because it had accepted the sins of all the Israelites passed onto it. Its throat was cut, and it soon bled all its blood. The priests then skinned it, cut it to pieces, and offered its flesh to God by burning it with fire.

The Messiah, who is the real substance of the sacrificial offering of the Old Testament, came to this earth, accepted our sins through the laying on of hands, bled on the Cross, and died in our place. Today, you and I have therefore wholly received the remission of our sins through the baptism of Jesus Christ and His death on the Cross. And we must wash away our actual sins committed in our everyday lives also by believing that these sins have already been cleansed away by the baptism that our Lord received and the blood that He shed on the Cross. We must know this truth and believes in it. We can be delivered from all our actual sins only when we believed that Jesus took all our sins upon Himself and washed them all away through His baptism. Whenever we commit actual sins, in other words, we must confirm our faith in the gospel of the water and the Spirit. And by ruminating over the truth that even these actual sins were already blotted out by Jesus with His baptism and the Cross, we cannot lose our salvation at any case, and can restore it at once whenever our hearts are attacked by a sense of guilt.

Because Jesus has already blotted out even the daily sins committed by the righteous who have received the remission of sin in their everyday lives, God permitted the laver to them so that these righteous, whose remission of sin came by the water, the blood and the Spirit, would be washed of their actual sins through their faith in the gospel of the water and the Spirit.

This is why God made the laver by gathering and melting the hand mirrors used by the women who had been serving in the Tabernacle of meeting, for these mirrors provide the reflection of the self. Whenever we commit actual sins and fall into despair because of our weaknesses, we must go to the laver and wash our hands and feet. The laver's role is to remind us that Jesus took the sins of mankind upon Himself all at once when He was baptized by John. It was to teach this truth to the righteous who have received the remission of sin that our Lord made the Israelites make the laver by melting the hand mirrors of these women, fill it with water, and allowed the priests to cleanse away all the filthiness of their hands and feet with this water.

We believe that Jesus is the Son of God, the Creator, and the Savior of mankind. And we must remember that the Messiah came to this earth in the flesh of a man and accepted all our sins passed onto His own body through the baptism that He received from John—that is, whenever we commit actual sins in this world, fall into weaknesses or our weaknesses are revealed, we must remember even more that the Messiah came in the flesh, was baptized and crucified, and thereby has already blotted out all our sins.

If we do not remember this and believe in it, even though we have received the remission of sin, we would yet again be bound by our actual sins and return to our old, sinful selves. As such, we must believe everyday that all our sins committed because of our weaknesses and shortcomings had already been passed onto Jesus through His baptism. Everyday, we must remember, believe again, and affirm that the Messiah took all our sins upon Himself with His baptism received from John and has washed them all away.

There is no one on the face of this earth who can receive the remission of sin by believing in Jesus without believing that He bore the sins of the world by being baptized by John and shed His blood. And even if people have received the remission of sin, there is not a single person who does not commit actual sins. As such, without believing in the baptism of Jesus, everyone would be sinful, and the will of God would never have been fulfilled to everyone. This is why God gave us His Son, had Him be baptized by John, and gave Him up to the Cross to bleed.

If we believe in Jesus Christ as our Messiah, we must believe that all our sins were passed onto Him through His baptism received from John, and that He bore all our condemnation by carrying the sins of the world to the Cross, being crucified, and shedding His blood. We receive our remission of sin by believing in the baptism of Jesus and His blood. All our sins have been blotted out by believing in this truth. We have reached righteousness by believing in the love of God with our hearts. Our hearts are now sinless, clean and spotless. But there are still shortcomings in our flesh. This is why we have to remember the baptism of Jesus everyday and remind ourselves of this faith always. Whenever our shortcomings and weaknesses are revealed, whenever evil thoughts rise up and we are defiled, and whenever our acts go astray, our Lord is pleased only when we remember that Jesus took all these sins upon Himself with His baptism received from John and cleanse our hearts by believing in this truth once again.

Whenever we commit sin, we must first admit our sins before God. We must then believe once again that all these sins were already passed onto Jesus through His baptism. We who have been cleansed by the work of Jesus' baptism must cleanse away our actual sins everyday by believing in this work. This is why we absolutely must remember and believe in the fact that we can wash away all our sins through the baptism of Jesus Christ.

We have now examined why God placed the laver between the altar of burnt offering and the Tabernacle. God placed the laver between the altar of burnt offering and the Tabernacle so that when we go before Him, we would go with clean bodies and hearts. Even after we became the righteous who have received the perfect remission of sin through the baptism of Jesus and the Cross, our hearts are still prone to be defiled whenever we sin, whether willingly or unwillingly. This is why we must cleanse away this filthiness at the laver when we pass the altar of burnt offering and go before God. Because we cannot go before God if we have even the smallest of all filthiness, God placed the laver between the altar of burnt offering and the Tabernacle so that we may be able to enter into the presence of God in cleanness, having washed ourselves with the water of the laver.

What Kind of Conscience Is a Good Conscience before God?

1 Peter 3:21 also defines Jesus' baptism to be *"the answer of a good conscience toward God."* Here, 'a good conscience' is the one that believes that Jesus washed away all the sins of

mankind, including all actual sins committed daily, with the baptism that He received from John at the Jordan River. To take our sins upon Himself, our Lord was baptized by John and thereby accepted our sins onto His own body. Because Jesus bore all our sins on His body, He had to die on the Cross. If we ignore and do not believe in what He did, then our consciences can only be evil. This is why we must believe in His baptism. We must have good consciences before God. Though in our flesh we may not be able to live perfectly 100 percent, at least in our consciences, we can and must have good consciences before the sight of God.

About half a century ago, when Korea lost everything in the ruins of the Korean War, a flood of foreign aids came into the country to relieve its plight. Even though orphanages were to receive such aids first, instead of being so, some unscrupulous people diverted them into their own pockets and built their own wealth. They had no conscience. When foreign countries gave powdered milk, flour, blankets, shoes, clothes, and other aid supplies, the supporters sent them so that the naked and hungry people in dire needs would be clothed and fed properly; they could hardly imagine that some evil public officials and swindlers would divert these aid goods.

People with good consciences would have distributed them fairly among the poor. Those who, instead of turning the foreign aids into an opportunity to build their wealth, distributed them fairly among the poor dying of hunger would have had nothing to be ashamed of before God, for they would have lived with good conscience. But those who did not do so would have been accused of being thieves by their own consciences. Of course, these thieves could still be washed of all their sins if they turn around and believe in the baptism of Jesus even now.

To take our sins upon Himself and to blot out all our actual sins, Jesus came to this earth and was baptized. Having thus been baptized by John, Jesus washed away our sins all at once. I would like to rebuke the unbelievers in His baptism, saying, "What, then, makes you to be so proud as not to believe in His baptism? With what confidence do you not believe? Are you good enough to enter the Kingdom without the faith in His baptism?"

If we truly want to be the people of good consciences, we must wash away all our actual sins with the baptism that Jesus received from John. To do so, we must believe in our hearts that Jesus took upon Himself all the sins that we commit in our entire lifespan and has washed them all away. This is why Jesus our Messiah was baptized by John before going to the Cross.

Jesus said to the woman who was caught in adultery, "I do not condemn you, either. I do not judge you, either." Why? Because Jesus had already taken this woman's sin of adultery upon Himself also, and because Jesus Himself would bear the condemnation of this sin also. He said, "I am the One who would be condemned for your sins. But be washed of all your sins by believing in My baptism. Therefore, be saved from all your sins by believing in Me. Be saved from all the condemnation of sin also by faith, and be washed of all your sins. Be cleansed of the sins of your conscience and drink the water from Me that lets you never thirst again."

Today, you and I believe that Jesus is the One who has saved us from our sins. Do you truly believe that Jesus indeed took our sins upon Himself with His baptism and washed them all away? Our Lord cleansed away our sins by being baptized. We can now go to God in good conscience. Why? Because our Lord took all our sins upon Himself and washed them all away by being baptized, carried these sins to the Cross, was condemned in our place by being crucified, and rose from the dead again. A long time ago, Jesus came to this earth, and through His 33 years of life, He took all our sins upon Himself and washed them all away with His baptism.

By taking even our actual sins all upon Himself and washing them away, our Lord has enabled us to go to God and become the righteous, and to be judged of all our sins through the sacrifice of Jesus Christ. It is by believing in this Lord, in other words, that we can call God as our Father and go before His presence. As such, those who believe in Jesus' works of the water, the blood and the Spirit are the ones who have good consciences. On the contrary, it surely is the evil conscience that does not believe in the Lord's righteous acts, His baptism and crucifixion.

Nowadays, Many People Do Not Take the Word of God Seriously Because of Their Superstitious Faith

Many liars, discarding the Word of God as if it were merely an ornament, only preach that we should also do good over our faith in God to enter the Kingdom of Heaven. And when it comes to salvation, they only speak of the blood of the Cross, and mistakenly think that they have to climb up some mountain to pray or fast in order to then meet God through their experience of the flesh. Although nothing could be more wrong than this faith, they are absolutely certain of it. They say, "I was tormented by my sins, and so I stayed up all night praying, 'God, I have sinned. I believe in You, Lord.' On that day, I was still tormented in the evening, but after I stayed up all night praying, when the dawn came, suddenly I felt as if a bundle of fire had been thrust upon me, and, right at that time, my mind was all cleared—all the sins of my heart were washed away white as snow. So it was at this time that I was born again. Halleluiah!"

Such thoughts are only man-made, ignorant and foolish thoughts that turn the Word God useless. You must remember that God will punish, by many folds, those who say such mystical non-sense and thereby deceive people and lead others to the fire of hell.

"My ears hurt so much. But I believed in what the Lord said, that we would be healed if we believe, and so I withstood my pain saying, 'Lord, I believe!' When I believed like this, then the pain was all gone!"

"I had a gastric ulcer, so every time I ate something, I got a terrible stomachache. So before I ate, I prayed, 'Lord, I am hurting here, but You said that You would hear whatever we pray for with faith. I still believe in Your Word.' Sure enough, I had no problem digesting!"

What are all these? These are the cases where people did not meet the Lord through the Word. These cases demonstrate the falseness of their faith that does not believe by the Word. These are not the answers to their prayers received through the Word, but just their mystical faith. They believe in God not by the Word, but in their mistaken confusion based on their own emotions and experiences. What is so regrettable and saddening is that there are so many such mystics among today's Christians.

Like this, pushing aside the Word of God and believing in Jesus blindly based on their emotions or experiences only amount to a superstitious faith. People who claim to believe in Jesus even as they do not believe by the Word need to examine themselves to see whether they are possessed by demons or not.

"I met Jesus while praying. Jesus appeared in my dream. I prayed ardently and my illness was healed." Anyone with a half-intact mouth can make such claims, but what is clear is that this is not the faith given by God, but it is the false faith give by Satan.

Through the blue, purple, and scarlet thread and the fine woven linen, our Lord has revealed Himself to us. Does our Lord reveal Himself to us in new and different ways in today's era? Does He really appear before us in an illusion or a dream? He is dragging huge chains at His feet, bleeding all over, has a crown of thorns on His head, and says, "You see, this is how I suffered so much for you. Now, what will you do for Me?"—is this how our Lord reveals Himself to us? This is all nonsense!

Yet there are still people who, after supposedly having this kind of a dream, make a vow before God, "Lord, I will become Your servant and serve You with all my heart for the rest of my life. I will build a prayer house here. I will build a church here. I will carry my cross on my back for the rest of my life and testify You throughout the whole nation and the entire world."

In fact, we can easily come across such devotional preachers in the streets or public places. With no exception, they are all mystics who say that they decided to live like this after seeing Jesus in their dreams or hearing the voice of the Lord while praying. But the Lord reveals Himself only through His Word; He does not speak to us in a dream or while we are praying, especially in this era when all His Word has been given to mankind completely. Dreams just come from the complicated realm of human sub-consciousness. These people have this kind of a dream because they have all kinds of imaginations about Jesus in their unrequited love and just think too much.

When your mind dwells deeply on some matter before drifting to sleep, you are likely to see yourself grappling over this issue in your dream also. Like this, dreams are made of your sub-consciousness. This is why if we think too much, we get all kinds of weird dreams. They all have nothing to do with faith, but they are merely a reflection of the physical changes or sub-consciousness.

This is why if people think a lot about Jesus bleeding on the Cross, in their dream He appears with a crown of thorns on His head. In itself, there is nothing wrong with such a dream. But to take this dream too seriously is a grave mistake. What if Jesus appears before them, bleeding all over, and actually says, "What will you do for Me? You shall live the rest of your life for Me as an ascetic. For Me, You shall not have any possession"? There are foolish people who actually give up all their possessions so that they can live like this. Is there anyone who was terrified because of a dream, who took it seriously, or whose life was changed because of it? None other than this is mysticism.

God meets us through the Word. He is not someone whom we can meet in a dream or a vision in our prayer. The Word of God is written in the Old and New Testaments, and it is when we hear this Word preached to us and accept it into our hearts that our spirits can meet Him through the Word. It is, in other words, through the Word and only through the Word that your spirits can meet God.

It is from the Word that we came to know that Jesus took all our sins upon Himself with His baptism; it is by hearing this Word that we have come to believe in our hearts. The answer to the question of why Jesus had to die on the Cross is also found in the Word. It is because Jesus took our sins upon Himself by being baptized that He died on the Cross and has saved us. By the Word, we come to know God, and by the Word, we come to believe in Him. That Jesus Christ is God is also known and believed by us only through the Word.

How Could We Have Come to Believe in God? Were It Not for the Written Word of God?

If there were no Word of God, how could we have come to meet and believe in Jesus, who has made all our sins disappear? If there were no Word of God, our faith would be nothing. "This is what I think"—we may speak out our thoughts, but this is not the truth, and when our hearts are filled with what is not true, then the real truth cannot enter into our hearts. The right thing to say is not, "This is what I think," but it is, "This is what the Bible says." When we read the Bible, the truth spoken by God comes into our hearts and corrects the errors of our previous thoughts.

What is your faith in the gospel of the water and the Spirit made of? Is it made of your own thoughts? Or did you become the born-again by coming to know and believe in it from hearing the Word? It is through the Word that we have come to believe in and meet God in our hearts. This is why the gate of the court of the Tabernacle was woven of the blue, purple, and scarlet thread and the fine woven linen.

The water held in the laver means the baptism through which Jesus Christ took all our sins upon Himself. *"Permit it to be so now, for thus it is fitting for us to fulfill all righteousness" (Matthew 3:15).* Through the Word of God, we came to know the baptism with which Jesus took the sins of the world upon Himself. Because it is from the Word that we came to know the baptism of Jesus who took upon all the sins that you and I commit throughout our entire lives, this Word has made us have the faith of baptism in our hearts. It is through the Word that we come to find out the truth manifested in the laver.

From the Word of God, we can find out that the laver was made of bronze. In the Bible, bronze means judgment. As such, the meaning of the bronze laver is that when we look at ourselves before the Law, which plays the role of a mirror that reflects ourselves, we are all bound to be condemned. This is why the laver was made of the mirrors of the women serving at the Tabernacle. The Lord has save us, who could not avoid but be condemned because of our sins, by coming to this earth, being baptized, and dying on the Cross. Through the written Word of God, we came to know that it was because Jesus was baptized that He took all our sins upon Himself, went to the Cross, and bore the condemnation of sin. And it is by accepting into our hearts and believing in this truth that we have been saved. What about you? How have you been saved?

In a certain denomination that follows mysticism, they claim that its members must know the exact date of their salvation, on which month and day they were saved. And a pastor in this denomination is said to have testified before many believers that he believed in Jesus and was saved when he climbed up some mountain to pray and realized that he was nothing. He claimed very proudly that he had never forgotten the exact date and time of his being born again. This certainly has nothing to do with the fine woven linen, but is only emotional. This pastor's faith has nothing to do with the blue, purple, and scarlet thread and the fine woven linen. The salvation taught by this denomination has nothing to do with the true salvation made of the Word of God, but it is only of their own making.

It's actually possible to hypnotize oneself. If people keep insisting that they are sinless, and think like this over and over again, then they end up being hypnotized by themselves and become sinless on their own. If they keep chanting this spell to themselves, then they may actually feel as if they really became sinless, but such feelings can never last long. So, in no time, they have to hypnotize themselves again, chanting, "I'm sinless. I'm sinless." How self-centered, untrue, ignorant, and superstitious faith this is!

The fine woven linen means God's Word of the Old and New Testaments. That the gates of the court of the Tabernacle, of the Holy Place, and of the Most Holy were all woven of the blue, purple, and scarlet thread and the fine woven linen tells us that Jesus has become the door of our salvation and our Savior exactly as written in the Old and New Testaments. I therefore truly thank God, for how certain is this salvation that God has spoken to us!

This is why when I pray, I do not try to appeal to emotions or put on a show. I just pray by leaving everything to God and trusting in Him. "Father, please help us. Make us preach the gospel through the whole world. Protect and keep all my fellow ministers and saints. Give us the workers who can serve the gospel, allow this gospel to be spread, and make the believers realize and believe in Your Word." This is all I say when I pray; I do not pray trying to stir up my emotions and crying, and none of this mumbo-jumbo is any part of my prayers.

Some people, when they just can't rouse their emotions no matter how hard they try, even think of their long dead fathers and mothers to ilk out tears and to feign their prayers to be taken seriously by others. Such invented prayers are like a bunch of garbage that would make God vomit. People also stir up their emotions by thinking of Jesus' crucifixion and keep shouting out blindly, "I believe in You, Lord!"

But does this really mean that such people's faith is strong? If you think about your sins and try to stir up your emotions, saying, "Lord, I've sinned. Help me live righteously," then it actually is quite possible to rouse yourselves emotionally. Because having such an emotional experience and a good crying session can vent out a lot of stress, many people, feeling refreshed, think this is what faith is all about. Though their lives are full of troubles, such emotional experiences at least make them feel better for a while, and so they continue their religious lives in this way.

You Must Believe that the Lord Has Come to Us through the Blue, Purple, and Scarlet Thread and the Fine Woven Linen

Our Lord came to us through the Word. You should therefore not wait upon your senses, but you must listen to what the Word of God says to you. What is important is whether or not you believe in this Word of God in your hearts. When you pray, do not try to concentrate on your emotions. Rather, you should control them down to an appropriate level. Why? Because there are many liars in this world who will approach those who like to be emotionally roused and inspired to take advantage of their emotional holes. Because people so often lose the intellectual parts by pursuing their feelings, when revival meetings are held under the banner of "Great Spiritual Revival," more often than not, the aim is only to stir up the participants' emotions.

However, now that I have been born again, I cannot hold such a revival even if I were to try, for preaching the Word of

God is not inciting people's emotions like these great spiritual revival meetings of the world. Because I have been born again of the Word of truth, I have long bid my farewell to my emotional aspect that used to intrude into my spiritual life.

We, the righteous who hear the Word of God, use our intellect, and believe in our hearts, never like to be emotionally stirred. We believe in the truth by quickly realizing whether or not someone speaks of the Word of God to us as it is, and by quickly discerning whether or not this person is speaking to us by truly believing in it. Because we who know and believe in the truth of the blue, purple, and scarlet thread and the fine woven linen have the Holy Spirit in our hearts, we all realize that emotional incitement is far from the truth, and we accept only the real truth into our hearts.

Jesus came to us by the blue, purple, and scarlet thread and the fine woven linen. How marvelous is this truth? How wonderful is the love of our Lord that has saved you? Through the four-fold works of Jesus written in God's Word, we all have come to believe that Jesus took all your sins upon Himself with His baptism, died on the Cross, and has thereby saved you with His fulfillment of all righteousness.

Do you believe this truth in your hearts? Those who preach the gospel must spread it within the fine woven linen, that is, God's Word of the Old and New Testaments, and its content must be the blue, purple, and scarlet thread. And those who hear it must accept it into their hearts and believe in it wholeheartedly.

The Water of the Laver Washes away Our Sins

Through His baptism, Jesus took upon all our sins on

Himself and washed them all away. The baptism of Jesus refers to the water of the laver; it has cleansed us, who were all bound to hell because of sins, and enabled us to stand before God. Because Jesus accepted all our sins onto Himself through His baptism, He could go to the Cross and wash them away by being crucified to death. Both the baptism of Jesus and the Cross testify that Jesus bore the condemnation of all our sins. Through the baptism and the Cross, Jesus fulfilled all our salvation.

Giving the prayers of repentance can never cleanse us of our sins. It is because Jesus already took our sins upon with His baptism that our sins have been all washed away. It is by hearing this Word and believing in what Jesus has done for us that we can be freed from the condemnation of all our sins. Thanks to the condemnation that Jesus had borne, we have already borne all our condemnation of sin through our faith in His baptism. Truly, we have been saved by faith. In a way, salvation is utterly simple. If we believe in the gift and love of salvation, we can be saved, but if we do not believe, then we cannot be saved.

Apart from the Salvation Fulfilled by God, There Is Nothing That We Can Do to Be Saved

We cannot do anything at all for our salvation, were it not for God. As our Lord decided to save us in this way even before the creation and fulfilled our salvation, everything depends on how God decides. God the Father decided to save us through His Son and the Holy Spirit, and when the determined time came, He sent His only begotten Son Jesus to this earth. When Jesus turned 30 and the time came for Him to fulfill these works of salvation, the Father then made Christ be baptized and die on the Cross, resurrected Him, and has thereby saved us. We are saved by learning and knowing what the Lord has done for us from the Word of the Old and New Testaments, and by believing in it in our hearts. Being saved by believing in our hearts is none other than accepting faith into our hearts.

Do you believe that this Word of the Bible is the Word of God? None other than this Bible is God Himself who has existed since the beginning, and His Word. Through the Word of the Old and New Testaments, the Word of God, we can know and meet God. And through the Word of the Old and New Testament, we can realize and believe that he has saved us through the blue, purple, and scarlet thread and the fine woven linen. Also, because those who actually believe in this truth are saved, they can testify that this Word has power for sure. We should not judge and measure the Word of God with our own narrow thoughts, but we must rather realize from it how exactly God has saved us.

From the Old and New Testament, I hope and pray that you would all now hear and believe in the Word of the blue (Jesus' baptism), purple (Jesus is King of kings), and scarlet thread (the Cross), and the fine woven linen (God's Word of the Old and New Testament). If you put aside the Word of God and judge His Word with your own measuring rod for the rest of your life, you will never be saved.

If you recognize yourself that you do not know the Word of God well, then you must listen carefully to what the predecessors of faith say. Whether they are pastors, workers, or laymen, when you listen to the Word of God preached by them, and when what they are preaching is indeed right before God, all that you have to do is recognize that it is right and believe it in your hearts.

Those who spread the Word do not spread it because it is so easy, but they do so because what they are spreading is right before God. This is why they preach the right knowledge before God—that is, the gospel of the water and the Spirit, the truth of the blue, purple, and scarlet thread and the fine woven linen. Regardless of from whom we hear it, if it is the true Word of God, then there is nothing else that we can do but accept it with a yes, for there is not a single jot nor a tittle that is wrong with God's Word.

We must believe in the Word of God. What is 'believing'? It is to accept. It is to trust. In other words, because our Lord was baptized for us, we entrust all our infirmities to Him and rely on Him. "Did the Lord really save me by doing this? I trust and believe in You." Believing like this is the true faith.

Among the theologians of this world, it is very hard to find anyone who knows and believes correctly. Even before reaching the laver, they are stuck at the gate of the court of the Tabernacle, unable to even enter into the court. When they give sermons on the Tabernacle, they make a conscientious effort to shrewdly skirt the gate of its court, and when they publish books on the Tabernacle, they insert illustrations that leave out the huge gate that took up over 9 m of the court's fence.

Occasionally, there are some who boldly preach about the gate of the court of the Tabernacle, but because they do not know the fundamental substance of the blue thread, they only say, "blue is the color of the sky." So they claim that the blue thread is the color of the sky that manifests that Jesus is God Himself, and that the scarlet thread refers to the blood that Jesus shed on the Cross while on this earth, thereby skirting over, very shrewdly, the truth of the gate of the court of the Tabernacle. What about purple? Purple tells us that Jesus is the

King of king and God Himself. The divinity of Jesus is already held in the purple thread perfectly, so that there is no need to reiterate the truth with another color of thread.

The truth of the blue thread is that Jesus came to this earth and took all the sins of mankind on Himself all at once by being baptized by John. But the theologians of this world, because they do not recognize this baptism of Jesus, can neither know it, nor preach it, but only utter their nonsense. Those who are not born again by not believing in Jesus who came by the blue, purple, and scarlet thread and the fine woven linen do not know that Jesus took all sins upon Himself through baptism and bore their condemnation. As such, they have become spiritually blinded and unable to solve the Word, and therefore they have religionized the Word of God by interpreting it arbitrarily based on their own thoughts. They teach, "Believe in Jesus. You'll then be saved. And be good and meek from now on." They have turned faith in Jesus Christ into a mere religion that only emphasizes their virtuous deeds.

Because people know that they cannot be good no matter how hard they try, they are easily deceived by such words that invoke the will of mankind to try to be good. Religions follow the same old pattern, "If you try, you can do," or "Try your best to become holy." The common theme running across all religions is that they rate the decent thoughts, efforts, and will of mankind very highly. What about, for example, Buddhism? Buddhism emphasizes the endless efforts and will of mankind and teaches its followers to try to become holy by themselves, saying, "Do not kill; seek the truth and be good." In certain ways, its teachings are quite similar to Christian doctrines. The reason why Christianity and Buddhism appear so closely related despite being at the opposite end of each other is because they are both mere religions.

Religion and faith are completely different from each other. The true faith is to recognize and accept into our hearts the gift that our Lord, who has saved us solely through the righteousness of God, has given us. Faith is receiving the remission of sin by believing in our hearts that the Lord came to this earth and was baptized to take our sins upon Himself, and that He bore all the condemnation of our sins by being crucified. Believing that the Lord has delivered us from all our sins and condemnation by saving us through the water and the Spirit is faith. Do you believe? We must truly believe in our hearts.

God Has Already Saved You and Me from All Our Sins

As such, all that we have to do is just believe this in our hearts and accept it. This is what the truly obedient children of God have to do before Him, and everything else is not that important. Because God has loved you, He sent His only begotten Son to this earth, made Him take your sins upon Himself by having Him be baptized, had Him crucified and bleed, and put Him to death by condemning Him, resurrected Him, and has thereby saved you from all your sins.

Then, if you do not believe in this truth, how would God feel? Even now, if you want to become His obedient sons and daughters who can please His heart, then you must believe that God has, through His Son, blotted out all your sins and saved you from them. If you believe in your hearts and in thankfulness, you must then confess with your mouths. Do you also want to believe in Him, but it seems to be too difficult for you to believe in your heart? Then, try to confess your faith with your mouth clearly. When you thus confess that you believe, then faith will be planted and grow little by little. Faith belongs to those who take it bravely.

Let's assume for a moment that I have a real diamond ring. Let's further assume that I would give it to you, but one of you refuse to accept it saying that he/she cannot believe that the ring is made of real diamond. Although the ring is a real diamond ring, because this person did not believe, it is not diamond for him/her, and so he/she has now lost the chance to get a real diamond ring.

Faith is like this. If an authoritative gemologist proved to people with his/her written statement that the ring is made of real diamond, they would come to believe so. God has told us in detail through His written Word that the salvation He has given us is true. And those who believe in His salvation because His Word testifies so are the people of faith. "It's hard for me to believe that it's actually true, but since You who are the Absolute One say that it's true, I believe so." When people thus believe, they can then become the people of faith, and the most precious gift becomes theirs as promised.

On the other hand, there is also a different kind of faith. Let's assume that a swindler imitated a diamond ring, and that someone bought it intoxicated by its brilliant colors, convinced that it was a genuine one. This person is totally convinced that he/she made a wise choice, but in fact, he/she has been cheated. When people believe in false witnesses who claim that the ring is made of diamond when it is not, then this fake diamond is the same as the real diamond for these people, for they believe blindly that the ring is made of diamond. But what they have, of course, is only a fake. Likewise, there are people who have false faith. Even though they are convinced of their faith, it is false, groundless and mystical, for it did not come from God's

Word.

God said, "Do not worship other gods but Me." The Word of God is God Himself, and the Word tells us that unless we are born of water and the Spirit, we cannot see the Kingdom of God (John 3:5). God is telling us that without first going through the gate of the court of the Tabernacle woven of the blue, purple, and scarlet thread and the fine woven linen, we cannot enter into the Tabernacle's court, and that those who do not first wash their hands and feet clean in the laver cannot enter into the Tabernacle. As only this Word is the truth, anything other than this is all a fake.

Only faith in the truth is the real faith, and faith in anything else is all fake. No matter how ardently people might have believed, what is not the Word of God is not the Word of God to the very end. When Jesus tells you that He has made all your sins disappear with His baptism and the blood of the Cross, all that you have to do is just believe. Since the One who says that He has done so is God, this faith in His Word is real. If our Lord has not really done this, then this is His wrongdoing, and your faith itself is not wrong. On the other hand, if the Lord has definitely done so, and yet you did not believe and therefore was not saved, then this is clearly all your own responsibility. This is why what we have to do is believe. We must believe what God speaks to us through His Church. Do you believe?

What is the Word spoken through the Church? It is the Word of Jesus Christ who came to us by the blue, purple, and scarlet thread and the fine woven linen. The Church spreads all the Word of God, that Jesus took our sins upon Himself by being baptized, that Jesus is God Himself, and that He bore the condemnation of all our sins on the Cross. Faith in this truth, that Jesus has thus saved us, is the faith of real diamond guaranteed by God.

When we first know the will of God and the spiritual meanings manifested in the Tabernacle and then speak of them, it is this simple. But if we were to pursue, unable to know them, only superficial knowledge about the external format of the Tabernacle, the original Hebrew word for it, or the historical background to it, then we will not benefit at all but only end up with a headache.

Believe in the baptism of Jesus. Jesus received the baptism that cleanses away all the dark, filthy sins that are even in our hearts. Baptism means to wash away sin, to pass on, to bury, to transfer, and to cover. It is because Jesus received such baptism that He took all your sins upon Himself. Those who do not believe in this now will all be put to death and cast out to hell. *"You shall also make a laver of bronze, with its base also of bronze, for washing... So they shall wash their hands and their feet, lest they die. And it shall be a statute forever to them—to him and his descendants throughout their generations" (Exodus 30:18, 21).* Not to believe is to be cursed. Not to believe is to be cast out to hell. If you do not believe, the curse of Jehovah and destruction will descend upon you, and you will be thrown into the eternal fire.

"So they shall wash their hands and their feet, lest they die." God said this to the High Priest, saying that it is an eternal law that he and his descendants throughout their generations must abide by. Anyone who wants to believe in Jesus as his/her Savior must believe in His baptism and the blood of the Cross. Faith belongs to those who take it bravely. Salvation becomes yours when you accept it into your hearts by believing. Truth can be beneficial to us only when we believe in it. We must believe in what God has told us. There is no obstacle to a heart that is greater than disbelief.

God said that when priests come before Him, they must first wash their hands and feet clean at the bronze laver, and yet there are too many people who have no faith to wash their hands and feet with the water of the laver. Everyone who does not have this faith manifested in the laver will all be put to death before God. Believe in the gospel of the water and the Spirit in your hearts and be washed clean, and thereby go before God, avoid your death, and receive His Kingdom as your gift. No matter how much you argue and insist before God, you will most certainly be condemned for not believing when you were given a chance. I hope and pray that no one among you would face death for not believing in the truth.

If you do not believe in the truth of salvation that has blotted out your sins with the baptism of Jesus and His blood of the Cross, you will be greatly harmed. Do you believe? We must give our thanks to God for saving us from our sins and condemnation through the laver.

The remaining part of the Tabernacle will be discussed in sequels to this book. I hope you all have the privilege of becoming God's children through the messages in these books. ⊠

TESTIMONIES
OF SALVATION

Testimonies of Salvation

Missionary Brucilla Johnson, USA

I bring you greetings and glad tidings in the precious wonderful name of our Lord and Savior, Jesus Christ. This is in reply of the question you e-mailed to me a few days ago: "Why did John the Baptist lay hands on Jesus in the Jordan River?"

It was the Law of Atonement in The Old Testament. It was the commandment of God for Aaron the High Priest to lay hands on the head of a sacrificial animal (goat), and confess the horrific sins of the children of Israel and their transgressions (Isaiah 53:3-6). Afterwards, the goat would bear and carry the iniquities and trespasses of the children of Israel upon itself and send it away by a suitable man to release the goat into the wilderness (Leviticus 16:21, 22).

During the era of Jesus shortly before His public ministry, John the Baptist laid his hands on Jesus' head in the same like manner. In order for Jesus to take away all the sins and transgressions of the world, He was willing and humbled to be baptized in this manner. He bored all our iniquities and transgressions upon His head and shoulders (the High Priest and goat) as it is written in Isaiah 53:3-6. The baptism (immersion of water) is this. Jesus took or bore upon Himself all the sins of the world, which were now to be purged, cleansed, washed and purified by the baptism ritual (John 1:29).

The real truth of this question is this: *we fall down, but we get up" (Psalms 37:23, 24). "All have sinned and have come short to the glory of God" (Romans 3:23). "No, there is none that doeth good. No, not one" (Romans 3:10-12).*

Oh! But praise God, Hallelujah! Glory be to God, *"For by grace we have been saved through faith" (Ephesians 2:8, 1 John 1:9).* The Lamb of God has borne and taken the wages of sin in this world upon Himself through His baptism and death on the Cross (John 1:29).

I am without sin having been saved by the grace of Jesus Christ through faith washed and cleansed by the baptism of Jesus Christ and the blood of the Lamb of God.

I am so elated and joyous in the readings of these books, which has enlightened and given me a deeper understanding in His word. These awesome, powerful tools have also given me knowledge and a word I really didn't know and wasn't aware of. WOW! Amazing!

Vannunthang, India

The Baptism of Jesus was for Him to bear the sins of humankind. In the time of the Old Testament, the Israelites had always given sin offerings that were blameless to be atoned for their sins. However, the animals could not atone for human sin.

Therefore, John the Baptist laid his hand on the head of Jesus when he baptized Him in the Jordan River. In Matthew 3:13-17, Jesus asked John the Baptist to baptize Him and said, *"Permit it to be so now, for thus it is fitting for us to fulfill all righteousness."* As the sin offering was blameless in the Old Testament, Jesus offered Himself up for the redemption of humankind. When Jesus was baptized by John the Baptist, all the righteousness of God that would redeem all our sins was fulfilled.

All our sins were passed onto Jesus and the works of the salvation of humankind was completed all at once. So if we believe in the baptism of Jesus which has saved us from the sins of this world, we will be saved from all our troubles and sins forever.

The baptism of Jesus cleansed away the sins of this world, and we have no more sin forever and ever. Everyone who believes in His baptism can enter the Kingdom of Heaven.

In John 3:16, we see that God gave us His only begotten Son, Jesus. The Son was sent to us. God wants us to be saved from the sins of this world. Because of Adam's sin, the entire humankind became sinful. In Hebrews 10:1-10, we see that the sacrifice of Jesus was for all our sins, and that it has saved us from all sins. Jesus was crucified because the wages of sin is death. So, even when Jesus Himself was not sinful at all, He still gave up His life for us.

Therefore, we have no more sin, because Jesus was already judged on the Cross for us. By His suffering I have been released from the sins of this world. Those who believe in Jesus' baptism and His death will be saved from all their sins once and for all. There is no more sin in the world! I have no more sin in this world because the baptism of Jesus and His death have taken away all my past, present, and even future sins! Amen!

Thanks to your books, I've come to realize that I have no more sin in this world, because I now believe that the baptism of Jesus and His death on the Cross have taken away all my sins forever. When Jesus died on the Cross, His final words were, "It is finished." He meant that the sins of this world were washed away all at once, and that those who believe in the baptism of Jesus and His death would be forever saved from all the sins of the world. Now we have no more sin.

After Jesus paid for our sins, we have no more sin for any time at all—past, present, and future. But we must have faith in God. We must believe in God and ask for whatever we need, and God would then help us just as He has given us our salvation. God wants to give us everything that we cannot get on our own. God can do everything. This means that there is room for faith in all parts and aspects of our lives. If we pray and take our problems to God, He will surely solve them all, because faith leads us to live in His grace. We have to rely on our faith even in the smallest things and affairs. In 1 Samuel 17:45, we see that by faith David solved his problem with five smooth stones. Romans 1:17 says, *"For in it the righteousness of God revealed from faith to faith."* I have no more sin. That's why whenever we face any problem, we can solve it by faith.

George Gogolashvili, Georgia

I want to say that after thinking and praying a lot about this matter, I came to decide that the faith in the gospel of the water and Spirit must be the only correct doctrine of God's Word for mankind's salvation. I may not understand yet some small issues, but in general, I can say that I believed in the Message, which was passed to me through the books of your mission.

I saw that the only way to be totally released from all sins is believing in their being washed away in the water of Jordan in Jesus' baptism and then eliminating them on the Cross of Golgotha. Only this truth could make my heart really free of any sense of guilt and trace of sin.

I just deeply regret that so many people and Christian believers in this world still do not understand this simple and saving truth! I will be trying to pass it to all whom I meet and who will listen. I believe that it was just God's appointed time for me to find such books and teachings and receive at last what I was looking for so long. It was again by His grace! I am deeply thankful to my Jesus, who completely saved me forever from all my sins and made me truly sinless and righteous!

Glory be to God! I am also praying for you and success of your mission, so that the gospel of the water and Spirit would spread everywhere with God's grace and power! Amen. ✉

HAVE YOU TRULY BEEN BORN AGAIN OF WATER AND THE SPIRIT?

PAUL C. JONG

Among many Christian books written about being born again, this is the first book of out time to preach the gospel of the water and the Spirit in strict accordance with the Scriptures. Man can't enter the Kingdom of Heaven without being born again of water and the Spirit. To be born again means that a sinner is saved from all his lifelong sins by believing in the baptism of Jesus and His blood on the Cross. Let's believe in the gospel of the water and the Spirit and enter the kingdom of heaven as the righteous who have no sin.

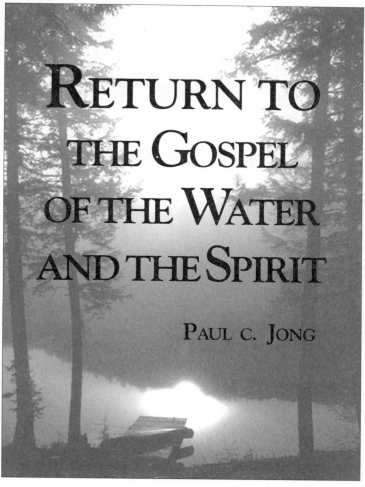

Return to
the Gospel
of the Water
and the Spirit

Paul C. Jong

Let's return to the gospel of the water and the Spirit. Theology and doctrines themselves can't save us. Many Christians still follow them and are not born again. This book clearly tells us what mistakes theology and doctrines have made and how to believe in Jesus in the most proper way.

The Holy Spirit who Dwells in Me

A Fail-safe Way for You to Receive the Holy Spirit

Paul C. Jong

In Christianity, the most significantly discussed issue is salvation from sins and the indwelling of the Holy Spirit. However, few people have the exact knowledge of these two things, while they are most important issues in Christianity. Nevertheless, in reality people say that they believe in Jesus Christ while they are ignorant of redemption and the Holy Spirit.

Do you know the gospel that makes you receive the Holy Spirit? If you want to ask God for the indwelling of the Holy Spirit, then you must first know the gospel of the water and the Spirit and have faith in it. This book will certainly lead all Christians worldwide to be forgiven of all their sins and to receive the Holy Spirit.

The words in this book will satisfy the thirst in your heart. Today's Christians continue to live while not knowing the true solution to the actual sins that they are committing daily. Do you know what God's righteousness is? The author hopes that you will ask yourself this question and believe in God's righteousness, which is revealed in this book.

The Doctrines of Predestination, Justification, and Incremental Sanctification are the major Christian doctrines, which brought confusion and emptiness into the souls of believers. But now, many Christians should newly come to know God, learn about His righteousness and continue in the assured faith.

This book will provide your soul with a great understanding and lead it to peace. The author wants you to possess the blessing of knowing God's righteousness.

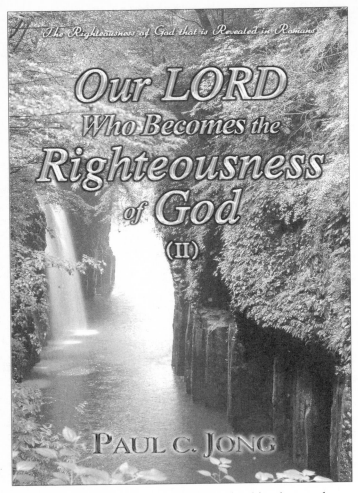

The words in this book will satisfy the thirst in your heart. Today's Christians continue to live while not knowing the true solution to the actual sins that they are committing daily. Do you know what God's righteousness is? The author hopes that you will ask yourself this question and believe in God's righteousness, which is revealed in this book.

The Doctrines of Predestination, Justification, and Incremental Sanctification are the major Christian doctrines, which brought confusion and emptiness into the souls of believers. But now, many Christians should newly come to know God, learn about His righteousness and continue in the assured faith.

This book will provide your soul with a great understanding and lead it to peace. The author wants you to possess the blessing of knowing God's righteousness.

IS THE AGE OF THE ANTICHRIST, MARTYRDOM, RAPTURE AND THE MILLENNIAL KINGDOM COMING? (I, II)

Commentaries and Sermons on the Book of Revelation

PAUL C. JONG

After the 9/11 terrorist attacks, traffic to "www.raptureready.com," an Internet site providing information on the end times, is reported to have increased to over 8 million hits, and according to a joint survey by CNN and TIME, over 59% of the Americans now believe in apocalyptic eschatology.

Responding to such demands of the time, the author provides a clear exposition of the key themes of the Book of Revelation, including the coming Antichrist, the martyrdom of the saints and their rapture, the Millennial Kingdom, and the New Heaven and Earth—all in the context of the whole Scripture and under the guidance of the Holy Spirit.

This book provides verse-by-verse commentaries on the Book of Revelation supplemented by the author's detailed sermons. Anyone who reads this book will come to grasp all the plans that God has in store for this world.

Paul C. Jong's Christian book series, which is translated into English, French, German, Spanish, Portuguese, Dutch, Greek, Danish, Swedish, Italian, Hindi, Malagasy, Malayalam, Telugue, Kannada, Nepali, Bengali, Bermese, Urdu, Thai, Japanese, Chinese, Taiwanese, Mongolian, Vietnamese, Indonesian, Arabic, Iranian, Javanese, Tagalog, Russian, Ukrainan, Hebrew, Slovak, Czech, Georgian, Albanian, Polish, Hungarian, Bulgarian, Romanian and Turkish, is also available now through e-book service.

E-book is digital book designed for you to feel a printed book on screen. You can read it easily on your screen in your native language after download the viewer software and a text file. Feel free to visit our web site at http://www.bjnewlife.org for e-book service, and you can get the most remarkable Christian e-book absolutely for free.

And, would you like to take part in having our free Christian books known to more people worldwide? We would be very thankful if you link your website to our site so that many people get an opportunity to meet Jesus Christ through the literature. Please visit our site at http://www.bjnewlife.org/english/nlmbanner.html to take our banners. In addition, we would be also very thankful if you introduce our website to the webmasters around you for adding our link.

The New Life Mission
Contact: John Shin, General Secretary
E-mail: newlife@bjnewlife.org